There is a remote summer lodge high on a wooded bluff overlooking Lake Michigan. A farm is down the road, and a village seven miles away. But otherwise there are only sky and lake, wildlife and weather—

And a young man and his wife on their honeymoon . . .

L. Woiwode's What I'm Going to Do, I Think is a hauntingly beautiful novel about youth growing up to the pain of loss, the puzzle of love, and the sense of despair lying near the surface of modern consciousness. This widely acclaimed first novel introduces an author of unique and memorable talent.

A best-seller since it was first published, What I'm Going to Do, I Think has also been bought for motion pictures.

Rave Reviews for
What I'm Going to Do, I Think

"Woiwode has staged the best three-way confrontation between a young man, life and the Michigan woods since Hemingway's Nick Adams stories. If a better first novel than this one appears in 1969, it will be a remarkable year."

—*Time Magazine*

"It is a deliberate idyl for our time, perhaps one of his generation's equivalents of the sweet-sad romances of Hemingway or Fitzgerald . . . It succeeds as literature must. It creates and exposes some lives, not millions of lives. But through the powers of art, it can inform us about all lives."

Webster Schott, *New York Times* (Sunday)

"There are few things more exciting than a writer interested in truth and coming across it, and Mr. Woiwode has produced here a novel of rare depth and understanding one would think beyond the ken of any writer so young."

—*San Francisco Examiner & Chronicle*

"A moving and powerfully promising first novel."

—*Cleveland Plain Dealer*

"Everything is right about *What I'm Going to Do, I Think*: the people, the writing, the setting, the situation and the structure that all makes them one . . . A small, beautiful work, bearing on every page the mark of an artist's hand, it is a first novel of genuine distinction."

Thomas Lask, *New York Times* (Daily)

"*What I'm Going to Do, I Think*, is going to be, I know, one of the year's best novels . . . Throughout the novel the language is brilliant. Be it lovers' small talk or the startling word paintings of the North woods, the result is the same accuracy and beauty. And there is much humor, both light and rich. Rarely has a young American author been able to write with such assurance and accuracy of both the male and female, both the young and old. His is a large and exciting talent."

—*Washington Star*

"Mr. Woiwode does something interesting with sex: he makes it interesting—without borrowing from Krafft-Ebing, the confessional or the couch. Any lovemaking that goes on this book (and there is a lot) is integral and meaningful, both to his characters and to the story. Cheers!"

—*Chicago Daily News*

What I'm Going To Do, I Think

L. Woiwode

BALLANTINE BOOKS • NEW YORK

An Intext Publisher

FOR

CAROLE,
NEWLYN,
and, not least,
WILLIAM TRIEBEL

BOOK ONE

THE BOY

ONE

IT WAS CLOSE to the end of the day. They drove through the woods, up the incline of the narrow clay road—the front tires taking their own erratic paths in the deep ruts eroded by spring storms—and came over the crest of the hill and onto a sight so arresting that the young man who was at the wheel went for the brake. To his left was a long meadow, to his right, at the edge of the woods, was a sprawling red-roofed lodge, and the lawn in front of the lodge, populated with tall birches, sloped downhill for several dozen yards and then ended. Hundreds of feet below, the pale green wrinkled surface of Lake Michigan stretched off for as far as his eyes could see, and the descending sun, just at the horizon, spread a gleaming channel of bronze across it. The angular shadows gliding above the channel, tiny in the distance, were gulls.

"Oh," his wife exclaimed. "What a perfect time to get here!"

"It's just luck we got here at all."

He was still angry at her for the way she'd driven. She sped through small towns, passed school buses, passed on curves, followed at the back bumpers of cars, as though she were bound by no laws, and when he couldn't take it any more and asked her to ease up, she pulled over to the side of the road and said, "You

3

drive. I'm bored." That any woman could possibly be bored in his presence, and especially her, his bride of only a month, was the lowest kind of insult he could think of. So for the final hundred miles of the trip to this peninsula on the northwestern shore of Michigan, he drove in silence, his anger growing more and more bitter because she laid her head in his lap and fell asleep as though nothing were wrong at all.

"I didn't think we'd get here, either," she said, and heaved a sigh.

"Then why'd you drive like a maniac?"

"I couldn't wait till we got here."

"What kind of reasoning is that?"

"Impatience."

"God," he said, and slumped in the seat. This long, exhausting trip was the first time since their marriage that they had really been alone together, and now, as he looked at the sunset on the lake and the isolated lodge, the knowledge that she was his wife, not just a close friend or mistress, was borne in on him, and he felt himself opening up, his emotions widening and deepening to include two people in their scope; but since he was still angry (or at least was feigning anger to remind her he'd been hurt) he didn't speak to her of his feelings, and his anger turned against himself.

"Well, anyway," he said, "we're here. Now what?"

"The first thing you have to do when you get here is go out to the bluff and look at the view. It's a must."

"Right. The bluff," he said, and reached for the keys.

"No. Wait. First drive down the lane to your right here, down to the lodge."

"Sure," he said, and tore up some turf as he backed around.

The tall grass in the center of the clay lane, unattended since the summer before, brushed along the underside of the car, cheerily heralding their descent down the slope to the lodge, which was built of massive logs and had a stone chimney at its far end. He stopped at the back door and shut off the ignition, and the silence of the uninhabited woods, alive with primitive secrets and its own undercurrent of sound, closed around them. Isolated, far from human activity, he felt closer to her. They were both silent. Then he felt his flesh was changing, shedding age, bruises, unpleasant experience, skins and shields of the past, becoming elemental as the woods around him, and as uncharted, returning to a state where he could rediscover, with her, the whole range of physical feeling. In the silence, in such proximity to her, he sensed a similar change taking place in her body. He waited for it to come to completion. Then he searched for words appropriate to the moment.

"Ellen—"

"The flowers," she said, pointing through the windshield to some tiger lilies showing in the thick grass. "Look at the flowers!"

"Yeah, well, all I can say is this yard's going to be a bitch to mow," he said, and got out of the car and slammed the door. He was jealous even of flowers. The air smelled of pine, decaying leaves, wetness and shadows, and was cold. He opened the door, pulled the keys out of the ignition, and with less dramatic impact (none of which was having effect on her, she was too busy seeing), slammed the door again.

She got out and said over the roof of the car, "Don't mow down the flowers!"

"You expect me to mow around each one? Your grandfather wants it all mowed."

The land was her grandfather's, the lodge was his, and so was the automobile; they had been offered to them for their honeymoon—"Since it doesn't seem you've planned that far ahead," her grandmother said, and they hadn't—once her grandparents had resigned themselves, with reservations and a show of great injury, to their secret marriage. He'd thought the gesture might ease some of the bad feelings between them, but he was doubtful that it would, very doubtful now. And

knowing that he had withheld from her grandparents
the most significant detail of all, the one weighing
heaviest on him, he felt like a man who knows he's
going to be dead soon and is willing to try anything
once. She was pregnant.

"And *those* flowers," she said, pointing to some
columbines that made a red streak along the edge of
the meadow. "What are those? I've never been up here
when there were so many flowers. Or else I never
noticed them."

She came around the car and took him by the arm.
"Promise you won't mow them."

"No. Not those. They're at the edge of the yard."

The yard, as he judged it, was that area of grass,
immediately surrounding the lodge, which was only
knee high. He took a scrap of paper out of his jacket
pocket, unfolded it, and ran his eyes over the instructions written in the slanting, energetic hand of her
grandfather:

> Go up on roof and check screen on chimneys. See if
> blocked up. Don't build fire till you do. Mow lawn. Clear
> off branches first. A lot of them fall. Call watchman (V.
> Weeks, 843-7448) and say you are there. Better tell who
> you are and why name is different. Fuse box is in back
> porch. So is water heater. Make sure water heater is full
> before you turn on juice. Otherwise can blow up. If
> water isn't running go to pumphouse up in meadow and
> turn on pump. Key to there is on chain with other keys.
> When on roof clean leaves out of gutters. Then the
> cleaning up inside and out. Ellen knows that. Ask her
> and do.

Reviewing the instructions, he sighed. Then his eyebrows arched high on his forehead, and he sighed
again, implying that she should be damn thankful she'd
married somebody like him, a person who was accustomed to this kind of work and could do a job that
would please even her grandfather. "Well, I suppose I
might as well get started," he said, and raised his eyes

so she could see all this mirrored in them. She was gone.

He looked around and finally saw her on a slight elevation at the opposite side of the car, sitting or kneeling, the crown of her head just visible above the grass. What the hell kind of game was this? He started toward her, angry and impatient, but when he could see her hands he stopped, then stepped back a step, as though he'd come upon a nest in the grass. Without breaking the blossom from the stem, she held a tiger lily in one hand and touched its petals with the fingertips of the other. Then she rose up, wholly absorbed, unconscious of his nearness, and started moving toward the columbines at the edge of the meadow. Her bearing—dignified and serene, with an even keel of self-assurance—also held him transfixed. He'd never seen her walk that way. He felt as he'd felt when they cleared the hill and he saw the lodge, the sun, the lake, and then that emotion emptied from him and was filled in by a fear just as great. He wanted to call out to her, to warn her, to run to her and protect her. He didn't know what he wanted to protect her against, but as she moved through the waist-high grass she seemed prey to some grave, unknown danger.

He turned away, went down to the door of the lodge, and started fumbling at its lock with the keys.

"Wait," she called to him. "Chris, wait! First you have to come out and look over the bluff!"

. . . 2

A week ago in Chicago, on the first hot day of summer, when the thick humidity and the heat waves swaying up from the asphalt made him feel he was moving through an aquarium, he boarded the late-afternoon bus for Madison, a stuffy submarine suffused with green sea light. He walked to the rear, where there were many empty seats, and placed two suitcases that contained most of his belongings, other than his books, on the overhead rack next to the john, then slumped down in a seat and lit a cigarette. His head ached. That morning, after three sleepless nights, he had passed an exam that enabled him to retain his $3,500 fellowship, and he'd just downed six beers in the Greyhound bar. Through the spattered window he saw a girl standing with her back to the terminal.

He sat up straight. Her face was impassive, she stood with the posture of a model, and there was no outward show of warmth or openness in her, but he felt her presence; it was as if only a threshold separated them and she was about to step over it. She wore a print dress cut low at the neckline, homemade, he guessed, and her hands were clasped at the level of her waist, her fingertips gripping the broad brim of a white hat whose wide circle was like a shield over her hips and thighs. She was fair, and the skin of her face was as white as the cleavage between her breasts.

Two tall males stood beside her, each of them with a piece of luggage in his hand, looking like cranes, he thought, with their spindly legs and big noses, or those storks pictured as carrying satchels, spectacles on their beaks. Both of them were chattering and grinning at her. College boys. Pale blue jackets, madras, tapered pants; the whole cardboard cutout. As they talked, she first turned to one, her blond hair falling in a fan over her shoulder, listened for a moment, gave him a slight smile, and then slowly turned her attention to the other —her lifted chin, prim lips, and straight nose showing in sharp profile against the dark brick. She must be the one leaving.

What did she remind him of? In rural Wisconsin where he was raised, young girls, Germans and Scandinavians, came to the country church in the summer wearing starched dresses and sat with straight backs in the pews, the sunlight gilding their hair, the down on their arms, and the down on the backs of their necks, and they looked like that. Made the service seem a jumble of fragments, maddening as the flies, a blurred jumble punctuated by shoulders, gold hair, a nape, the surprise of the gospel, scraping and rustling, and then seeing the bodies full-length. Hands smoothing and rearranging a skirt. A shoulder strap tucked. What a hell of a reason to go to church.

She reminded him of Ellen. The resemblance had more to do with her manner than the physical, but that was it, Ellen: poise in a sheath of simplicity. The same patience and courteous attention, the strong profile, the identical aura. The hat held as if in modesty. She would board one of the other buses, sure as fate (there were half a dozen others lined up on the lot, all with their motors going), and he'd never know what she was like.

He slumped back in the seat and glanced at the ring on his finger, the gold band worn thin by age, dented and scratched and turning the color of bronze. It was three years since Ellen gave the ring to him, an eighth of his life, and for a full year of that time it was all he had of her other than memories. The ring was her mother's, one of the few material things Ellen treasured and the single physical object of her parents' that she owned. Her grandparents had burned her mother's and father's possessions, their clothes, their books, the photographs and movies of them—everything that bore their image, their imprint, their signature or touch. They were killed in an accident when she was a child. He'd never learned what really happened. If he made any reference to it, her body tensed and her eyes widened, brimming with a terror beyond tears, a terror that never showed in her at any other time, and it would have been unmerciful to ask anything more, so he never did.

She referred to it simply as "the accident" and dated the events of her life from that time. "That was just before the accident," she would say, or, "Oh, yes, now I remember; it was three years after the accident." When she gave him the ring, she said, "This is all I can give, other than me, and it's yours, too. Take it, take it!" He sat unbelieving, afraid, reluctant, so she took him by the wrist and, after several tries (his hands were slim and delicately boned), she found that the ring fit the third finger of his right hand. She slipped it in place. "No," she insisted. "You *must* keep it. For me."

Now it was on his ring finger.

He never would have believed that she could be so positive and insistent. When he first saw her, she seemed isolated by a grief no one could reach through. It was his junior year at Madison, and he was doing everything he could to keep it from being a bore— painting scenery for plays, trying to learn the rudiments of the banjo, auditing classes with freak instructors, and attending the beer parties, the professional parties, the pot parties, the pill parties, the parties that themselves became a bore.

She appeared at one of them, wrapped in a long

black coat, and sat in a corner with her back against a radiator, the coat still on, and lit one cigarette after another and let them burn down to her fingers without once taking a drag. It was a stand-up, BYO, bottle-in-the-hand party, where the crowd moved in slow revolutions around a packed apartment. People stopped in front of her, trying to make conversation. Some offered drinks, she refused, and they shrugged their shoulders and walked off. Late in the evening, when he was bolstered with beer, he came up in front of her and stood there, silent, until she had to raise her eyes to him. Her eyes. They were large, wide, tentative, with whites white as milk glass, and because her lashes and eyebrows were pale the whites looked even more enormous and unprotected; and the color of the iris seemed to lie in layers, a blue that met his stare, a green pulsing beneath the blue, trying to reach surface, and beneath the green a deeper blue he retreated from. Then her eyes went blank and distant. He lifted up a strand of her hair, fine and blond, wrapped it around his finger, and pulled hard.

"You want to be left alone," he said. "Right?"

"Yes."

"Me too," he said, her hair still in his grip.

She moistened her lips as if to speak, to protest, and he moistened his. Then he went down on his knee and kissed her forehead, her cheek, her mouth, and each of her eyelids. He stood. "You need to be kissed there," he said, and turned and walked away. A few minutes later she got up and left.

She began to show up at the parties he went to, wearing the same black coat or similar unflattering apparel—bulky sweaters and long skirts, one-piece dresses, ill-fitting men's clothes—and remained aloof, sitting off at the edge of activity, in a corner, or on a windowsill with her legs drawn up, staring out at the night, or on the floor or on a counter top in a kitchen, where nobody went except for drinks. A couple of times he caught her staring at him.

One night, wedging himself between her and a refrigerator (she was against a stove), he sat on the floor beside her, and before he could speak she broke into a torrent of words about the night sky, the constellations, about Cassiopeia and Sagittarius, about Orion, who reminded her of the Stoics, and phrases such as "translucent metaphysics" and "solitary as sleep" and "at those times I feel quixotic and ephemeral" fell from her tongue like everyday language. Her cheeks flushed and her eyes grew larger and more dark, the green rising up in them, shimmering. There was no more distance in her. She was speaking to him. Then they were interrupted by a heavyset fellow with horn-rimmed glasses and sideburns down to the bottom of his jaw, who said, "Hey, babe, I'm cuttin' out. You want the ride home?" The stranger walked off and she excused herself and got up and followed. He was furious.

The next time, he monopolized her; he stayed at her side the whole night, listening mostly, while she told him of her interest in philosophy and languages. She was friendly, but somewhat distant and formal, even pedantic at times, and he wanted her to be as open as she'd been before. He questioned her about astronomy. It no longer interested her. He tried to get her to talk about her friends. She had none. He offered her a drink of his beer. She said no, she never drank. That was precisely the reason she should try it, he said, and finally persuaded her to take a sip.

"What an outdoor taste!" she said. "It's like plums fresh from the tree."

"Watch it," he said. "That's a quart."

"I didn't realize it would taste so good."

"You've never even tasted it?"

"Never. And my grandfather makes it. Isn't that un*natural*?"

"Your grandfather's a brewer?"

"He used to be a brewmaster, but he started a plant of his own several years back and it's done fairly well.

He's very proud of it. Oh, that's his. The one you have now."

He was opening a new quart. He looked at the label. *Auld Meister.* "Well, I'm glad we could all get together tonight," he said, and drank to that. She took a small sip from the first bottle, and he settled back beside her.

"If your grandfather's a brewer, there must have been barrels of it around the house, and you claim you didn't even taste it?"

"No."

"You mean you had that much self-restraint?" Testing her.

"There was never any in the house, to my knowledge. We're not allowed to drink."

"It's in the veins?"

"We're Christian Scientist."

He looked at her, and she gave him a solemn nod, her eyes wide. My God, he thought, a sense of humor, too? "Christian Scientist, you say?"

"Yes," she said.

"Making *beer?*"

The same nod. He covered his mouth with his hand. An older woman he respected told him once that the only thing that ruined his good looks, which she called primitive Cro-Magnon (he had a big broad forehead, deep set eyes, and high cheekbones), was the gap between his front teeth that showed when he laughed; and he laughed easily, especially with beer in him, and now he couldn't stop.

"But we *are*," she said, and when she became insistent about it, and then offended, setting her beer down so hard it foamed over, and then indignant as he continued to laugh, he realized it was the truth, the *truth*, and he forgot about his hand, his teeth, everything, overcome with laughter, and finally, to catch his breath, he had to slap the side of the refrigerator. Then, for the first time, she must have seen the humor in it too, because she suddenly burst into laughter herself. He stopped and stared at her in awe. He'd never heard such rich laughter, laughter that covered so much of the scale, cascading from high to low, and was colored with such darkness and light.

A few hours later, when he was drunk, he led her, half drunk, to his rented room. For an hour she fought him, fending him off with fingernails, elbows, and knees, and finally passed out. He sat on the edge of the bed and took off his clothes, his head nodding as consciousness slipped from him, and then stripped her naked. The cool air woke her and she fought him again, with a determination he'd never felt in a woman, until, sobering, seeing in her large eyes the look of a cornered animal, he began to feel compassion for her and to resent himself. He dropped on his back into unconsciousness.

In the morning, she was sitting at the window, fully dressed, with her coat on and a lighted cigarette in one hand. Her head was bowed so low that her hair shielded her face.

"You aren't crying?" he asked, rising on an elbow.

"No."

"Oh."

"I've been waiting for you to wake."

"Oh," he said, and covered his groin with the sheet.

"Did you ever see outside?" she asked.

"See what?"

"Your view."

"Sure."

"It's nice."

"Just backs of old buildings," he said.

"But they're all in whites and grays. The alley's purple. It's European."

"You've been to Europe?"

"No. I'm going."

"When?"

"Soon."

"Oh." Why should that make him, who had no claim on her, feel hurt and abandoned?

"That garage with the doors swung back, the iron poles against them—are they always that way?"

"Always."

"I love it. It's like a Utrillo. I feel dimensional, at the center of one of his canvases. One of his red ladies."

"In a black coat?"

"He'd paint me red."

"Before he tried the cure, or after?"

"Cure?"

"It didn't work. He died raving, brains eaten out. Booze."

"Oh." Her head sank even lower, and there was a long silence. Then she murmured, "I feel I've been abused."

"I know," he said, his voice as regretful as hers. "I'm sorry. I've never been that way."

"You've been others?"

He left that open.

"Why were you?" she asked. "The 'booze'?"

"I wanted you."

"Why me?"

"Why not?"

"What for?"

"For you."

"What part of me?"

"All parts. You."

"Who's that?"

"You. Everything you know about yourself. All you've imagined."

"What about what I don't know?"

"That, too."

She extinguished the cigarette with methodical care, laid the long stub in the ash tray, and placed a pack of Benson & Hedges on the windowsill. "You're out of cigarettes," she said. "I wanted one of your Camels and looked through your clothes. There weren't any. Was that presumptuous?"

"No, no, of course not. It was perfect. It assumes something."

"What?"

"Just that you felt you could do it."

"Maybe I did it in fury," she said.

"Maybe you did."

She rose, shoulders drawn high and close, head lowered, hands in her pockets, and went across the room in a slow, uncertain, sidling step, a sad sashay. She opened the door and stepped outside. All he could see was the end of her coat sleeve and her hand on the knob. The door began to swing in, and her arm, her shoulder, then her face appeared, eyes averted, and he could see she had been crying. He wondered how long he'd lain there, spread-eagled, while she was awake, and at that moment he loathed his body. Her eyes lifted, traveled slowly over the sheet, and met his, where they held for a long time.

"You're insidious," she said, and in one deft and graceful movement she disappeared and shut the door.

He didn't see her for a month. He watched for her on campus and at parties but with no luck, and after a while he gave up looking and kept to his room, where he busied himself with his badly neglected studies. The first frost came and then the first snow. Several times he picked up the telephone book, found her number, dropped a dime in the phone, and started to dial, but always hung up before he reached her. He was sure she didn't want to hear from him, and he couldn't blame her. Besides, a few curt words from her over phone wire was all he needed to make his sense of loss more keen, for he did feel a loss; he hadn't realized how much it meant just to be in the same room with her. He found himself composing letters in his mind—playful, bantering ones, angry ones, and long mournful ones, exaggerating his sadness—and though he hardly knew what she was like, the letters were addressed to her.

One morning, after a heavy snowfall, when he was squinting against the glare, he saw a woman moving down the street in the sad sashay he'd seen only once—her!—leaving prints in the snow that were like grace notes to him, sudden music, a precursor to birdsong and spring. He ran up and touched her shoulder. She turned. When she saw who it was, a smile so radiant it seemed the reason for the brilliance around them appeared on her face. The past, everything that had happened, was covered over, he saw, as the ground was covered, was white, and they could begin again.

Still smiling, she said, "I'm supposed to be angry at you."

"Why?"

"You didn't call."

He took her for coffee, and began the long delicate task of courting her—a task he'd learned, from his blunders in the past, to carry out with aplomb, patience and detachment; but when he realized he had the power to free her from her sadness, and saw her transformed from a retiring, sober, and somewhat pedantic student of languages into an uninhibited participant in life, as full of curiosity, passion, and exuberance as a child, he was so moved by the transformation and so proud of himself for bringing it about that he fell in love with her, and first the detachment went, then the patience, and at last, in a flurry of jealousy, the aplomb. But by that time she had given him the ring and was living and acting like his bride. She accompanied him everywhere, even to the doors of his classrooms, she kept his room and desk in order, she laundered his clothes, she ate her meals with him, and when she had early classes (which he never had), she came to his room and got into bed with him and slowly brought him into the world of the waking. Golden mornings. Her hair rayed like a nimbus around her face on the pillow.

Then she took him home to meet her grandparents.

He shifted and strained in the seat of the bus like a man trying to throw off chains. Why had he been so insistent that they get married legally, for real, when she was getting so much pressure from those two?

—I think I want to get married, she would say.

—What do you mean 'think'?

—I do, but in a while. Maybe after I've finished school and have a job and you have your doctorate.

—That's a *while*?

—It isn't long.

—Hell, I'll never get it.

—Yes, you will. I know you will.

—You just want time to play around.

—I want to be settled.

—You want money.

—Quit! I just want you.

—Then let's get married.

God, for months that conversation had gone on. And there were others, too, as circular and pernicious.

—You're back in your old thing, he would say.

—What thing?

—Your slumped-over, catatonic, 'I dare you to find me and bring me out' thing.

—I can't help it. I feel trapped.

—Which is my fault.

—I didn't insinuate that.

—You said it outright.

—I did not.

—It's what you meant.

—It isn't!

—Then get out of this.

—I can't.

—*Why?*

—I need your help!

—God, I'm sorry. Here. . . .

The bus driver called out the destination once more, for the last time, and started climbing the steps of the bus, helping his bulk along with the aid of the metal rails, then dropped into his seat and raced the motor, making steel panels vibrate and screws buzz. The girl outside placed the hat on her head and, ignoring the protests of her two companions, took the pieces of luggage from them, then leaned from the waist, so that her breasts wouldn't touch them, and kissed each of them on the cheek. In a wash of astonishment that cleared his mind and made him more attentive, he saw she was boarding this bus after all.

Surprisingly, there were few other passengers on it, and most of them were sitting near the front. She walked several seats past them, glanced at him, and chose a seat, by herself, near the rear of the bus. The driver, who had lurched out of his seat and was following behind her, helped her put her luggage on the rack. Since the beer, which was supposed to be dulling the eruptions of his mind, wasn't doing any good, was, indeed, making his headache worse, he decided he might talk to her.

The bus pulled out. By the time they reached the Expressway, the sun was beginning to set, and he felt the approach of emotion, limiting as the night, that he'd felt every evening at this time when he and Ellen were apart. His persistence and her grandparents' frantic disapproval of him finally drove her off, to New York, where she lived for a year while he was finishing his last year at Madison. And then, as though Fate meant to reunite them but made a miscalculation, she returned to Madison two weeks after he'd moved to Chicago.

He knew no one in Chicago; he'd won a fellowship to a school there. He lived in a run-down neighborhood, near a Catholic seminary that was like an externalization of his desolateness, and each day rode the El to school and from school to the Loop, where he worked part time for an accounting firm. The place he stayed in was a two-story frame house, once a family dwelling, whose large rooms had been divided into cubicles that rented for eleven dollars a week. Most of the occupants were old men who had grown up in the neighborhood and were now on Social Security. At the head of a flight of stairs that creaked and leaned toward the left was a single bathroom (a sink, a stool, a shower stall made of Masonite) that served the whole building.

His room was unfurnished. He found a discarded lamp and some curtains in a garbage can, and installed them. He bought a mattress and laid it on the floor, and he slept there and worked there, holding a board across his knees for a desk. He placed his books in stacks according to subject. He ate one meal a day—most of the time a hamburger or a bowl of soup—in a cheap restaurant, and lunched on candy bars and raisins the rest of the time. He allowed himself cigarettes and, every Saturday, a case of beer, and saved most of his money. At the pressure of a fingertip his gums bled, and he grew thin and weak. Every evening at this hour, when the light at his window failed, he drew the curtains and lay down facing the wall, and Ellen's aura and presence and scent filled the room. But as semidarkness turned to dark, he grew afraid, shook himself free of her, and switched on his lamp and went to work.

They began to write to one another, each of them trying to take the entire blame for what had happened, and toward the end of the winter she came to visit him. He rented a suite for them at the Blackstone (no extravagance too extreme for her), and one day took her across town and showed her his room. "How ascetic!" she said. "True," he intoned, as proud of the way he lived as he was sorry for himself. She visited him again at Easter, when magnolias were in bud behind the seminary walls, but this time she was distant and depressed and cried at the sight of his room, cried at sparrows foraging for food in a gutter, cried on the El (causing passengers in the car to stare at him as though he'd slapped her), and cried at the airport—he insisted she fly—when he saw her off. Several weeks afterward he received a telegram:

> HELLO LOVE. ITS SPRING AND ALL SPRING MEANS.
> CALL IMMEDIATELY.   ELLEN

Two weeks later they were married.

And now he was on this bus, barreling through the night, going from that unpleasant past, which at least was over, into a future that could be worse. He shifted his weight in his seat. There was no way he could get comfortable. A single person—a colored man whose sleeping head swayed and bobbed with the motion of the bus—sat in the row of seats between him and the girl. He scooted over and started out of his seat, figuring, what the hell, why not talk to her? But, as he rose, there was such pressure on his skull he felt he was lifting a sandbag with his head. The beer. Finally, the beer was getting to him, now when he didn't want it to. Damn. He took several unsteady steps forward, the sandbag teetering, then swung around and went on sea legs to the john, where he urinated, his hip banging against the metal door. The beer, and the lack of sleep, kept closing in on his mind until there was only a pinpoint of consciousness to see through. Shapes at the periphery were vague and distorted. A white tile? A towel? The face of an animal? What?

Then the whirling water, whining and spiraling down, enticing him to give up. That dark place. He shook his head, shouldered open the door, and started toward the front of the bus, grabbing the backs of seats for balance, then stopped short. The pinpoint closed. His shoulders sagged, and he fell sideways into an empty seat.

... 3

When he woke, it was totally dark out, and some
reading lights were on at the front of the bus. Two seats
ahead of him, a single light cast its slash of brilliance
onto the glistening crown of the girl's head, which was
turned to stare out the dark window, and in the window
was a reflection of her that he stared at. The beer was
still with him, but now he felt as giddy and reckless as
he did depressed. What role should he adopt? The
naïve boy with shining eyes, bushy tail and all, a coup
for her? The silent, inscrutable starer—make her so ill
at ease she has to do the work? The witty dazzler?
Hell, he'd never pull that one off, not in his shape. The
beast? Hell with it. Hell with them all. Let the beer
dictate his tack.

He pulled himself up, tottered a couple steps as the
bus made a turn, then went forward and dropped into
the seat beside her, and at the whoosh of the cushions
she swung toward him, startled, her green eyes wide.

"Hi," he said.

"Who are you?"

"Ticket inspector. Did I scare you?"

"Yes, you did."

"Sorry. Just wanted to talk. Grew cold in the back
there."

"The whole bus is cold."

22

"Cold night." There was a promising start.

Her nose was more pointed than it appeared from a distance, but her long, curled eyelashes and full upper lip —the kind that made you want to press it flat against teeth—more than compensated for this minor imperfection. She didn't seem put off by him, judging from her sidelong look of interest, and suddenly he felt depressed. "You remind me of Ellen," he murmured, staring straight ahead.

"Ellen?"

He raised the hand with the ring on it. He let it drop. "My wife."

"Oh. You're married."

"No, no. I'm putting you on. Do I look married?"

"It's hard to say."

"Do I? Tell me, do I?"

"You seem young, boyish—a lone-wolf type, maybe —but that doesn't mean you're not married. You could be and you couldn't be."

Oh, god, he thought, a mediator, an agreeable one, a pushover.

"What do you do?" she asked.

"Student," he said. "Perpetual student."

"A graduate student?"

"Yeah." He looked up and found her studying him. "You?"

"Undergraduate," she answered, lowering her eyes from his frank stare.

"Northwestern?"

"No, an Eastern school."

"Which one?"

"Radcliffe."

"Radcliffe!" he said, and made wide eyes. "Jesus, pardon me while I get on my paws and crawl back where I came from!"

She put her fingers to her lips and stifled a small laugh.

Flattered, he wondered, or just dumb?

She turned her large eyes, which were still shining

with amusement, on him and said, "You've been drinking."

Maybe not so dumb. "A few beers," he said. "A few beers, a few laughs. Ha. Ha."

"I noticed you."

"You mean my dance? My waltz from the john to the barroom floor?"

"No. When I got on the bus."

"You did?"

"Why lie?"

"Well, why didn't you say hello?"

"It's not the way I was brought up."

"How was that?"

"Puritanically. To be a young lady." She made quotes around the last word with her index fingers, and then grinned.

"Are you?"

"What?"

"A lady?"

"I try."

"Puritanical?"

She laughed, showing teeth as small, short, and square as a child's. "Definitely!"

"Hey, we're moving along like a couple of bats out of hell!" And better get some reins on quick. "My forebears are from the East," he said.

"Oh." She let it fall faint and cold as a snowflake.

"Right. A Van Eenanam was a— Oh, my name's Van Eenanam. Chris." He turned and paused for her.

"Sue McIntyre."

"A Van Eenanam was a scribe in New Amsterdam, Old New York, the Peter Stuyvesant thing. *Nieuw* Amsterdam. Ha! My grandfather traced the family that far and stopped. He figured that was good enough for him, and what's good enough for him is good enough for me. *Her* family," he said, exhibiting the ring again, "they trace back to Sir Philip Sidney." He flapped a limp wrist. "The fairy queen," he said in a high, gay voice, and quickly covered his mouth with his hand. Damn teeth. "Proud as hell of it, too."

"Then you *are* married."

"Oh. Ah. Well, in a way."

"Either you are or you aren't."

"Must we mince?"

"It's one way or the other."

"Right. Why lie, huh? Well, she and I have gone through the formalities, but it remains to be seen if I'll be shotgunned by her family. The one time I was exhibited to them—her grandparents, she lives with her grandparents—they declared me off-limits." He wagged his finger at her. " 'Don't ever let us catch you laying eyes on him again!' "

"Apparently she did."

"And then some, Sue. There was a bit of the shotgun hanging over the wedding itself, in case you're interested, and they don't even know we're married, much less that. Christ! One look at me and they decided I was a wastrel, a Clyde, a, a . . ." As he searched for a fitting expression, his hand kept making a circular motion close to his shirt, as though he were unreeling ribbon from its front, and in this indecisive delay, caused by the fog of the beer, he felt he was losing his hold on her.

"Why did they think that?" she asked.

"Who knows? I didn't run at the mouth like now. Got my hair cut so you could see ears. And I played the quiet and sociable young fellow. Listened deadpan to everything they said—about the Pope and the Communists taking over the world, how the City Fathers are poisoning us with fluoride—and agreed with every bit of it. Her grandfather's judgment: 'Spineless. Doesn't have an opinion of his own.' "

"Oh, that's too bad," she said, and there was a true note of commiseration in her voice.

"Yeah, I guess. He assumed I hadn't worked a day in my life and never would. Hell, I was brought up a farm boy, or 'form buoy' as they say where I come from."

"Where's that?"

"Near Madison. Rock Creek. Ever been there?"

"I'm afraid not. I've—"

"Nobody has. Hick town."

"What does your family think of it?"

"What's that?"

"What does *your* family think of the marriage?"

He hadn't expected this, and the sudden change in direction made his ribs and forearms ache with anxiety. "My parents?" He had to take some quick breaths of air. "They don't know. I haven't seen them for a couple years. We write."

"Oh."

"Nothing dramatic," he quickly added. "I'll let them know. It's just that I'm not a form buoy any more."

"They expect that?"

He shrugged his shoulders. He was ashamed of his parents, who were uneducated and poor.

She had turned away and was looking out the dark window, her straight hair eclipsing her face at the cheekbone. He thought he noticed a flush in her throat.

"Why are you riding this bus?" he asked.

"It's taking me to Madison, where I pick up another."

"I mean, why a bus? I hate the damn things."

"Why are you?"

"Perpetual student's curse. Also, I'm a tightass."

"I don't have much money, either. And besides, I wanted to see the countryside in different states. I've never been out of Massachusetts."

"I'll be damned. Cloistered life?"

"Sort of."

"Family's doings?"

"My father."

"Wanted to keep you for himself, huh?"

"Perhaps. That, and being poor." On this her voice became distant and weary, and he felt sorry for her.

"So do you work to pay for school, or what?"

"That, and I have a scholarship."

"And now you're going—"

"To Saskatchewan."

"What for?"

"To teach Indian children."

"Indians!"

"For the Canadian government."

"Jesus, how'd you get sucked into that?"

"I saw a brochure when I was in a bad mood and I thought it would be a good excuse to get away, see the country, so finally I applied and was accepted. It surprised me. At first, I didn't know whether I really wanted to go. The reservation is supposed to be in wild country."

"And you'll live there?"

"Yes."

"How? I mean, in a schoolhouse, or barracks, or tepee, or what?"

"I don't know many details, really, until I get there, except I'll be teaching English to Indian children, and I'll get paid a little for it."

"Some balls!"

"Pardon?"

"Pardon," he said. "That must take courage—get-up-and-go."

"I think mostly a desire to be on my own."

"Jesus, do all women want that?"

"I don't think so. I do because of my situation—at home, I mean—and just for now."

"Ellen did the same damn thing," he said, and the air around him dimmed. The beer? He also felt out of breath. "Wouldn't take help from her grandparents. Oh, they thought it magnificent! Frail Girl on Her Own, Big Capitalistic World, Survival of the Fittest. That crap. Of course, before a couple months were up they saw to it she had a few conveniences. Record player. Air conditioner. Car. Little things." His vision dimmed again and his head, which felt crushed down at the hairline, burdened by the same sandbag, began nodding. "Christ!" he said.

"Do you always talk this way?"

"What's that?" He hadn't heard her.

"Your talk. Vulgar language. Clipped. That way. Blunt, then intimate, then so cold."

"Oh, that. Mostly when I'm swacked."

"Swacked?"

"Smashed, gooned, juiced, bombed, stoned, zorched, my head wedged, out of—"

"You're that way now?"

"A hair's breadth."

"How long since you've had sleep?"

"Three days."

"Three days!"

"Beg pardon. Just caught a nap behind you there, accidental one, on my way up."

"Are you all right now?"

"On and off, Sue. You know how it is. If I pass out, just roll me in the aisle so somebody steps on me when this thing stops. Have to be awake. Have to meet Ellen, for Christ's sake."

"Who is this *Ellen?*" she asked, and her voice was so altered and sharp that his head cleared and he sat up straight.

"I told you," he said, a bit indignant. "My wife."

"All night you've been comparing us, and no woman likes to be compared with another, especially if she makes a person act the way you do."

"How's that?"

"Bitter."

"Oh, that's not her. That's her grandparents."

"Using foul language every time you mention her name."

"Foul language?" he said, more to himself than her. "Is that right?"

"Yes."

He shrugged his shoulders. "Because I'm a bastard, I guess."

"You do run loose at the tongue sometimes, as you said, but I'm sure that's because of your condition. Your eyes look bad."

"I'm a bastard," he insisted.

"I don't think so."

"I said I'm a bastard!"

"Hush. The people."

"What about this," he said, and put a hand to her jaw and kissed her on the mouth, purposely pressing his elbow against one breast. She sat rigid, motionless, her hands folded in her lap, as though she weren't being kissed for the first time. He drew away. "What about that?" he asked. "That's what I *really* wanted to do all night."

"That doesn't make a bastard of you," she said, and slowly turned her large eyes on him. "And besides, I remind you of Ellen."

"I just said that. It's not really true. I mean, it's not like, it's not . . . It's what you *radiate*."

"And that's?"

He looked into her eyes. "Sun. Outdoors. Virginity."

"That sounds pleasant enough. And flattering," she said, but she looked ill at ease instead of flattered, and turned back toward the window.

"Let's see," he said, and took her by the chin. "Your bone structure's different. And lips. Your top one is fuller. Everything's different but the hair, as far as I can see, and hair is just hair." He moved his face closer and turned her head from side to side until her neck muscles relaxed and she began to pose for him, eyelids lowered. "Beautiful," he whispered, and kissed her again. Instead of resisting, as he expected, she moved closer and placed her hand on the back of his neck.

Then, abruptly, she pushed him away. "No," she said. "The people."

"They're all up there," he said, and shut off the reading light.

"The driver can see."

"Here." He slipped his hand between the seat and her buttocks and drew her forward so that she was half sitting, half lying, her legs straight.

"I can still see his eyes," she said.

"Haven't you ever been on a bus? You can see his eyes from every seat. It's the angle of incidence, an optical illusion, bus-mirror parallax. It doesn't mean he's looking at you."

"But I know he is."

"That's vanity." He drew her down lower, and pressed that lip flat. He'd never felt a woman warm so fast. Soon she was out of breath and struggling in the seat to get closer against him.

"This is what I want," he said. "This, this."

"Please. No. What will he think?"

"He'll like you more."

"How will I face him."

"Don't. When we stop, pull your hat over your eyes and run."

"He'll think I'm trash and you will, too, and I'm not. I've never been this way. I was never allowed— Oh!"

"You're not wearing a bra."

"I never wear a bra in the summer, never, never, I've never worn a bra in summer!"

"Nnnn."

"Oh, this is torture!"

He felt he'd been struck a blow from behind, and in a sunburst of blue his muscles went slack and his head sank to her breast.

"Oh, thank you," she said. "Thank you."

He started to ask her what had happened, who had hit him, why they had hit him, but when he tried to speak no words came. She was stroking his hair and neck and murmuring, "Thank you, thank you, that was good of you. I don't know what I would have done. Thank you." And then he understood that his mind was giving out. That dark place. He tried again to speak, and produced a sound like "bok" and another noise, but his mind kept driving him deeper, past his voice, down through his defenses and experience, taking him way to the bottom, where he thought, Jesus, Jesus Christ, if we'd been anywhere but here I would have had her, and that would be adultery. Which made him drop deeper into unconsciousness. He retained his sense of touch and his hearing became acute and distorted, amplifying tiny sounds, but all he could smell was an odor of lilacs—from where? not her, she wore a musk perfume—and all he could see was black. But there was dimension to the blackness, as though he were sitting at the rear of an empty theater staring at a dim screen. Occasionally images flowered on the screen, glowing, and then came into focus, and he felt, through some frayed network of his nerves, that if he didn't add subtitles to the images something final and irreversible would happen.

First he saw:

—his head, detached, lying on a woman's breast, whose face was invisible—

BOY FINDS MOTHER

Then he saw:

—the screen door, covered with plastic, that led to his rooming house in Chicago—

THIS DOOR CONDEMNED

Then:

—a girl from childhood, scraping down the street in her mother's high heels, wearing a red dress that dragged on the walk—

SISSY TURNS WHORE

And then:

—blond hair falling in a fan over a low-cut dress—

STORKS FLANK VIRGIN AT DEPOT

"What?" she asked, and he realized he must be talking out loud.

"Those two at the bus station," he said. "Boy-friends?"

"Oh, no." These vowels seemed prolonged, and her voice reverberated and came from a distance, as though she were speaking from the end of a marble corridor—"Owowo Nowowo. They're from Harvard."

"Trailing you? After you?"

"They live in Chicago."

"Not lovers?"

"I have none."

"Good. Never have any."

"Why?"

"Wait for me."

—her body spread on the ground, limbs tied to stakes, a brown body mounting her—

NO!

"What is it? Are you all right?"

"Don't let the Indians get you!"

"I won't."

The reverberations grew, began echoing between his ears. "Wait for me."

"You have Ellen."

"Maybe."

"You love her."

"Yes."

"Then you have her."

"*Wait for me.*" This echoed in his head until he was no longer sure he was talking to her or had ever talked to her, and the steady stroke of her hand on his hair was a room away. There was a rush of images—tree roots, egg crates, balled paper (his heartbeat picking up as each one went past without a title), a culvert, angle-worms, a fingertip, an inkspot, clothes ripping, clothes

being ripped down a seam through which he fell head-
long. Into oblivion.

Then hands were at his cheeks, trying to lift his
head, dropping to his shoulders, shaking him, while the
refrain "Wait for me, wait for me" kept ringing through
his mind. The fingers of the hands traced a familiar
pattern over his features, and he knew he was awake.
He opened his eyes and saw the inside of a bus, with a
row of overhead lights shining down on him. The bus
was empty except for one face, with a broad smile on
it, in front of him.

"Ellen."

"You're here!" she said. "You're home, you made
it!" She leaned over and kissed him on the mouth, and
then moved her lips to his ear and whispered, "I
thought I'd never last until you did."

TWO

THE BRONZE CHANNEL on the lake widened as the sun went down. She put her arm around his waist and led him closer to the edge of the bluff. He looked over. It was a sheer drop for fifty feet and then a deep wash like a dried riverbed—a hundred yards across—was visible, falling away for an additional two hundred feet. The tan clay of the wash was scored and streaked with gulleys, runnels, potholes, small ravines, and was barren except for some stunted shrubs and a few frail silver maples—tentatively holding the erosion in check—that were leaning over backward. Far below, a border of trees separated the wash from the lighter-colored strip of the beach, which, from their height, was no more than a white line before the green of the water. A gust of wind, guided up the wash, swept over the bluff and took his hair back from his forehead and stung his eyes, and the leaves of the silver maples took orange on their undersides from the sun.

"What a perfect time to get here," she said again, but in a quieter tone, to him.

"Do you want to jump?"

"Oh!" she said, scoffing, and held him tighter. "It's exciting enough just to see."

"Safer, too."

"Do you like it?"

"Yes," he said.

"Really?"

"Of course."

"You're positive?"

"What do you want me to say? It's beautiful, it's spectacular, it's breathtaking, it's dynamic. I'm impressed."

"I'm afraid you think I forced you to come up."

"I could have said no."

"You wouldn't," she said, and looked out over the lake. "You're too considerate."

He winced.

"It's just that I love it so much," she said. "There's no other place we possibly could have come. You'll understand, you'll see. Here I'm elemental."

"Oh." His attention was somewhere else. He pointed to a long, low ridge of land that lay far out in the water, straight ahead of them, silhouetted by the sun. "What's that?"

"Manitou. Manitou Island. Actually there's a North and a South Manitou, but the southern one is smaller and lies behind the one you can see. That's North Manitou."

"Is it inhabited?"

"Yes, by a few people. But the only way you can get to it is by plane or boat. It's about fifteen miles away. A boat with mail and provisions goes over several times a week."

"Does it take passengers? Could we go across?"

"If you'd like. I went once and got sick."

"I thought you never got sick."

"The waves were big." It was apparent that this recollection made her uneasy. "Up there," she said, pointing north, "are the Fox Islands. You can't see them unless it's this clear. I don't think anybody lives on them. That one looks like a mountain peak."

To the right of the wash, as far north as he could see, the steep fall of the bluff was forested. About a half mile down the shore, a point, banded by a beach, curved out into the water. Near the end of the point, an area of water was stained brown in a shape too small and too regular to be a drop-off or cloud shadow. "And that," he said, pointing to the stain. "What's that?"

"Hooper Cove."

"No, no. That square thing beside the cove. Straight out from that big rock. See?"

"Oh, that. That's a wreck. Submerged. A big tanker ran aground in a storm once."

"When?"

"It's been there as long as I can remember."

"Has anybody tried to salvage it?"

"Part of it used to be above water, and I think somebody came out with torches one winter, when there was ice, and cut that part off and took it away."

"What about what's below. Have any skin divers been down?"

"I don't think so. They're just farmers here, and it's been sunk so long nobody thinks about it any more."

"Have you ever looked at it?"

"I've been swimming by it."

"What's it like?"

"Just a steel hull with some holes in the top where the cutting was done."

"How big are the holes."

"Bigger than doors."

"Have you ever gone through them, inside it?"

"Of course not. Why?"

"My God, who knows what might be in there!"

"What, for instance?"

"Who knows? We'll go down some day and check it out, all right?"

"If you want."

"How do you get to the beach?"

"There's a trail leading through the woods, at the edge of the wash, there to your right. You can see where it starts."

He walked over to it. A clay path, littered with twigs and dead leaves, slanted down the face of the bluff, then turned off to the left and was obscured by ground hemlock and trees. For this evening, that would have to wait, but now there was a renewed clarity and dimension to the place, the lake, to her at the edge of the bluff, to the islands she was staring at; and even the scenery, which reminded him of much of Wisconsin, took on a new depth. That wreck. Why should it excite him so?

Why not?

He went back to her side and stepped a little ahead of her, so he could see toward the south. A growth of cedar and spruce traveled up that side of the wash, starting in a broad swath at the bottom and gradually narrowing into a V whose tip didn't quite reach to the top of the bluff. There must be another wash on the other side of the trees; they grew on a high mound, which was fringed at its edge with drooping roots and stood in the wash like an island in a forking river. A sharp dorsal of clay curved down from the lip of the bluff to the point of this island. There was a flat sandy area in front of the island, and he noticed some burned logs there, and was about to ask her if they picnicked in that spot, or had fires at night, and, if they did, how they got to the place, when suddenly he said, "Jesus," and shoved her back with his arm.

"Chris, what is it?"

"Look," he cried, and in the stillness his voice rang over the lake. "Look!"

He raised his arms as though holding a rifle, and in its imaginary sights he followed the thing he'd spotted, a large clumsy animal—a porcupine? a badger? a beaver? a woodchuck!—he followed a woodchuck hurrying up the dorsal of clay, sending small rocks scattering down the wash as it scrambled for its life toward the island of cedar.

"Blam!" he said, centering it in his sights. "*Blam! Blam!*"

. . . 2

They had not planned on having to counsel with a preacher. They no longer believed in the formalities of the faiths they were brought up in, if in the faiths themselves, and neither of them had been in a church for years, but they felt uneasy about a marriage ceremony in a courthouse or office or kitchen, conducted by a judge or justice of the peace. "That's so gross and public," was her opinion. "Too slam bang," he said. So while they waited for their blood specimens to be evaluated by the state, he began making phone calls from the motel room they'd taken in Madison. First he tried the nondenominational chapels, the congregational churches, the quasi-religious brotherhoods; few of them answered their phones, and most that did sounded suspicious of him. Others sounded suspicious to him. Finally he reached a certain number and talked happily for a few minutes, and then in morose monosyllables for a long time. He hung up.

"The Bahais are out," he said.

"What's that?" She was in the bathroom.

"No go with the Bahais."

"How come?"

"You need signed certificates from the family of each participant and the council, whatever that is, only convenes once a month. They just met yesterday."

"Oh." She emerged from the bathroom with a white towel, just wide enough to reach from her underarms to her thighs, wound around her.

"How about an out-and-out church?" he said.

"As long as we don't have to convert."

"What's something neuter?"

"Some Christian Scientists I know were married in the Presbyterian Church."

He dialed the First Presbyterian church and was informed by a cheery secretary that the pastor was on a lecture tour and would be back in two weeks, at which time the pastor would be more than happy to meet with them and discuss their prospective marriage, but when he pressed her with the urgency of the matter, she said, well, prehaps in *that* case, her voice growing stony, the assistant pastor could help, and switched him to a different line.

"Reverend Nelson Hartis. May I serve you?"

"I believe so, sir. My fiancée and I would like to get married."

"Bless you!"

"But we have a rather unique situation here."

"Ah."

Watch those thoughts. "Right. My fiancée is a Christian Scientist."

"Ah, yes, yes, I see. The Scientist faith has no provision for the sacrament of matrimony, isn't that correct?"

"True."

"Well, we've married many, many young Scientists— the hand of the Lord is one and the same, you know— and they've all seemed well satisfied with the way it was handled, and some of them, in the end, have even turned to our church. Just last Sunday I saw a young couple, Scientists whom I married this winter, sitting in the congregation. So your fiancée needn't feel troubled. Are you in regular attendance?"

"No. I'm from out of town."

"You're Presbyterian, however."

"No. I'm not. That's another thing." Why say that? Why not lie?

"Oh. What faith are you?"

"I claim none."

"We don't marry atheists!" the minister said, and broke into hearty laughter.

"Oh, I'm not one of those. It's just that I was brought up Catholic, you know, pressure of family, and once I broke from that I haven't claimed any specific faith. I'm still looking. In fact, I've attended the Presbyterian church quite often, and many times wished I belonged to it. That's why we'd like to be married there."

"I see. Well, these are things that can be ironed out in good time. Were you planning on a June ceremony?"

"No. We were thinking of the end of this week."

"Whoa, now. That's impossible!"

"Impossible?" He put as much crushed disappointment into it as he could. "Why?"

"Well, here you are, two young people of faiths that are hardly reciprocal, asking me, a minister of a third faith, a man in whom God's care has been entrusted and who my parishioners look to for guidance, asking me to marry you, total strangers, on the spot! The least we ask of nonmembers is that they study with us for several weeks, or months, until they fully understand the gravity and seriousness of the state they're entering into."

"We realize that. We're well educated, and both very religious, as I mentioned, and we've been engaged for three years."

"Holy smoke, *three years!*"

"That's what I mean. We've been putting it off and putting it off, because we both wanted to finish school first, but now we feel we've put it off too long, and, well, you know how long engagements can get." He let that rest for a while in the silence of the wires. "I realize the pressure it must put on you, such short notice, and all, and I'm sorry about that, but it's only because I have to get back to Chicago."

"Chicago?"

"I go to graduate school there."

"And your fiancée?"

"She goes to school here."

"And after you're married?"

"There's only about a week of school left."

"Three weeks here."

"Right." Sweat came out on his forehead. "We plan to commute until then."

"Is that wise?"

"I don't think there's any way of getting around it."

"I see."

There was a long silence.

"What's your name?"

"Christofer Van Eenanam."

"Goodness! How do you spell that?"

He spelled it for him.

"And your wife's? Pardon. I'm sorry!" There was some more hearty, low-ringing laughter. "Good Lord, I have you married already! What's your *fiancée's* name?"

"Ellen Strohe." He spelled that, too.

"Can you meet me tonight— Let's see; choir practice, and that, and that . . . Can you meet me in my office—it's in the new brick addition at the back of the church—at, say, eight thirty tonight?"

"Sure."

"You and"—some rustling of paper—"and Ellen. Ellen, too."

"Certainly."

"This is indeed, as you said, a knotty problem. I think we should all sit down and hash it over."

They reaffirmed the time and place, and Chris hung up. "Whew!"

"What is it?" she asked. "How did he sound?"

"Chunky. Bald. Fortyish. The homesy type. Dedicated, but agreeable as hell."

"Then he'll do it?"

"That remains to be seen. We meet tonight to hash it over."

"You're sure you want to go through with it?"

"I have for three years."

"The church thing, I mean."

"What have we got to lose? I can't go back to Chicago anyway until I'm certified syph-less and we get the license."

"Oh, God!" she exclaimed, and he jumped from the bed as though it were burning.

"What is it?"

"What can I wear?"

"Oh, for Christ's sake, is that all." Trying to relax, he sighed, and slowly sat down again. "Well, not Levi's."

"No, I mean—you know." She blushed. They were both shy of openly naming her condition. "If I wear a shift or anything loose and comfortable, he'll think, he'll *assume*—"

"The right thing."

"—and if I wear anything tight . . ."

"What?"

She smiled, and looked up from lowered lids. "He'll think me a brazen woman."

"You mean," he said, and took hold of the towel tucked at her breasts and jerked it so she spun in a circle and unwound from it, naked. "You mean you don't want the Reverend to see *this*."

She continued to turn, lifting her arms above her head, making a graceful pirouette of it, and pirouetted again and again, caught up in the youth and grace of her body, spinning around the room, the light from the blinds lying in pale stripes across her, stripes that slid over her skin as she lifted and fell with each pirouette and then, as she dropped onto the bed, lay lateral across her. "No," she said, and lifted her arms. "No. Here. That's for you, just for you now."

. . . 3

She wore a shift after all, a pale paisley print with a lace collar and long sleeves, but she belted it with a linked chain so that her slim waist was emphasized and the curves of her hips and breasts were subdued by the loose, gathered material. They arrived at the church at eight twenty-five, entered the new addition (cinder block painted beige), and located a door with the plastic shingle *Rev. Nelson Hartis* nailed to it. Chris knocked. There was no response. Praying? He waited until eight thirty and knocked again, then again, then once more, harder. "Are you sure you had the right time?" she asked. "Positive. I wrote it down." He searched through his pants pockets, his suit coat, his billfold, but couldn't find the slip of paper. She leaned against the wall.

"Do they wear garb?" she asked.

"What's that?" He hadn't heard her.

"The black suits and white collars."

"Oh. I don't know. I've never been a Presbyterian."

He stared at the clock suspended from the ceiling of the corridor, hardly listening to what she said, growing more and more nervous with each jerk of the second hand, unable to pace because he thought it might look bad if the minister appeared, and watched ten minutes go past. The knot of the unfamiliar necktie constricted

43

his throat, which was dry, and he kept putting his right hand into his jacket pocket or clasping it with the left, trying to conceal the band of white skin that was visible since he'd removed the ring.

"I better do the talking," she said.

"Should we forget about it?"

"It's up to you."

"Five more minutes. If I make it through this, I'm going to jump up in the air and click my heels."

"Promise?"

"To find out whether I'm still in one piece."

They heard hurried footsteps moving through the main, vaulted part of the church, and in a few seconds double doors winged outward at the end of the corridor and a young man of medium build, in a sport coat and bright tie, came toward them with a brisk step, his blond crew cut and the lenses of his glasses flashing each time he passed an overhead light. "Am I sorry!" the man said, still coming toward them. "But we're in hot water here. Our organist just quit, just up and quit right in the middle of practice and I had to carry on as well as I could, and we need somebody to play at a service tomorrow—I'm not good enough, or my wife— and my superior's not here and, oh, what a mess! I've searched around and sought advice and made phone calls and still have no replacement. We might have to enlist a Nazarene. Well!" he said, standing between them now, his hands clasped in front of him. "You must be Ellen"—he bowed toward her—"and you must be Christofer."

"It was nice of you to remember our names," Chris said.

"Oh!" The man placed his hands, fingers outspread, on his jacket front. "I'm Nelson Hartis."

They shook hands, and as Chris stared into the minister's eyes, perfectly round and pale blue, as unabashed and open as his manner, he felt now was his chance to get out of it all—this meeting, responsibility, the marriage, everything—to run for it, and he thought he saw a faint reflection of his feeling, like light glancing off water, appear in the minister's eyes. But the minister smiled and said, "I hope you don't mind my saying right off that you're one of the finest and healthy and adult-looking young couples I've met." He then unreeled some keys from a spool at his belt, unlocked the door, and swung it open. "Come in," he said. "Come in, come on in! I'm bashful, too."

His desk was littered with notes, monogrammed stationery covered with loopy handwriting, books open at markers, and balled paper. "Sermons, sermons, sermons," he murmured. "I have to do all the sermonizing now." He sat down in a swivel chair, impatiently elbowing some of the clutter aside so there was room for his arm to rest, and indicated two other seats; one standing alone in the center of the room, and the other beside his desk. Chris, who had a vulnerable back (if he ever got it, got it for good, he knew it would come from behind), took the chair beside the desk and moved its back against the wall.

"So you were brought up Christian Scientist," the minister said to Ellen.

"Yes."

"When I was in seminary we had to study comparative religions, for cases just such as yours, and I remember it as being one of the faiths that interested me most. Very unusual and self-sustaining. Very unusual. You still follow it faithfully?"

"Well—" she said, inclining her head and folding her hands in her lap, assuming her demure pose, while Chris thought, that's it, be the saint, don't complicate things.

"—lately I haven't."

"Oh. I understood . . ." The minister glanced at Chris and Chris looked at Ellen.

"Oh, I subscribe to the tenets," she said, and flashed a smile. "It's just that I don't read the lesson every morning, the minute I wake, dreading something disas-

trous will happen if I don't, and I'm sure all doctors
aren't dirty old men."

The minister chuckled.

"And I've not become disillusioned; man's mere existence, to me, presupposes a greater existence, as this
galaxy does others—how expand our knowledge if
we're limited by man and not reaching toward an Infinite? But lately I guess I've become more eclectic and
more a realist."

"How's that?"

"Too many Christian Scientists are out of touch and
one-minded. They believe theirs is the only way, and
they become disdainful and superior. I'm sure you've
seen the type. They don't even notice dead animals. Or
there's the other extreme, the ones who are overly
complacent and assume that as long as they go to
church and read the lesson everything will work out, all
will unfold, as they say, and happen as it was ordained
to happen without the least effort on their part. I can't
be that way. I believe we're in a real world and have a
real commitment to it."

" 'Unto Caesar what is Caesar's'?"

"Not so much that as 'I am that I am,' which I
interpret not as a pompous declaration of self, but an
outcry—the cry in the wilderness, if you like—to remind us our uniqueness is malleable and must be self-
expanded to do the most good. For ourselves and for
others, too."

"A unique interpretation," the minister said, tapping
his forefingers together. He swiveled to Chris. "And
what do you think of all this?"

"About the same way."

"You mean you two have talked this over?"

"Oh, yes. Many times. For three years. I've read
Science and Health." His face paled.

She rescued him, launching into a long speech about
One God, in whom all men and therefore all churches
rested, with which the minister seemed to agree, and
they bantered Biblical quotations back and forth. Was

she trying to snow the minister? Chris couldn't tell. When she got caught up in conversation, only the moment, the passion of talk, was important to her. Whether she was trying to snow him or not, she was. Chris watched the minister's blond eyebrows rise above the black frames of his glasses as she spoke of the wholly personal relationship to God, which to her was most important, and which she felt no church represented since everybody was an individual, a church in himself, you might say; and in her speech she managed to make reference to Thomas Aquinas, St. John of the Cross, Spinoza, Malraux, and Camus.

"I'm not up on all these mystics," the minister said. "Have you considered just having a civil ceremony?"

"I think they're *un*civil," she said. "I was at one once where two people raised their hands, mumbled something, and paid ten dollars, and it was so godless and arbitrary and businesslike. I wouldn't feel we were married. I'd feel, as that couple must, that we were merchandise—two bundles a busy clerk tied together."

The minister's belly began to heave.

"With cheap string," she said.

The minister broke into his hearty, low-ringing laughter. "I'll have to remember that," he said. "I'll have to use that in a sermon."

"After all," she said, "it's a sacrament, isn't it?"

"Yes," the minister said, growing solemn. "Yes, it is." He turned to Chris and seemed perplexed and nervous, as though he were more at ease with women. "Now, you're sure about your background?"

"What's that?" Chris said.

"Your Catholic upbringing."

"What do you mean?"

"That there's no hidden danger there."

"Danger?"

"That it's no scar that might cause strife between you."

"Oh, no. No, as I think I mentioned, I gave up the

church—not faith—a long time ago, way back in high school."

"Why was that?"

"Why does anybody?"

"Yes," the minister said, and his staring eyes didn't blink.

"I just couldn't take it."

"Oh?"

"I couldn't go along with most of the dogma."

"What, in particular," the minister asked, and leaned back in his (distractingly silent) swivel chair and made (appropriately enough) a steeple of his forefingers.

"Oh, I don't know," Chris said, and shrugged his shoulders. "The infallibility of the Pope . . ." There was a long silence. She couldn't help him here. He rummaged through twelve years of catechism (Holy Christ, was that all he could come up with?), and was about to mention confession, Latin, the transubstantiation, Fatima, anything.

"Yes," the minister said. "That particular one's a stickler for lots of Catholics."

Thank you, Chris almost said aloud, Thank you, thank you.

"The Godhead is the only Supreme Being," Ellen declared.

"That's true," the minister said. "Do you agree?"

"Oh," Chris said, trying to erase the image aroused by that strange word, Godhead: a big purple one. "Oh, sure. Of course."

Using the end of his thumb, the minister hiked his glasses higher on his wide nose, crossed his arms, and stared at Chris as though he sensed his uneasiness and was wary of it. "It's hard to believe, isn't it, unless it's instilled in you from birth, that a human, any human, could be infinitely perfect, infallible, completely without fault?"

"I don't believe Mary Baker Eddy was," Ellen said.

The minister's laughter eased the tension in the room.

"For instance," Ellen said, "she never accounts for the phenomenon of death. She evades the topic, really, by saying that death is Unreal, a manifestation of Material mind, and that the Material and the Unreal don't exist. It's a closed circle. Because of it, I've never understood death. If everything is a part of Infinite Mind, or God, as she claims, and Infinite Mind is synonymous with Infinite Life, as she claims, how can there be death? Jesus said, 'Consider the lilies of the field, how they grow; they toil not, neither do they spin: And yet I say unto you, That even Solomon in all his glory was not arrayed like one of these.' Then why do lilies die? I'm sure all this is sophistry, but it's because I love flowers."

"Of course," the minister said, stroking one of his rounded cheeks. "Of course," he repeated (in reference to *what?*), and turned once again, as though to get down to business, toward Chris.

Suddenly Chris said, "Technically, I suppose, you could think of me as a Christian Scientist, if you want, if it would simplify things, since they don't require baptism or any kind of formal conversion."

"Now there's a thought," the minister said.

"And he has read *Science and Health*," Ellen said, "and gone to church with me."

"I assume you know the Ten Commandments and follow them as Christians."

"Yes, of course," they both said, and Chris started a quick mental review of them. He couldn't remember the second one.

"Well, then," the minister said, "I think it's about time we got down to bare facts. Why do you want to get married?"

Chris and Ellen looked at one another, looked at the minister, and before either could speak, he said, "Certainly. Because you love each other. But why at this particular time?"

"As I mentioned," Chris said, "we've been engaged for three years, always vacillating back and forth—"

"Why the vacillation?"

"Just as to when would be the right date. First we thought when I graduated from college, then when *she* graduated, then we thought maybe we should wait till I got my doctorate."

"Was this because of the financial security involved? Don't be afraid to mention it. Heck, it's part of marriage. It's one thing besides religion that every couple should go into deeply, and I'm afraid enough don't. They get all carried away by the romance of the thing— marriage, I mean. Marriage should be that way, and it's wonderful if you can keep it so, but it's also hard fact. My wife and I—" He moved books and papers aside, revealing a photograph of a youthful, low-browed woman, and as he paused to study her face it was as if a fourth person had entered the conversation. His voice altered to accommodate for her. "My wife and I have been married six years and still find ourselves in hot water over finances. I think she thought all ministers are rich. Well, not so, not so."

Chris noticed that the minister's coat was ill-fitting, and there was shine on the knee of his slacks. Chris looked at the photograph. What did she think of him as a minister? a husband? a man? Her eyes were close-set and must be as gray as in the photograph. That cold even stare.

". . . seem enlightened, and you're both certainly intelligent, so I suppose it's something you've gone over soberly and in plenty of detail."

"Oh, yes," Chris answered. "And things have changed. I just won a fellowship, a big one, to a school in Chicago."

"Then how is it that you're here now?"

"It's a research fellowship. I work under another man, who sets up projects, and once I've finished a project I'm more or less free until the next one is prepared." Though this was true, Chris's voice took on such an unnatural tone as he spoke that it sounded like a lie even to him. He lowered his eyes and a rivulet of sweat streaked down the side of his rib cage.

"I see. So you came up here and all of a sudden decided to get married."

"It's not sudden. A three-year engagement? And we've been thinking about it more seriously these past months, ironing out minor problems"—the minister's language was infectious—"planning on dates, and so forth."

"Why not wait till school's out?"

Chris looked at Ellen. No help. "Well, we could, I suppose. But this week when we saw one another, even before we spoke, there was this feeling between us. We both knew that now was the time."

"Do you feel it was divine guidance?"

"Yes."

"I see. Well, were you thinking of a large ceremony, or a small one?"

"Small. Very small."

"Because the church itself couldn't be made available on such short notice. We do have an auxiliary chapel, however, that will seat over a hundred. How many people did you expect?"

"Just us, I guess. Whatever witnesses are needed."

The minister leaned forward in his chair, looking scandalized. "No *family?*"

"No, I don't think."

"Not even parents?"

"I have no parents," Ellen said. "I lost them in an accident."

"Oh, I'm sorry," the minister said, and Chris saw that for the first time in her life this might be an asset.

"It was a long time ago," she said.

"Well, I'm very sorry. You must have strong sustaining faith to keep so bright and cheerful as you are. But don't you have relatives or guardians that you'd like to have present, or who'd like to see you get married? It only happens once, you know."

"There are just my grandparents," she said, and her

voice became colorless and faint. "My grandfather's always busy at his office. He owns a big business. My grandmother has women's clubs and church leagues she has to attend. She's chairman of two. She handles many projects."

"Well, that's too bad!" the minister said, and his rounded cheeks flushed with indignation. He studied her for a long time, and then, in a voice so gentle and soothing she could have been a lost child, said, "What is your age, Ellen?"

"Twenty-one."

"Well, you're certainly of legal age to do as you see fit." He turned to Chris. "And your age is—"

"Twenty-three."

"And your family?"

"You know how the break is when a family's strongly Catholic. Bad. I haven't seen them for two years. I consider myself independent."

"I see. Well, perhaps your marriage might be a way to build new bridges."

"That's what we want," she said. "We want to do it quietly, on our own, to show our strength."

"You mustn't do it in rebellion."

"No, not that. I was away from home for a year. I've had rebellion. I want peace."

"I can see how marriage might be a haven for you, but you can't expect it to heal old wounds."

"I don't. I expect it to be difficult at times, but not too complicated—and unselfish. And I hope the unselfishness will be an example to others."

The minister looked at Chris with more directness, his pale eyes bright—reevaluating him, Chris felt, to judge if he was fit for her—and Chris gave back the most piercing, manful stare he could summon. The minister's eyes fell, he swiveled to his desk, unbuttoned his sport jacket, and hiked his glasses higher. He picked up a piece of paper, held it at shoulder level without looking at it, then let it fall and sail off to one side. "Oh, all right," he murmured. "I'll do it."

"Oh, thank you!" she said.

"God, that's great." Watch the tongue.

"Could it be on Friday?" she asked.

"Whoa, now. Hold up a minute. There are a few things that need to be gone into first." He turned to Chris and folded his arms. "Now, you must not lust after your wife."

"Oh, no."

"There's a great difference between an object of lust and the love for spouse, and you . . ." There was a long explanation with particular details, drawn mostly from teenage sensations and experience, and Chris listened with lowered eyes, feeling as trapped as he had in confessionals, and murmured assent. For the first time, he noticed, the minister became formal and strained. Did people only lecture on what they feared? Then the minister talked about the importance of religion in family life and in bringing up children, and his free-wheeling manner began to return. ". . . and I can't stress enough the importance of daily prayer. Just this afternoon my wife and I had an argument over something as silly as a phone bill, and I'll confess there were harsh words between us. Now this may sound childish to you, but when two people live on such intimate terms the smallest details can be the most maddening, and today I got so angry—I'll admit it, you'll feel the same way sometime, so don't be surprised—that I just wanted to walk out on her, for good. But then I went to her and said, 'Is this what we want?' 'No.' 'Is this what God wants?' 'No.' So we got down on our knees and prayed together and from then on the day's been wonderful! Now I want . . ."

Chris lowered his eyes in embarrassment. He remembered taking his grandfather, a wiry, taciturn man, by the elbow, and helping him kneel on the hard floor of their farmhouse to pray the rosary during Lent, and watching his grandfather's head with its rich thatch of white hair nod gently at each naming of Jesus, and wondering what his grandfather, who didn't have long to live, really thought of religion and death. Then, one afternoon, Chris was summoned from high school to the hospital where his grandfather lay dying. The hospital room was filled with relatives and friends, as though their massed presence could sustain another life, and when Chris appeared his grandfather beckoned to him. Chris went to the bedside. His grandfather took him by the hand and then made an impatient gesture with his head. Chris bent his ear close to the old man's lips. "Chris," he whispered. "You got sense. I don't know where I'm going to go. If I get to purgatory, I'll be there for a long time, if I get there, so you pray for me, ya? They won't. I got so old they think I'm a saint. You got more sense." The pressure on Chris's hand became emphatic. "*You* pray for me." That afternoon he died. He was the one who had held the family together.

"... a lot of young couples, and I like to tell them to think of their marriage in terms of a sculptor, such as Michelangelo, working at his art. Suppose he chiseled a face, a beautiful face, one that could never be matched, in a big piece of marble. Now the face is all he has and he's working to create a complete person with body, limbs, and what adornments he wants. Now suppose he sees a piece of raw marble, perhaps of better quality than the one he's working with, or so it would seem, and perhaps he would like it. But would he throw aside what he has, the finished face—who knows what hidden flaws might lie in the other—and begin all over with the new piece? No, I think not. Not if he's sensible and smart. I don't think he'd risk losing the beauty he's created. So it is in marriage. We work to improve and perfect the creation we begin at the altar, and we work daily with all our diligence and skill, and our artwork is never done." The minister had fallen into what Chris assumed was his tone for sermons, and now he looked from one to the other as if to gauge his effect, and then added, "Not until God calls us." He seemed uneasy mentioning the name at such close range. "Well," he said, suddenly using his feet to propel his chair backward. "Let me just end by giving you these."

He leaned over to a bookcase, his chair groaning in protest for the first time, and took up two pamphlets from a shelf, then pedaled himself forward and handed one to each. *Our First Month Together*, the cover read.

"In these you'll find prayers and spiritual food for each day of the week. We like to think that after the first month it becomes a habit with the young couple."

"Thank you," Chris said, and slipped it into his pocket.

"Well, I have your names and ages, and I suppose you know about the license and will take care of that?"

"Yes."

"So all I'll need right now are the names of the witnesses. There have to be at least two."

Chris looked at her, startled, and she lowered her eyes. If she had no one in mind, who? Finally, Chris gave the name of a married couple he'd been friendly with a year ago, hoping they still lived in Madison.

"And, Ellen, you say you'd like the service to be on Friday?"

"Yes, if it could."

"About what time?"

"At sunset."

"Let's see," the minister said, and shuffled through some papers, then threw up his hands. "Why not? I know I'm free then. Fridays are dead for me. That's when I work up my sermons. All right, we'll meet on Friday, then, at seven, is that good? Good. And you bring along the license and your witnesses. Come right to the office here. The chapel is just down the hall. Now let's say the Lord's Prayer."

They bowed their heads and said the Lord's Prayer with him, and as they stood Chris almost cried out with relief, it was so good to be on his feet, free, flexing muscle. They were at the door, ready to leave, when the minister said, "Oh. Oh, yes. One more thing." He went to his desk, pulled open the top drawer, and handed a book to Chris.

"We ask all our young couples to read this before the ceremony."

Chris turned the book over in his hands, searching its white cover, which had a cross of magenta in its center, for a title or author, but there was only the cross.

"It deals with practical matters that may not have occurred to you," the minister said, and seemed impatient for them to leave. "I'll ask you both to read it through and return it to me on Friday, and if there are any questions you can ask me then. Otherwise, just be here at seven." He smiled and shook hands with them, and said, "God bless you."

They had only gone a couple of steps down the corridor when the office door closed behind them with a click. It was a quarter to eleven. They walked the length of the corridor in silence, without looking at one another, and Chris pushed open the plate-glass door. The outside air was chilly. Chris stopped and breathed it, watching insects dive through the light of a pole lamp, beneath which her car was parked, at the far end of the lot. She laid her hand on his sleeve.

"Just let me stand a minute," he said.

"What's wrong? Why were you so tight?"

"Who knows?"

"He was okay."

"A bit persistent. I think his mother was frightened by a nun."

"He reminded me of a jolly P.E. major. But he's not as naïve as he pretends. He suspects, I think."

"Maybe that's why I was tight."

"But he was so natural about it. He's going to do it."

"I wonder what his superior would say."

"Unconditionally, no."

"Is he just being a good Joe then, or what?"

"He's kind. And I think he believes he's doing the right thing."

"Divine guidance?"

"Just the right thing."

He turned to her. "El. Do you really believe all that?"

"What?"

"You know. Religion— *You* know."

"Oh, that. In Christian Science you learn a kind of lingo. It rolls off the tongue."

She was lit from behind and in the darkness he couldn't see her features, but there was darkness in her voice also, as though she were naming a loss.

He opened the cover of the book. "Holy God," he whispered. He lifted away the dust jacket. "Jesus! 'Practical matters that may not have occurred to you'!"

"What is it?"

Chris glanced over his shoulder. "Is he coming?"

"No."

"I read this when I was ten. Found it in a closet."

He showed her the cover: *Sane Sex Life and Sane Sex Living.*

"Oh, no!" she said. "Before I started college, Grandpa *made* me read that."

They started giggling.

"We better get out of here," he said, and they started toward the car, crunching over crushed rock.

"Wait," she said, and took him by the arm. "Wait. You promised."

"What?"

"The leap in the air. The kick of the heels." She was giddy.

"You really want it?"

"Yes!"

During his scenery-painting days, he'd been enlisted to do the opening to a dance scene that the male lead of the musical couldn't do—a high-flying leap, high as the dancer's shoulders, with a sudden side kick to it, whose momentum carried him halfway across the stage; followed by another leap that took him behind a teaser, from which point the male lead emerged, dancing at ground level with his partner. Ellen came to every performance, and he imagined he could hear her "Ah!" above the rest of the audience.

"Here," he said. "Hold the comic book."

He took some short sprinting steps, getting the feel of the ground, the feel of his legs and muscles, then broke into stride, the air brushing like gauze over his ears, and when he reached top speed he suddenly leaped, feeling free, a light beast, a deer, a gazelle, a winged thing, and then KICKED and came down. She trotted up to him, a broad smile on her face, applauding quietly. "Beautiful!" she said. "It's the best you've ever done it."

After they had gone a ways toward the car, he started saying, with each alternate step, "Oo— Oo— Oo" and getting the weight off his left foot quick. He sat down on the front bumper of the car and took his boot in his hand. "Crushed rock!" he said.

"What is it?"

"You better drive. I think I sprained my goddamn ankle."

THREE

"YOU WOULDN'T," she said. "You *couldn't* do it!"

"No, no, of course not. I was just playing, for God's sake."

He was alarmed by the way her eyes had widened, overlarge, brimming with fright and defense, as though his imaginary shots at the woodchuck were an attack on her.

"It would ruin this place," she said. "Violate it. Everything here lives in its natural state. Nobody ever hunts."

"Not even in the fall? Or winter?"

"We've never been up then."

"I bet they do."

"They shouldn't. It's private property. And the area is so wild it maintains its balance naturally. Ravens come down from the Upper Peninsula, and even eagles have been seen."

"Bald eagles?"

"Yes."

"I'll be damned," he said, feigning interest to keep up the conversation and mitigate her fear and mistrust.

"A lot of the farmers around have identified them. One used to nest just past the cove."

"Did you ever see it?"

"We were never up early enough."

"Maybe we'll see one this year."

"Maybe."

The sun had sunk lower and the surface of the lake, riffled by wind, was pink from horizon to shore. The beach was now bright red, the cedars blue, and the wash was welling up with lavender shadow. Bank swallows began spilling out of holes at the lip of the bluff and went swooping after insects. The gulls were moving inland. Large clusters of them passed overhead, crying to one another as though lost, their voices high, brassy, childlike, as senseless and unsettling as fingernails raked over classroom slate.

She lifted her head to watch, and said in a gentle voice, but as though to chide them, "How raucous!"

When there was silence, she looked over the lake again. "It's the only place we could have come. *Here's* where we make our beginning. The month apart doesn't count."

"What about the year?"

He was sorry he said it. She lowered her head and drew her coat closer around her. "That's over," she said. "It's over now. It has no place here, either."

It's in me, he wanted to say. "I know. I didn't mean it. It's nothing, it's over, you're right. Let's forget the damn thing."

"Please."

"I'll never mention it again."

More gulls came over, flying so low that their sharp cries fell around them like metallic shafts.

He took the scrap of paper with the instructions scrawled on it out of his pocket: *Fuse box is in back porch. So is water heater. Make sure water heater is full before you turn on juice. If water isn't running go to pumphouse up in meadow and turn on pump.* Her grandfather. That was a scene he didn't want to repeat. The old man, who had been deathly silent for several days, suddenly said to Ellen, "Think of your mother. Have you no respect for her memory? Running off like this and marrying—" It took just one flash of his eyes on Chris to convey the sum of his contempt. What the hell, Chris wanted to say, we all have our little faults, but he sat silent, more intimidated and withdrawn than he'd been with the minister.

He shrugged his shoulders and tried to shake it off (he and Ellen were alone now, away from them, it made no difference), and brightened his voice. "Well, to trivialities. We'll want hot water for showers."

"Wait," she said. "Come here first. Look at the sun."

He went to her side and put his arm around her. The sun was half set, a bowl overturned, staining the expanse of the water. The wind had risen and it was growing cold. From far below he heard a faint sound; aroused by the wind, by the movement of the moon, by whatever aroused it, the water was beginning to stir and break in small waves on the beach.

"Here I'm elemental," she said.

"What?" He'd just seen three big black birds flap out of a tree near the point where the wreck lay submerged and fly out of sight around the cove, soundless.

"I'm elemental here," she repeated.

"Oh," he said, and looked at the sunset. "Yeah. Nice."

. . . 2

There was the question of who should tell her grand-parents. "I think it would be easier on them if they heard it from me," she said, as they drove from Madison toward Milwaukee the day after he'd arrived by bus. "But they're going to be furious," he said. "Or worse. I don't want you to have to face that." They deliberated and debated, taking and changing sides, both of them growing more and more nervous, and finally he declared, "No, no, that's no good. *I'll* do it." He suddenly turned solemn. "It's my place." He wouldn't be argued out of it. He became intractable and even more solemn. Then she said, "Of course. You're right. It has to be you." She was at the wheel, and she pushed her weight against the back of the seat as if in relief.

They were driving through the county in which he'd been born and raised, and he watched the countryside go speeding past, seeing as if for the last time the neat pattern of pasture, field, and summer fallow, the houses and farm buildings so trim and well-kept they seemed covered with a coat of fresh paint, and the Holsteins, like jigsaw cutouts to be fit into memory, grazing on the rolling land. And as he watched it all go past, filling slowly with a sense of loss, he tried to formulate an opening line. "Anybody, when they've reached a certain age, should have the freedom to act as they see fit, and we—" Christ, that sounded like the Constitution. "Since you've last seen me I've changed, I've been very busy, I've finished school, I almost have my Master's, I've won—" No use getting self-righteous before they knew why he was there. "For three years now Ellen and I have been in love—" He'd be stopped by laughter or a scream. Love? "Before you started calling anybody names—" Say. A bit defensive?

Then again, he might have to be; the one time he'd seen her grandparents, during an Easter vacation, he'd been pleasant and ingratiating and that hadn't worked. To begin with, he was rendered speechless at the sight of their house. From the manner in which Ellen dressed, and from the simplicity of her few personal articles, he had assumed that she came from a background similar to his. The house, situated on a low wooded hill of several acres, was a labyrinth of more than seventeen rooms. A gray-brick tower with a balcony rose like a battlement at its west end. There was an open, glassed-over garden in the north wing where plants, flowers, and trees grew. One section of the house, which included a kitchen, a den, an office, and a dining room, was stark and modern. This section was termed "lived in" and throughout the rest of the house the carpets, tapestries, and furnishings were antique, and of a different period in each room: there was the Louis Quinze room, the Colonial room, the French Provincial, the authentic Early American, the Late Stuart. Others.

During the day, when Ellen was talking with her grandmother in the kitchen, Chris wandered mindlessly through the maze of the multilevel house, staring at paintings, picking up *objets d'art*, looking at books, studying the furnishings—trying to remember which was the way to the kitchen and which to the john, while he waited for Ellen's grandfather to return from work so the two of them could talk. In every room Chris entered (he assumed the old man's office, his library, the basement, the bedrooms, and the exercise room were off limits), he noticed the same thing; in spite of the lavish décor and the impeccable arrangements, there wasn't a single ash tray. No ash trays anywhere. It didn't bother him, he wasn't a heavy smoker and he'd stopped a week ahead in training for the time he was to spend here, but didn't they entertain people who smoked?

When he got tired of wandering, he went up to the tower, a sitting room, and looked out at the view. On one side of the wooded hill was a park where children were playing, their bright cries sometimes reaching him where he stood, and on the other side was a country club and golf course, with the buildings of Milwaukee visible in the distance. The dimness of the rooms. The stillness of the house. A pall of old age and opulence. Up a boxed stairway. Down a circular one to another level. Onto a platform used for dining. Down a long hall. Up a couple of steps to the garden, a fountain splashing in its center.

Occasionally he heard laughter as pleasant as Ellen's, but in a higher scale it never moved out of, and staccato, and he wondered what Ellen could have said to make her grandmother laugh. She was a slight, nervous woman, with sloping shoulders, large gray eyes, and gray hair coiled in a tight bun. She had a thin face and a long thin neck, and she always held her elbows tight against her sides. When she was in the house, no matter what else she wore she always wore the same garment over it—a man's sweater, maroon, with buttons up the front, that hung below her hips.

She showed Chris her lineage chart, chattering along in a gay but nervous manner, her large eyes flashing away from his when they met, and didn't give him much opportunity to speak. She smelled of soap and lilac sachet. As she pointed to the branch of the family that reached back to England, Chris noticed the skin of her hands; it was so thin it had a glazed appearance, and pigmented spots of gold and rose showed beneath its surface. That was the only occasion they really talked alone. She kept Ellen close to her the rest of the time (afraid of all those dark rooms?), chattering to her as gaily and as nervously as she had to him, but at the end of each of her long speeches to Ellen, she would say, "Not so?," leaving a space for Ellen to respond. The few times the old lady asked him a direct question, he answered in an offhand, boyish manner that seemed to please her. Once, when she was standing at the work counter chopping nuts, saying to Ellen that women nowadays got no joy out of menial tasks, that it was a thing that should be instilled in them when they were young, as it used to be, and that it was an art, a rewarding art, she glanced at Chris and he gave the old lady a wink. Her voice caught in her throat and she blushed scarlet.

He made one serious mistake with her. After he'd been visiting for a couple of days, she asked him what he thought of the house (he learned she'd helped plan and decorate it) and waited with a smile on her face, knowing she'd have to be complimented, but perhaps wondering if Chris could be original. He described several of his favorite rooms, remarking how tastefully everything had been arranged, naming particular pieces of furniture and color combinations; he mentioned that he liked the uncluttered, efficient part of the house they lived in, and said she must have used a mathematical equation to arrive at such a perfect balance between the two parts. "And I notice you have some valuable first editions." (One of his part-time jobs had been in the stacks of a library.) "I like the way you shelve them in rooms where the décor dates from about the time they were printed." From her pleased smile, he saw that this apparently was a detail few people noticed. "But," he said, returning her smile, "where are the ash trays?"

The smile went and her face took on a pale, stony cast. "Oh," she said. "You *smoke?*"

Had he for three days? The only way out, as he saw

it, was farther ahead. "Just in the mornings. Right when I wake up I like to have a big black cigar."

Her face got stonier, and she turned away and stalked into the kitchen and came back with a large brass ash tray, carrying it like cat litter. "Here," she said.

"No, no, no, I was just joking!"

"Here."

"A cigar like that would kill a man!"

"Here!"

"No, please, I was—"

"I'll *drop* it."

He refused to take it and protested enough so that she finally carried it back into the kitchen. That night, after a silent, mirthful scuffle in a john with Ellen, he went into his bedroom and saw that a plant stand with a spindle leg had been moved next to his bed. On its marble top was the brass ash tray.

When Ellen's grandfather returned from work, at seven or eight, slapping his hands together, slapping his hat over his coat (to remove dust, dandruff, the dregs of business?), and then, when the coat was removed, slapping his suit jacket and pants legs, he first went down to the basement and vacuumed his shoes. Then he came up to his office. Then he went to the library or den. Chris maneuvered around halls, stairs, and passageways, trying to position himself so he could be run into, but her grandfather usually kept a room or a level ahead of him. He was a stocky, heavy-jawed German with bright, bulging eyes and square patches of bristly eyebrows. He was totally bald, his broad dome sloping back from the bristly brows, and there was a network of raspberry vessels in the center of his cheeks. About the time Chris got discouraged and gave up his flanking movements, the old man would appear from somewhere, rubbing his hands together, then give a clap and cry out, "Well, boy, what have you got to say!"

The first night he put an arm around Chris's shoulder and led him to a couch and began to talk about his

brewery. He told Chris that every union boss should be
shot, that it was impossible to hire a common laborer
any more who did not think he owned a share in the
business (*bissiniss*, it sounded like; he had a German
accent), and about a new opening device for beer cans
he had invented that had made some of those cocksure
major brewers sit up on their big fat asses. Chris
blinked at this, but the old man himself didn't seem to
be listening to his talk. It was as though he used it to
gain detachment, because his bright, bulging eyes, the
blue of a blue bottle, kept flashing over Chris with a
personal interest that had nothing to do with what he
was saying; and from the vantage point of his real self
he seemed to be sizing Chris up. Then, just as Chris's
mind went blank and his eyes glazed, the old man
broke into an abrupt series of questions.

"What nationality's your dad?"

"Dutch."

"*Deutsch?*"

"Dutch."

"And Mom?"

"Finn."

"What do they do?"

"Farm."

"Farm?"

"Yes."

"Where?"

"Rock Creek."

"What size farm?"

"Eighty acres." Chris was prepared to expand on
this, to explain that his family had worked the same
land for a hundred years, yet their farm was one of the
most desirable properties in the area, that he'd always
felt closer to his grandfather, who had died, than to his
parents, but at that point the old man slapped him on
the leg and said, "But what's that between us, boy!"
and started talking again about his business. The blank-
ness of futility, and an uneasiness too, a growing one,

about the way the bright eyes were evaluating him. Then the questions:

"Do you like school?"

"Yes."

"What do you do there?"

"Study math."

"What else?"

"History, some——"

"I mean, what do you *do?*"

"Read. Work in a lab."

"That's it?"

"About."

"You mean you don't go out—for eats, to parties? Anything like that?"

"Not too much." Chris assumed the old man had statistics on how much beer was consumed on the campus in a week.

"I hear they have some sexy parties!" the old man said, and winked.

"I guess."

"You don't go?"

"Sometimes. Not too much."

"You keep that busy?"

"Usually, yes."

"Don't they have organizations there; political parties, church groups—all that you could join?"

"Oh, sure."

"What do you belong to?"

"An honor society."

"That's all?"

"I've worked with the theater group."

"An actor?"

"No, I——"

"Oh, so you're the *dancer* Ellen told us about."

Chris blushed. "That was just once, a bit part, just that one time. Mostly I work backstage. I can build, paint, do——"

"Aren't all those theater people——" The old man hunched down his head, raised his hands level with it, and wriggled his fingers as though playing tremolo on a piano. "You know. Fairies?"

"Oh, I don't think so. They're just students who—"

But the old man was off on another topic, politics this time. And now Chris noticed something different. As the old man rested within his detachment, keeping the barricade of talk between them, a wiliness began to shine in his eyes, a sly, wild humor. My god, was he being played with, Chris wondered, and a word (from an Elizabethan play?) that up until now had been only a vague shape covered with hair came to his mind: bearbaiting. Now, staring into those eyes, he felt he understood, in an emotional sense, the meaning of the word. But no sooner had he thought that than the old man became warm and avuncular, offered to show him some old photographs of Ellen, and led him off to the library with an arm around his shoulder.

Then, after they had looked through some family albums (with many pictures missing and parts of others clipped away), and had stepped out into the hall, another sudden grilling came:

"What faith are you?"

"Pardon?" His accent made it sound like "fate."

"What *faith* are you?"

"Oh. None, I guess."

"You mean you don't believe in God!"

"I didn't say that."

"In my book, any man that doesn't admit he believes in the Supreme Being is a chickenshit."

"I didn't say I didn't."

"Would you?"

"What?"

"Say it, say it!" the old man cried, his eyes brightening with the sly look. "Aw, don't let me scare you, boy," he said, and punched Chris on the shoulder and walked off. Then he went to the basement. Then to his office. Then he went to bed.

For three nights this continued. Her grandfather would ask him if he worked. Chris would remind him of his job in the lab. "No, no, I mean *work*, boy!" Then he would laugh and pat Chris on the thigh and say, "The Lord says you shall reap what ye sow," and would begin talking about Christian Science, whose truth had been revealed to him by the Grandma. On this subject he became unsure and repetitive, the barrier dropping from between them, or else shining-eyed and lyrical. Once, however, he got lost completely, couldn't find words, started groping as badly as Chris, and suddenly jumped to his feet and said, "Am I fit?"

"Sure."

"Do I look fit?" He passed his hand over his glossy skull. "Except this?"

"Certainly."

"Sock me."

"What?"

"Sock me in the gut."

"No."

"Come on, sock me! Are you chickenshit?" The old man started feinting and shadow-boxing, moving his heavy frame over the floor with the grace of a light-weight, and then stopped in the center of the room and broke into laughter, throwing his glossy head back so far that big wrinkles furrowed his bull neck. He came over to Chris and took him by the shoulders. "Boy," he said, giving Chris a slight shake. "Say, boy, I *like* you."

If Ellen came into the room during these proceedings, her grandfather would spring from the couch and cry, "Here's my girl!" and go to her and hug her and swing her from side to side, saying into her hair, "So long at *Schule*, so long at *Schule*, and why? For why?"

"Oh, Grandpa, don't!"

The old man would let go and step back. "*Look* at her. Look at this Ellen of mine." His eyes, bright with pride, would begin to gleam with emotion, tears brimming up.

"You're a marshmallow, Grandpa."

"What!" It was ritualized family talk.

"You're a marshmallow inside."

"Just for you, Ellen. Just for my girl."

Then they would face off, place hands on one another's shoulders, and begin to dance, her grandfather waltzing with his light step and singing in a rich baritone, " *'Du, du, du liegst mir im Herzen! Du, du, liegst mir im Sinn!'* . . ." For Chris, whose family was quiet and solemn and reserved in its show of affection, this was such an unusual sight, and there was such gaiety in the old man's face and in Ellen's laughter, that he felt his own eyes brim up as the old man's had.

Chris was supposed to stay on for the entire vacation, but after the third day had passed, Ellen's grandfather took him aside. The old man looked preoccupied and morose. Then he became apologetic. He said they hadn't been expecting anyone to visit, and he and the Grandma had planned a trip, a family trip, to see some friends up North. "You understand, don't you, boy?" he said, and patted Chris on the back. His voice and eyes seemed filled with genuine regret. "Have you ever flown, boy?" he asked.

And then he offered to pay Chris's plane fare home.

. . . 3

A. J. STROHE, the metal signpost read. She turned up the drive. Chris had not remembered the drive as being so long, nor bordered with so many trees, but time, as he'd learned, either contracted or expanded the shape of the past. It would not let it be. Insignificant objects— a shell fragment picked from a beach, a nestling's feather, a blue rubber ball—grew so massive the mind couldn't cope with them, and old landscapes, no matter how limitless, shrunk until you no longer fit into them. The house they moved toward, he noticed with detachment, was more formidable than the house he held in his mind, and then he felt he'd gone white with a wash of panic. He looked at Ellen. She seemed as tense as he was, guiding the car with care up the hill, her face set. "If they offer the lodge," she said suddenly, "let's take it."

"I don't want anything they offer."

"I know. But if they do, let's."

"It's a bad way to start."

"But you'd love it, I know you would, and I want to go there once more if I can. Last summer was the first time in ten years I didn't go."

"Why was that?" He knew.

"Oh—" Her arms lifted at the wheel, then fell. "I wasn't here when they left."

"You mean you were cattin-ass around New York."

72

"Don't," she said, and her face flushed. "Not now. It's going to be hard enough."

"Okay, okay, I'm sorry. Really. What the hell."

He stared out the window. Children, dressed in bright clothes, were playing on swings and bars in the nearby park. Was he dead wrong, or did designers, manufacturers, dyers—the whole works—did they purposely make the color of children's clothes brighter every spring?

She stopped in front of a three-car garage and put her hand on his thigh. "Chris?"

"I'm sorry," he said. "Christ."

"I am, too. About that. But we can't be down now. They'll misunderstand."

"They'll probably—"

"Oh!" she cried, startling him. "Winston. There's Winston!"

A tan and white dog as large as a Saint Bernard was coming in a clumsy plod toward the car, its enormous head lowered and swaying from side to side, its tongue hanging loose and dripping strings of saliva. It was her dog, as he'd learned during his other visit and from her reminiscences, and he could never understand why she cared so much for the ill-formed, odorous, shaggy thing —so old it seemed close to death. She got out of the car and ran to it and hugged it, pressing her cheek against its neck, which was as wide as its broad back and big head, and Chris caught phrases such as "... been so long, Winston, *so long* ... Pretty Boy, I thought I'd never ... Yes, you, you ... love you even more." Chris got out of the car and walked over to them. The dog was on its haunches, groaning and swinging its head around like a seal.

"This is Chris. Remember Chris, Winston?"

With a preoccupied glaze in its eyes, the dog moaned and shifted around on its haunches, trying to get a hind leg into position for a masturbatory scratch.

"I'll talk to you later, Pretty Boy." She stood up. "I'll go ahead and get them in a good mood. Then you come." She took him by the hand. "Don't worry. It'll work out. Just be yourself."

Then she went running into the house. Chris heard her grandmother's cries of delight, her staccato laughter and Ellen's cheerful voice, and then Ellen's laughter, cascading down the scale. He stood at the screen door for a long time, staring at the scrolled S on the pushbar, and finally opened the door and stepped inside. There was a high mirror, a bright rug, a milk bottle with a slip of paper in its neck, and some fur-topped boots. He felt like a housebreaker. He leaned against the wall. He'd never learned what Ellen's grandparents said to her on that trip North, other than never to see him again, but he could imagine; he could see her grandfather being jovial and candid with her (much more so than he'd been with him) in his devastating way. And her grandmother, with her sense of righteousness, her firm religion, and her ability to dramatize unforgivable hurt. Whatever was said, from that time on Ellen's confidence in him was undermined, and the arguments began.

—Forget the metaphysics of it, for Christ's sake, and just give a straight answer.

—I think I want to get married.

—What do you mean 'think'?

—I do, but in a while. Maybe after I've finished school and have a job and you have your doctorate.

—That's a *while?*

—It isn't long.

—Hell, I'll never get it.

—Yes, you will. I know you will.

—You just want time to play around.

—I want to be settled.

—You want money.

—Quit! I just want you.

—Then let's get married.

—Give me time to find myself. I have no self any more!

—If you don't have a self yourself, then *I'm* your self.

—Then why do I feel empty and useless even when I'm with you?

—That's your own goddamn fault.

The arguments grew even more irrational and violent. He became brooding and sullen, and she reverted to her sad sashay and silence. Then one night in the late spring, after too much wine, there was a face-off in which they brought up each other's worst faults—the personal ones that can't be changed and need never be mentioned—in detail after detail, both of them pale and trembling, and he vowed never to see her again. He stayed away for a week, and a few days before the end of the term his phone rang. "Yes?" he said. "Ellen." There was more distance to her voice than was caused by telephone wire. "Yes?" he said. "I'm leaving for New York. Will you come see me off?" And since he'd been so petty and demanding for so long, he was gentle, concerned, and unselfish when he saw her off, and told her that perhaps a separation was best for a while, that now she could be at peace, that all he wanted, since he loved her, was to see her at peace; and then he watched her go, praying that she'd been so moved by his magnanimity that she'd return the next day. She didn't. She was so lost and alone in that bus station that if he'd grabbed her by the arm she never would have left.

He shoved away from the wall and started toward the kitchen, the source of the voices, staring at the floor as he went. He heard her grandmother say, "Oh, a visitor. Oh, how nice!"

He stepped into the kitchen. Her grandmother was holding Ellen by the arms and when she saw him she let them drop. "Well!" she said. "What are *you* doing here?"

"There's no use beating around the bush." There was one he hadn't thought of. "I might as well come right out with it. Ellen and I are married."

She swung to Ellen. "*Married*?"

"Yes," he said.

"What do you mean, 'married'?"

"Just that," he said, and although he was speaking to the old lady she continued to stare at Ellen, who stood before her with lowered eyes.

"When?" she demanded. "How?"

"In Madison. About a month ago."

"A month ago! Ellen! You mean that for all this time you've been deceiving me!"

"She hasn't been deceiving you. We just decided not to tell you until now."

"Why? *Why*?"

"We wanted to be together when we told you, and we both had to finish school. I go to Chicago now."

"How could you do this without my permission!"

"It's what we should have done a long time ago," he answered, and since her grandmother hadn't taken her eyes from Ellen, he began to feel bodiless, like a spirit speaking through somebody else.

"A month! He left you on your own for that long?"

"Yes," he said.

"What kind of a marriage is this?"

"Oh, Grandma—"

"Is it *legal*?"

"Of course," he said. "It was in the Presbyterian Church."

"You mean there's nothing can be done?" she asked Ellen.

"What do you mean?" he said.

"You mean you have to *stay* married?"

"For God's sake, yes," he said. "Why do you think we did it?"

Her grandmother turned to him. "Don't you dare talk to me in that tone."

There was a long silence as the old lady stared at him with eyes like an animal at bay, and he could see a shimmer start around her silver eyelashes.

Finally Ellen said, "Where's Grandpa? I want to say hi to Grandpa."

"You stay right here till you've explained this. You know perfectly well he's not home."

"Where is he?"

"At the office."

"But it's Saturday."

"Don't play dumb with me, Ellen. Where is he every Saturday?"

"I thought he'd be home by now."

"He'll be back soon enough," her grandmother said, and glanced at Chris as though his doom would be dealt then. "Now then, Ellen, you tell me exactly what's been going on."

Only when Ellen repeated what he had said, embellishing it with descriptive color and romantic detail, did her grandmother begin to understand it was the truth. The shimmer around her eyelashes condensed into tears. "You mean, you—" she would begin. "This is what you— But how could— Oh, Ellen!" The tears had brimmed over but she apparently wasn't aware of them because she took out a handkerchief and blew her nose several times, hard, but the tears continued to run down her cheeks, dropping onto the front of her sweater.

"Don't be sad, Grandma. Not when we're so happy."

"How can you be? How can you after what you've done!"

"But we're in love."

"Love!" The sudden contempt in her voice could have frozen stone. "What's *that*?"

"Oh, Grandma, you know—"

"I don't understand how you can even look one another in the face! Have you no shame, either of you, not even you, Ellen, after the way you were brought up? Think with what horror God looks on this!"

"But we were married under His eyes."

"Don't say that, Ellen, not in front of me. Not after the way you've sneaked behind my back to do this."

"But we were!" Ellen then described counseling with the minister, the solemnity and humor of it, and how the ceremony itself, in the small chapel at sunset, was so austere and moving.

"You needn't be so jubilant about it!" her grandmother said.

"But I am."

"Then stop throwing it in my face like this! You're in my house now!"

Chris stood pale and speechless, and Ellen bowed her head. "Oh, Grandma," she murmured, "why do you have to be this way? Why can't you just accept it?"

"Accept it? I'll never accept it. I want you to understand that right now, Ellen, and you, too, mister. I'll *never* accept this." Her frail frame convulsed, she covered her face with the handkerchief, tried to blow her nose, and began to sob and gasp for air.

Chris started toward her. "I'm sorry, Mrs. Strohe. Maybe I should—"

"Don't speak to me," she said, turning eyes that were bright and hostile on him. "Don't come near me. I want nothing to do with you."

There was a sound of the back door being closed. Chris turned.

"It's Grandpa," Ellen said.

Her grandmother called out in a loud, tearful voice, "Before you start your rituals, you better get up here!"

"I know," the voice in the distance said. "I saw her car. Where is she?" Rapid footsteps approaching. "Where is this Ellen of mine?"

Chris stepped out of the doorway and off to one side so he could face him. The old man hurried into the room, his hat and topcoat still on, and at the sight of Chris he stopped, then stepped back a step. "Well," he said. "Well, *boy* ..." His brow furrowed and he glanced at Ellen, then at his wife.

"They're *married*," she said, and the scorn she put into it sent a chill through Chris.

The old man studied Ellen for a long time, then Chris, then Ellen again, his face dead of expression, his eyes dull, and then he began to nod his head in a slow regular rhythm.

"Last month," Chris said.

The old man took off his hat, ran his hand over his glossy skull, still staring from one to the other, his head still nodding, and took off his coat and folded it, laid it on the table, laid his hat on top of it, pulled out a chair and sat down, and said, "What a hell of a thing to happen on a man's birthday."

"Oh, Grandpa!" Ellen went to him and kissed his forehead where there was a reflection of the kitchen. "I'm sorry. I forgot. Let's have a party. I'll make a cake for you. We'll celebrate."

"No," the old man said. "I think I've had enough for now."

"Don't you be sad, too, Grandpa."

"How can he help but be?"

"No," he said, staring ahead with sightless eyes. "No, it was bound to happen."

"It was *not* bound to happen," the old lady said.

"The Lord gives and the Lord taketh away," he mumbled.

"Is that all you can say?"

The old man lifted his eyes and looked from Ellen to Chris. "You did it," he said, and his eyes dropped. "Congratulations." He looked at them again. "And God bless you." He let his eyes drop. His coat was folded with the lining exposed, breast pocket up, and Chris could see, beneath the brim of his hat, several metal tubes, the aluminum kind used to encase expensive cigars. So that was why the ash tray. At that moment, as though the old man sensed Chris's discovery, he turned to Chris. "Where are you going to stay?"

"We haven't had time to decide," Chris said. "I just finished school."

"Why don't you stay here?"

"Aloysius! Don't be a fool!"

"Why not? We got plenty rooms. The house is empty—" The old man looked at Ellen, and his bristly brows lifted so high in appeal that wrinkles appeared in the top of his head. "Maybe for a week?"

"Let them go! Let them live their married life, with no means of transportation and no place to stay, and most likely not a cent!"

"We just wanted to come up and explain things," Chris said to the old man, "and we hoped you'd understand. Then we thought we'd move to Chicago. I have money."

"Chicago?"

"That's where I go to school now. I also have a job there I can go back to any time."

"Chicago," her grandfather said, staring at Chris, his head nodding again. "I see. You got big plans."

A great sob came from her grandmother. "Oh, Ellen," she cried, "you're the only one I have left, and I've always looked forward to a big ceremony for you!" She hurried out of the room with the handkerchief to her face.

Ellen watched her retreat, then leaned against the work counter as though giving way under it all, her face pale and contorted—from anguish or physical pain, Chris wasn't sure which—and just as he was about to go to her, a tear gathered on one of her gold eyelashes and dropped to her cheek. "If that's what she wanted, if she wanted a big ceremony, it's her fault I didn't have one!" And with that, Ellen ran out of the room.

"Women," her grandfather said, staring at the floor. "They get so emotional about stuff like this."

Then the old man picked up his hat and coat and went down to the basement.

Chris felt as unwelcome in the house as he had in the conversation, an expendable appurtenance, and besides he didn't know where to begin to search for Ellen. All those rooms. He needed to smoke—as he assumed her grandfather was doing in the basement—but didn't. He hoped the histrionics were over. He couldn't take much more. He glanced around the kitchen, at its slate floor, ceramic tile, built-in appliances of bronzed enamel, its walnut cabinets and walnut table, and the luxury rendered him even more immovable. He eased himself into a chair. He pressed his fingertips against his eyelids and stared into his personal void. There were not even the usual shifting colors in that infinity of blackness.

In about half an hour, Ellen came into the kitchen, her face swollen and flushed, the white whorls of a bedcover imprinted in one cheek. She took his hand in hers. "Don't feel bad," she told him. "She didn't mean it."

"Are you all right?"

"Yes."

"Are you sure?"

"Yes."

"You got so pale, I thought—"

"I just needed a nap."

"You're sure?"

"I think the driving did it."

"And the upset."

"And that."

"Were you sick?"

"No. Queasy."

"Oh."

"She'll apologize. She's invited us to stay."

"Is that sensible?"

"Whatever you think."

"What do you think?"

"It would probably be better," she said.

She took utensils out of the cupboard, gathered together some ingredients, and started making a cake for her grandfather. "They don't usually celebrate their birthdays," she explained. "Grandma believes birthdays make you timebound. But Grandpa likes to be remembered."

The smell of baking drew the old man from the basement. He went to Ellen and put his hands on her shoulders. "Oh, my girl," he crooned, "so good, so good of you. You've always been so good to me." He looked at Chris, paled with embarrassment, and let his hands drop, gesturing with them. "Chocolate is my favorite," he said, as if to explain, and came and sat at the table with Chris. There was still a dull, distant cast to his eyes, as though he were immersed in symbolic, wordless thought. He folded his fingertips into the palm of his hand and studied them. He took out a nail clipper and snapped off his nails with an intense, preoccupied air. He examined each nail. He swung out the small file and cleaned his nails one by one. He scraped everything together, the edge of his hand squeaking on the table surface, brushed it all into the cup of his palm, carried it to the sink, and dropped it into the garbage disposal.

When the cake was finished, Ellen's grandmother came down from the other part of the house looking haggard and old, her face pale and set, her hair no longer neat in its small bun, her elbows held tight against her sides. The four of them sat at the table and her grandfather bowed his head and said grace and asked that the marriage be blessed. Her grandmother began an apology to Chris, formal and cold, but couldn't go on after a few words. She excused herself and left the room.

"It's been hard on her," the old man said. "The suddenness. She's so high-strung. Tomorrow she'll apologize."

The three of them sat picking at their cake.

"I'm sorry it isn't much of a birthday, Grandpa."

"It's a birthday."

The old man got up and went to the basement. Ellen cleared the table, and she and Chris washed and dried the dishes in silence. Her grandfather had begun his nocturnal wanderings. This evening, however, they lacked their usual elusive pattern, and each of his circuits ended at the kitchen, where he stood in the doorway and studied them, a quizzical look on his face, then seemed to remember something and wheeled away to the other part of the house. Occasionally he asked a few questions.

"How could you leave this girl, this Ellen, for a month?"

"I had to finish school and requalify for my fellowship. I felt it was my responsibility."

"Oh."

"As a husband."

"Oh."

On his next circuit, he would say: "You have a fellowship?"

"Yes."

"How big?"

Chris told him and he seemed surprised.

"And a job?"

"Yes."

"Where is it?"

Chris told him.

"Oh."

He disappeared but was back in a few minutes.

"Where is this fellowship?"

Chris told him, and they went through the same series of desultory questions. Although the old man nodded and appeared to be listening, suddenly, in the middle of an explanation, his preoccupied look would grow more intense, his brow would furrow, and he'd turn and walk off before Chris could finish. Several times he took Chris by the shoulders, and said, "Well! Boy! . . ." But his bright gaze failed and turned inward, his hands slipped from Chris's shoulders, and he was off on another round.

They got their baggage out of the car and went up to the bedroom. It was large and furnished in the period of Louis Quatorze. Ellen turned on a lamp at the vanity and looked around. "I don't know why Grandma insisted we take this bedroom," she said. "There are four others. It's not mine and it's so big and cold. And the bed's terrible. It's lumpy, it sags in the center, and it squeaks like a porch swing."

"Squeaks?" he said. "Maybe they want to keep tabs on us."

Ellen used the bathroom first, and then undressed and got under the covers. Chris washed his face, getting off all the nerve oil he'd exuded, and rinsed it with ice-cold water, a mistake, because the freshness of the water made him ache for a cigarette. He went back into the bedroom. Ellen was propped on one elbow, her breasts exposed, watching him. He sat down on the edge of the bed, exhausted, at his limit, and reached for his boot. His back muscles were so tense it was difficult to bend.

"If they're so loaded," he said, "why don't they have servants, a maid and butler? Why don't they have a valet for me?"

"A cleaning lady comes once a week, that's all. They hire a catering service when there are a lot of guests. They're parsimonious."

"Parsimonious!"

He tugged at his boot. The bed did squeak. So badly that he got up and hopped over to the bench of the vanity to keep from upsetting her grandparents unnecessarily with the sustained jiggle of springs. The ankle he'd sprained was still sensitive and weak. He got off his boots, and was almost undressed, when there were sounds at the door. He jerked up his pants and Ellen flopped on her stomach. The door opened and her grandfather wandered into the room wearing his preoccupied look and a pair of silk undershorts, barefoot, his barrel chest with its matting of white hair bared, and walked across the room without glancing at them. He stopped in front of a pair of French windows. "These stick," he mumbled. "A house like this and the doors stick. They go out to a porch, Ellen knows that." He fiddled with the latch and finally they came open. Staring outside, he said, "Well, now you can sun yourself when you get up or have a smoke if you want. It'd be best smoking out there. The Grandma can smell it a mile off." He opened and shut the doors several times, then wandered across the room, bent over with his back to them, and started playing with the latch of the door he'd entered. "Ya," he said. "This has a lock. You can lock it if you want." Then he wandered out, leaving it wide open.

Chris turned to Ellen.

"Don't ask me," she said. "That's how he is."

Holding up his pants, Chris shuffled over and shut the door.

In the morning, the atmosphere was changed. Ellen's grandparents returned from church invigorated and at ease, giving off a serene air, as though they had circumstances under control and could be expected to act themselves. Before Chris had a cup of coffee and was fully awake, Ellen's grandmother took him aside and made a long apology, which was sometimes flighty, sometimes nervous and self-deriding, but the old woman stared him in the eye through the whole of it, while he murmured that he understood, that it was so sudden, that he was sorry it turned out the way it had. She concluded, "And I'm ashamed. It was foolish of me to lose my head over something so petty," and then turned and walked off. Whenever she spoke to Ellen during the day, she prefaced her remarks with, "Now that you've gone and eloped, dear . . ." Or, "Now that you're a married woman, Ellen . . ." Or, "Now that you have a *husband* to support you . . ." And she wouldn't let Ellen help in the kitchen. "Oh, no!" she said. "No, you better rest while you have a chance, dear. You'll get more than you want of this in a couple of months, believe me."

Her grandfather said he wanted to talk to Chris and ushered him into his office while Chris thought, This is it, he's going to ask if she's knocked up. First, the old man wanted to know how Chris expected to support her. Once again, Chris told him about his fellowship

and the job. Her grandfather said that that was hardly
enough to send one person to school, and he knew it
was important to Ellen that she finish school. And
Chris should also take into consideration the fact that
Ellen had expensive tastes and was used to buying
whatever she liked. Chris said he had saved some money. Her grandfather wanted to know how much. Chris
told him, and the old man made pop eyes of overplayed
awe. Chris looked down at the ring. Her grandfather
was telling him what a fine girl Ellen was, that Chris
should be thankful for her, that he himself had raised
her since she was a child, as though she were his own,
but maybe he'd spoiled her a little by always seeing she
had the best, huh? Chris started to say he thought she
had good sense. But the old man was talking with
shining eyes of the time when she was seven and won a
spelling contest, of how she stood in front of the judges
and contestants in a yellow dress and wasn't afraid, and
it was spring, and her hair that year was in long curls
and the same color as her dress. Then he broke off.
"You're sure about these finances?" Chris paled and
was about to produce his bankbook, when her grandfather said, "Aw, don't let me badger you, boy. I can see,
just looking at you, you're really moving up in this
world."

They ate dinner in the kitchen, in a silence that Ellen
tried to relieve, but her grandparents would not be
moved by her ebullience. Chris felt an unsettling, electric transformation take place in the room, as though
her grandparents were letting her talk herself out while
they maneuvered into a predetermined position. Her
grandfather folded his napkin and placed it beside his
plate. "So you're still a graduate student?"

Chris answered, once more, for the thirtieth time,
yes.

"Where at?"

Chris told him.

"Isn't that the place where they're having trouble
with the Commies?"

Chris said he thought that was being played up in the *Tribune*.

"Can't this school business go on for good?"

Chris explained, again, that he nearly had his Master's.

"I've known grown men," the old man said, talking to Ellen now, "that have gone to school their whole lives—the boy here has probably seen the kind—and come out still not knowing their elbows from a hole in the ground. And some of these long-time students get so strange, don't they?" he asked, leaning toward Ellen, his brow deeply furrowed as though he didn't comprehend. "Aren't they the ones that go half nuts, let their hair and beards grow out like beggars. You know, those raggle-tag ones—beatniks, or something—that run around with homemade signs, yelling and screaming their heads off, about the gover'ment, usually, and are always boozing and smoking drugs and trying to get out of the draft, which most of them get out of, I understand—maybe the boy here can tell us—because they're fairies."

Chris stood up and slapped the table. "That's it! I refuse to be belittled!"

"Sit down, boy," her grandfather said, without looking at him. "I wasn't talking about you."

Like hell, Chris almost said aloud.

Then, leaning closer to Ellen, the old man began to reminisce about her good sense of judgment, evident since she was a little girl—his voice mellow and soothing—and about how he respected her judgment, and had always been pleased with the way she handled her life.

Her grandmother got up and went to the sink.

There had been bad times, sure, her grandfather continued, but she had always lived up to her strong ideals, and there was never a time she couldn't come to him for help or advice. Except this time. Why? Maybe he was getting old and they were moving apart, huh? But he never, never would have imagined that she could do a thing like this without thinking of her parents.

Though Ellen sat with lowered eyes, Chris could feel the terror rising in her.

"Think of your mother," her grandfather went on in his gentle, consoling tone. "What would your mother think? Have you no respect for her memory. Running off and marrying—" The eyes on Chris. "Oh," he said, as if in self-deprecation, "I don't expect you to honor an old man like me the rest of your days, but before you went ahead and got *married*, it seems to me you would've at least thought of *her*. My Mary Elizabeth, my poor girl."

Ellen lowered her head to the table and let out a long wail.

Chris started to go to her, to put a stop to this, when a piercing tearful voice at his back struck him like a scattering of birdshot:

"It's not your mother I pity or myself I pity, it's *you* I pity! Look at him! What is he!"

FOUR

WHILE SHE was gathering twigs from the yard for a fire, he went around to the back door of the lodge, unlocked it, and stepped into a small enclosed porch. In front of him an identical door of broad raw plank, gray and furry with age, led to the lodge itself. *Make sure water heater is full before you turn on juice.* Back in a far corner, behind a pile of fireplace logs, a bicycle, boxes, a lawn mower, paint cans, and a ladder, all neatly in place, he saw the water heater. He rearranged things in order to get at the faucet which, thanks to his rural heritage, he knew could be found at the base of the heater. A damp mold clung to the bottom of some of the cardboard boxes. Where the enamel of the water heater was chipped away, a metallic fungus was growing. He turned on the faucet and water splattered onto the floor. He felt there was somebody watching him—her?—and gave a glance over his shoulder. Nobody. He shut it off.

As he straightened up, a cobweb passed over the back of his head and he whirled around and slapped at the air. His heartbeat picked up. He whirled and hit out again. The cobweb was dangling from the hair at his nape. Brushing and slapping at the back of his head, dodging out of range of the unknown, he made his way out of the corner, tripping over a box and upsetting the bike. He looked over his shoulder again. A broom rake described an arc along the log wall and hit the floor, its tines jittering.

"What else?" he said, and took a couple of steps toward the equipment. "What the goddamn hell else, huh?"

Innocent and immobile, the equipment maintained silence.

He took out the key chain again, unlocked the inside door, and swung it open as though he expected someone to be there. An iron cookstove, presaging the time period they would be living in, faced him across the darkened room. There was also an electric range just inside the door (schizophrenia), and an old-fashioned Frigidaire that stood off the floor on high legs. The log wall beside the stove was lined with wooden shelves, where dishes and canned foods were stacked, and a plank work-counter extended out from the wall. In the center of the counter was a sink, with a pair of brass faucets perched above it on bare pipes. The counter pointed toward a dining wing attached to the left of the kitchen. A deer's head gazed down on the dining area from the gable end of the wing, and the wing, with high windows on three sides, looked like a pleasant, sunny place to eat. When there was sun. He placed the keys on the work counter beside the sink and turned on a faucet; a trickle, an explosion of air that blew dust from the sink, then a torrent of orange water, pausing, coughing, an old bull clearing its throat, followed by some spattering explosions, then settling into a steady flow, its color rapidly clearing. Satisfied that the water was running, he shut off the faucet and went out to the back porch and turned on the juice.

He flipped a switch inside the door and the kitchen light went on. He let it burn (it was getting dark out and he felt uneasy in the unfamiliar place) and went through a hall that led off the right of the kitchen and stopped still, awed and for some reason filled with misgivings—was her grandfather trying to put something over on him?—at the sight of the main room. It was at least thirty by forty, and all the furniture was stacked and covered over with old sheets and had been pushed off to one side, making the room seem even more spacious. There was no ceiling; the log rafters and log beams supporting the high peaked roof were exposed, intensifying the raw, unfinished smell of the building, a mingled aroma of mildewed wood, damp varnish, wet canvas, and creosote. The far wall was dominated by a fireplace of fieldstone, and its mantel-shelf was one big log split down the middle. Above the fireplace, the mounted head of a moose looked down on him with amusement, an inscrutable smile on its big-lipped mouth, apparently enjoying his reaction to the place.

"Grandpa shoot you?" he asked.

Or maybe the moose was smiling to cover its own shame, finding itself bodiless, hanging from a wall, helpless to do anything about the hairnet of cobwebs spanning its antlers.

On both sides of the fireplace, projecting from a mortar chink between the logs, there was a peeled and varnished tree limb; a preserved possum, its glassy eyes turned toward him, hung upside down from one of the branches. A raccoon was frozen in the act of climbing the other. In the silence of the room, its air dim and still, colder than the air outside, the sheets in a white bank against one wall, he felt he had stepped into the silence of a winter month, when there were no human beings here and animals had free rule, or back to another, earlier time, when man's place on earth was not established or secure. Disturbed, he turned away, planning to check the front entrance to his left, but caught sight of something behind him and swung around and found himself staring into the face—black eyes, fur, muzzle, fangs—of a bear! His weak-kneed retreat, cut short by something behind him, brought things into perspective. Resting at eye level was a bear skin; the dark mass underneath it was an upright piano.

The thing behind him was a rocking chair, now rocking under a sheet. He looked around to make sure Ellen hadn't been witness to this shameful performance. There were many large windows looking onto the woods and, at the front of the building, over the lake, none of them with curtains. There was no sign of her. He sat down in the rocker. What was it? For the past month he'd been alternately furious and scared. What was at him? Come out, come out, wherever you are. Explain. Show yourself. A frontal attack. Come on. Nothing. A blank wall. He closed his eyes and put his hand to his brow. He rocked. JFK in the Oval Room. He got his from behind.

He stood up. The rocker with ebbing urgency nudged him at the back of the knees. Beyond the piano, there was a door leading to the left. He went over to it and entered a room and the stern set of his face gave way to bashful appreciation. The bed was huge. Its frame was made of small straight logs stripped of their bark, and it was as high as a hospital bed. It faced a pair of windows that looked onto the lake and another pair of windows, along its far side, offered a view of the meadow.

He sat down on the bed, bouncing, testing its mattress, and at that moment, as though the object of his desire had materialized, the crown of her blond head moved along the bottom of the front windows. He went to them and looked out at her. She stood beside a birch, facing the lake, her head held at an angle of inquiry and interest. A nuthatch clung to the birch a few feet above her. It hurried up the tree a ways, turned upside down and, hopping around the tree, disappeared, then came hopping into sight, found itself almost on a level with her eyes, and went in a dipping flight into the woods, *yank-yanking* with fear. She lifted her hand and her fingers made delicate, restless gestures in the air, as though there were something tangible where the bird had been that she was testing, touching as she had touched the tiger lily.

His wife. Wife with child.

He made a fist and raised his hand but, sensing that a sudden knock on the glass would startle her, let it drop. He studied her for a long time—the hair that had been rayed out on his pillow, her strong straight shoulders, the curve of her slim calves showing below the hem of her coat—and then found himself knocking on the glass in a strong sustained rap that thrilled him in proportion to the scare he imagined he was causing her. She turned with composure, as though she'd known he was there, and her broad smile broke over her face, illuminating it, lighting her eyes with such deep joy and trust he had to look away.

He pulled out the list of instructions and made a show of studying it: *Go up on roof and check screen on chimneys*.

"Right," he said.

But as he came into the main room he saw something that made him stop. Scattered several feet back onto the plank floor were splinters and bits of broken glass. There was a missing pane in a front window.

"Jesus." With the glass scattered inward that way, it had to be broken from the outside. The windows were hinged and in pairs, as he discovered on examining them, and they swung outward. The hook holding the two sashes together was still secure. But if somebody unhooked it when he came in, why couldn't he as easily hook it when he went out. If he was out. Chris looked around.

At the end of the room where the piano stood, a split-log stairway, with a log railing along one side, led to an attic above the bedroom. Why should anybody be up there? If a transient, a bo, an Indian, any undesirable was living in the place in secret, wouldn't he use the bed downstairs? Certainly. *He* would. Then he noticed something else, and went out the back porch and around to the front, where she was gathering twigs.

"Do you like it?" she asked.

"Very much."

"Really? I hope so. It's my favorite place. A trapper originally lived here, I told you that. He and an Indian built the cabin and all the furniture inside out of trees from the woods. When Grandpa bought the place, he called it the last symbol of the frontier (not in those exact words), and vowed he'd never change a thing. He hasn't, and he got it shortly after the trapper left. The trapper built it for his wife before they were married—natives still call it honeymoon cottage—but once they moved into the place, the trapper's wife, who was from the city, went out of her mind with loneliness, they say, and before a year was up she left him. He never found her, and he could never come near the place again."

"I wonder if your grandfather had that in mind when he shipped us up?"

"Oh, no! It means more to him than that big house. I was afraid he'd never offer it."

"First he wanted to see how we stood the rack."

"Don't."

"Well, what the hell? Okay, forget it. Oh. Are there any beds in that attic?"

"No. Mostly junk. Why?"

"What used to be on those deer-foot pegs above the front door?"

"Guns."

"They're gone."

"Oh, Grandpa buried those in the woods. That's one thing he did do. He doesn't believe in firearms. Why? Why do you want to know?"

He turned her so she could sight down his extended arm to the window. "See that? I think somebody tried to break in."

"Oh."

"I doubt if it's serious. Nothing inside looks disturbed. I'll mention it when I call the watchman and maybe he can tell us what happened. Here," he said, and took the twigs from her. "You go in now. I'll do this. I know the trip tired you."

"But I love it outside! I've never been up this early in the summer. Summer here is *spring*. It's like another world, with the trees in another stage and all the plants and flowers different. I've never felt so much at home or at peace as I do now, outside here"—she took him by the arm—"with you."

"But we have almost a month. And anyway, tomorrow there'll be more light." He put his free arm around her. "Come on," he said, adopting a husbandly tone—imperative yet benevolent, chummy and superior. "The water's running, so I don't have to go to the pumphouse, the heater's on, so pretty soon we'll have hot water, and now I'm going to get out a ladder and check those chimneys and then build us a big fire."

The porch door was locked. He handed the twigs back to her. He searched through his pockets. He walked over to the dining wing, cupped his hands, and peered through a window. On the counter next to the sink, splayed out like a many-legged obscene thing, basking under the kitchen light, were the keys.

"Shit," he said. "Do you have a set?"

"No."

"So what do we do?" The nearest town was seven miles.

"Clausens, in that farmhouse back at the turnoff, have a key to the front door."

"Well, to Clausens, then," he said, and turned and started toward the car, and then stopped, his back to her.

"No," she said. "I don't have an extra set for it either."

"That place is a mile away!"

"A mile and a half."

"What now? I can't leave you here alone. It'll be pitch dark in a half hour. Can you walk that far?"

"I'd love to. There's going to be a moon."

"But can you? You know—"

"Oh, of *course*. I'll be all right," she said, and even this much reference to her condition made her blush and lower her eyes.

"Isn't there a flashlight in the car?" he asked.

"In a clamp under the dash."

He got it out and gave her his arm and they walked up the driveway with the tall grass in its center and across the corner of the meadow, where bank swallows were swooping after insects and a bat was flapping in erratic patterns in one spot like a cloth on a wire caught in a wind. They came to the steep clay road at the edge of the woods. He stopped and turned on the flashlight. Nothing. He slid its switch forward, depressing the button as he did, and banged it against his palm. He slid the switch forward, held the button down, and whacked it hard on his thigh.

"Oh, hell," he said, and stuck it in his back pocket.

"Doesn't it work?"

"Would it?"

He took her by the elbow and started down the rutted, rock-strewn road. With each step they took into the woods it grew darker, and the sound of night insects swelled around them and made the darkness seem even more dense. He squinted against it.

"A hell of a lot of good your moon does in trees."

"As long as we keep on the road we're all right."

"To do that, we'll have to get down soon and feel."

He took the flashlight out of his pocket and banged it again, and this time it came on, but with a light so feeble that the clay of the road, except where the small circle of the beam fell, took on a violet hue. He directed it in front of her feet and in its dim light the domes of buried stones glowed as though phosphorescent. He stepped on something loose, his weak ankle gave, and he said "Oo" and landed on his tailbone.

"Chris! Are you all right?"

"Yes."

"You didn't hurt yourself?"

"No."

"You're sure."

"Positive. Just let me sit a minute."

He let the beam shine between his knees.

"What a perfect time to get here," he said. He got to his feet and took her by the elbow and they walked on in silence. From the feel of her arm he could tell she was hurt that he had mocked her exclamation, and he was sorry. He didn't want to curb her openness; it was one of the traits he liked most in her. He liked this place, too, more than he told her, and would have cared for it as much as she did if they could have come to it alone, free of indebtedness, free of the magnanimity and auspices of anyone, especially her grandparents. "Since it doesn't seem you've planned that far ahead, I suppose you'll want to use the lodge for a honeymoon place," her grandmother said. "That is, unless you look on honeymoons, as you seem to on proper marriages, as old-fashioned and beneath you." Then her grandfather scribbled down the instructions and handed them to Chris. "Whatever you can't handle," the old man said, "the neighbor, Clausen, will do for you." Chris started to remind him that he'd been raised on a farm, but her grandfather held up a hand. "Don't worry about that," he said. "*I'll* pay him. He sends me bills." The old man left the table and came back in a few moments with his hat and topcoat on. "You can take the car, Ellen," he said, and glanced at Chris. "That car's yours." And then he left for his office.

They postponed going, hoping to reconcile her grandparents (or get even with them, it wasn't clear which), but made little headway. On the morning they were to leave for the lodge, Chris woke in the squeaky bed and found Ellen propped on her elbows, straddling one of his legs, stroking his chest with her fingertips.

—Bald as an egg, he said.

—I love it. It's like the armor Centurions wore.

—A bit firmer.

—Oh? she said, and pulled herself up and pressed her breasts against him. It gives, she said.

—You like it to give?

—Just that much.

In the kitchen beneath them he could hear the voices of her grandparents in a subdued argument. A frying pan banged in anger.

—Mmmmm, she hummed, then whispered in his ear, *Feel* you. *Feel* you today. Mmmmmmmm, I can feel you all the way down.

—A little thing I like to keep handy. Club lions to death, et cetera.

—Never for me?

—Shhh. In *this* place?

She giggled.

It began as a burlesque, with him on top of her bouncing the mattress, making the springs jiggle and shriek, both of them trying to suppress their laughter, the voices in the kitchen rising to get above the noise of the bed, more utensils and pots being banged, throats cleared, a loud, inflectionless dialogue starting below while they bounced harder, and then Ellen's expression changed. She drew him down and kissed him and he could feel her wet against him.

—I'm being so forward, she whispered. God, do you think I'm being forward?

Then they tried to be quiet and kept the bed almost motionless until he saw her start, and then the bed went, the room and the place, and there was only her, her, and the white silence that enwrapped them as they went together to the end.

He lay back. The rest of the house was so silent it was like a mold poured with wax. When they went down for breakfast, her grandmother would not say good morning to Ellen (she hadn't spoken to him for two days) and she kept her back to them. Her grandfather greeted them both, but stared at the floor, and Chris noticed that the network of bright vessels in his cheek was colorless.

VAN EENANAM COMES FROM UNDER TO
TAKE ROUND NUMBER THREE

"The light," she said. "The light!"

"What's that?"

"The *flash*light."

"What about it?"

"You're shining it everywhere but in front of us."

. . . 2

As the trees thinned they could see a row of golden windows, farther in the distance, flash between their trunks. They came to the edge of the woods and were hit by a chill wind. Chris fastened the snaps up the front of his leather jacket. "This way," she said, and they cut across the slope of a meadow where hay was lying in windrows, scenting the night air, and went downhill toward the lights of the farmhouse, stirring up insects that sought the weak beam of the flashlight and went spiraling up it. They entered an orchard, and as they walked through the low, evenly spaced trees a dog started barking close to the farmhouse. A yard light went on. The dog, a large collie with a shaggy ruff, came running up and slid to a stop and edged toward them in a crouch, its teeth bared, its hackles up, and barking so hard it almost choked. Chris stopped and drew back.

"It's all right," Ellen said. "He and Winston play together. There's something wrong with the poor thing. Watch." She took a step toward it and went, "Rarf," and its ears flattened and it took off running sideways, yipping as though it had been hit.

"Nice dog," he said.

He knocked on the door of the back porch and a woman's face appeared, pale behind the glass. Her eyes, large and watery, were magnified by the lenses of her glasses and had a fishlike, evasive look. She caught sight of Ellen over his shoulder and smiled a tight-lipped smile. She opened the door. "So it's you," she said to Ellen. "I was sure I saw a car go up a while back, but the thought never occurred it might be you. You're here for the summer?"

"Yes," Ellen said.

"You're here early." She glanced at Chris out of the corner of her watery eyes.

"Yes, we are. Oh! This is Chris. We just got married." She tried to suppress a nervous laugh.

"Oh."

"Yes. Last month. Chris, this is Anna."

Anna drew her clasped hands tight against her stomach, so Chris merely nodded and said, in his best country manner, "I'm pleased to meet you."

"Are your grandma and grandpa up?"

"Not yet. They'll be here in about a month. At the regular time."

"Oh." Anna glanced at Chris again. "Well, why don't you come in. It's chilly out."

"We just wondered if you still have a set of keys to the lodge," Ellen said.

"You forgot yours?"

"Not exactly," Chris said. "I locked them inside."

"Oh."

"I haven't even seen the place yet," Ellen said.

"I didn't know the door was self-locking," Chris explained, shifting his weight in uneasiness. "It locked on me."

"Yes," Anna said. "That can happen."

Yes, it can, he thought, feeling uncomfortable under her eyes. There was something ambiguous and furtive about them, and even when she looked at him directly he felt he was being spied upon.

"Well, come in, come on in," Anna said, and stepped aside for them. Chris let Ellen precede him and went up the wooden steps into the porch, which was large and enclosed and was used, he saw, more as a work area and storage room than as a porch. Baskets of fruit and vegetables sat on the floor, and winter clothes and work clothes were draped over the tops of cream cans and heaped in one corner. There were stacks of newspapers, a tractor tire, a washing machine with galvanized tubs, and a butcher's block with tin cans of sorted nails on it. One narrow path, marked off by frayed rugs laid end to end, led through the center of it all. Anna ushered them into the kitchen. It was also part bathroom. There was a sink, a mirror, a toothbrush rack, and a water heater in the corner to the left. An androgynous appliance—half cookstove, half electric range—sat forward of the sink, and a cat was on the floor beside it, eating scraps out of a milk carton that had been slashed in half lengthwise.

"Sit down," Anna said, indicating a long table at the other end of the room. Chris pulled out a chair for Ellen and sat down himself, staring at the clutter of religious pamphlets on the tabletop, the worn and greasy oilcloth, a lazy susan ringed with glasses of assorted condiments (which were attracting flies), a jug of milk, more religious pamphlets, and a bowl of something brown. There was another cat, a gray one, at the head of the table, sitting in a cleared area where a place had been set, its vibrissae dripping with milk. It tried to lick off the drops, then boxed at its nose, then turned its gold eyes on Chris, unperturbed.

"Did you drive all the way up today?"

"Yes," Ellen said.

"And you haven't been in the cottage yet?"

"*I* haven't."

"Then you must be starved. Let me fix you something."

"That's all right," Chris said. "We ate on the road. We have to be getting back."

"Don't bother," Ellen said.

"Please," Chris said. "Really."

"No bother." Anna's voice was prim and unequivocal, like an efficient schoolmarm's. She went to the cupboard and reached up and her tall, long-waisted body, flat at the chest as well as behind, made a straight, graceful line. Her brownish-gray hair was braided, the braids coiled around her head in a crownlike shape, and there was a light shading of hair above her upper lip. Over her black dress she wore a man's flannel shirt, and she had on brown opaque stockings and squat-heeled shoes. She got down two glasses and wiped them out with her apron, all the while staring at Chris with her magnified, watery eyes, and then set the glasses in front of them and filled each to the brim with milk from the jug.

"Have you seen any eagles this summer?" Ellen asked.

Anna clasped her hands in front of her, compressed her prim lips, turned her eyes up, and then looked at Ellen and said, "The last time I saw one was two years ago this May, right after a rain. It was going west toward your bluffs, flying low over the trees."

It seemed she had held the answer in readiness for the two years. It was the kind of loneliness Chris had seen only in rural women, an accumulated catalogue of precise detail—a reserve that was drawn from for the benefit of others, rather than a state that was inflicted on them. She reminded Chris of his grandmother. It was warm in the kitchen. He unsnapped his jacket, put his elbows on the tabletop, and shifted his weight around on the seat of the chair, absolutely at ease.

Anna cleared room for plates, made sandwiches of peanut butter, lettuce, and tomato, and gave them each a portion of homemade applesauce from a crock on the cabinet counter.

"How long will you be staying?"

"Probably till Grandma and Grandpa get here. About a month."

"You must come visit us," Anna said.

Then she watched from the stove while they ate.

Chris had been in kitchens worse than this (the other

rooms were probably as well-kept and unused as in a
museum; the kitchen was the center of a farm) but he
was afraid Ellen was put off by it, so he ate the sandwich as quickly as he could, and drank down the milk,
which—he closed his eyes against it—had small black
specks, like soot, skating on its surface.

"You *really* must be starved," Anna said, and in
spite of his protests made him another sandwich. Chris
noticed that Ellen was eating slowly, with elaborate
daintiness and attention to detail, as she did only when
she was famished and wanted to appear polite. They
hadn't eaten on the road. He was hungry too, he realized, and ate the second sandwich (bologna and lettuce
and mayonnaise) with a slowness that was gratifying
and almost obscene.

"Thank you," he said.

Anna went to the cabinet, pulled open a small drawer that contained nothing but keys, hundreds of them,
and began pawing through the metallic tangle. Chris
judged it would take a half hour.

"Here," Anna said. "This is it." She held the key in
front of her eyes, pointed end up, and stared at it with
the fascination of a child staring at a candle flame.
"Yes. This is it. This is the one." And then she laid it
down in front of Ellen.

They rose and thanked Anna again for the lunch and
prepared to leave, but she became voluble, talking to
Ellen about the winter, how severe it had been, and if
they had come a few weeks earlier they never would
have made it up the hill with a car. Chris went to the
doorway, restless, unnerved, anxious to get back to the
lodge. Anna seemed to sense this, and turned her eyes
on him and began asking what he did, where was he
from, was his family Lutheran, did he like the lodge,
did he like the area, and he gave her curt answers and
kept saying, "Well, we better go now," and edged closer
to the door of the porch. Finally he made it there, and
he and Ellen were standing on the steps, saying good-

bye, when they heard a vehicle winding up in low gear and then backfiring as the driver decelerated.

"Oh," Anna said. "That's Orin. He'll want to say hello."

They waited on the steps. Headlight beams traveled over a barn, a stone silo, a machine shed, went swinging out over the orchard, then turned and came toward them, blinding, and stopped a few yards away. The lights burned for a while, as though to study them, then went off. A blue pickup.

"Ya," said an elderly, febrile tenor. "Ya. The Strohes."

A tall thin man with stooped shoulders came toward them. His bib overalls were so big at the waist and back and legs that they seemed to be standing still while he shuffled ahead inside them. He stopped in front of Chris, squinted his pale blue eyes several times, and made a thumb toward the pickup. "Over to Traverse City, oh, thirty-five miles," he said, as though resuming a conversation in the middle, "over at the cherry factory there, they make this juice. New juice." He paused, looked them both over, and the yard light glinted off his glasses. "Just this year. Apple cherry, they call it. Good juice too!" he declared, as though they had refuted him. He had a heavy Norwegian accent and his voice kept dipping up spondaic waves of inflection. "They can it there, the big cans you can buy in the grocery store, and they do a good job, I'll say." He paused. "You maybe seen it in the store." These pauses of his you could drive a convoy of pickups through. His long face was weathered and finely wrinkled, and his lips kept drawing back in a half smile, as though the juice amused him, they amused him, everything amused him, and any moment he would explain why and everybody could laugh, but meanwhile they had to be content to watch the creases of humor appear around his pale blue eyes, and watch the gold-filled teeth at the front of his mouth flash in the light each time his lips twitched back. "They got the whole set-up there, for processing it and canning it and all," he said, and bowed his head and shook it once as though this was hard to believe. "Ya, it's a thing you should see, a real corker, I tell you. Then they got a storehouse that they stack the cans in for storage, the cases they're shipped in. Big place. Big as the barn. Bigger, too!"

"Why don't you make your point!"

Startled, Chris turned to Anna to see if it was actually her voice that had come out so hard and sharp. Her large eyes were brimming with contempt. Orin inserted some fingers under the band of his striped cap and scratched at his gray hair, the tentative smile still playing over his face, then slipped his hands under the bib of his overalls and turned and walked toward the pickup.

"They don't want to hear about your cherry factory or your apple juice or your bargains!" Anna went on. "Here they are, just married, just arrived here, and right away you're going on about that before you even say hello. What makes you think they want to hear it? All you know is cherries and hymning and hawing and bargains and sloth!"

Say, Chris thought, and turned again, and saw that the look of contempt in her eyes had grown to fury. He never would have expected that from her. Being Orin's wife for thirty years? Living in such isolation with him? The religious pamphlets?

Orin, however, didn't seem to hear her, or if he did, it made no difference. He came back from the pickup, the smile still wavering, creasing his weathered cheeks, and handed Chris a #10 can, with no label on it, that was bent in the center like a stubbed cigarette.

"They got all these canning processes they got to go through, and then stacking them in that storehouse they just give the boxes a toss. It makes you hurt to see it, I tell you, but them it don't bother. They make plenty on it, so all they care is to keep it moving. The buyers, though, they don't go buying these," he said, and took the can from Chris and studied it. "Broken cases, they call them, because some of these bended cans, the juice runs out, you see, and then the labels get dirtied up or come off some of them in the case, but it sure don't hurt what's inside the others any." He squinted at Chris. "You ever had this, this apple-cherry juice?"

"No."

"Well, if my partner could get us something to open this with and a glass, too, I'd show you. Good juice, I'll say that! Well, partner, what do you think?"

Anna turned and stalked into the kitchen. Orin stood grinning at them. The collie, whining in its throat, came slinking out of the darkness, ran up to Orin, began nudging at his crotch, and then went up on its hind legs, placing its front paws on Orin's overalls bib, and tried to lick his face. "Oh, ho ho," Orin said, scratching its ruff. "Oh, you dog, you." Suddenly, in an altered tone, he whispered, "Git, now," and the dog ran off, whimpering. Anna returned with an opener and one tumbler, and passed them through the screen door. Orin sat down on the steps, pierced two triangular holes in the top of the can, poured out half a tumbler, and motioned for Ellen and Chris to sit down. They sat on either side of him, and Chris could feel Anna's disapproving eyes on his back. Ellen tasted it first. "Oh, it's great!" She took another dainty sip. "Here, have some," she said, and handed the tumbler across to Chris. "Hey," he said. "It *is* good. I've never tasted anything like it." He finished it off. Orin took the tumbler, rose, shuffled over to an outside spigot, rinsed the tumbler clean, and came back and sat down and filled it to the brim. He held it up to the yard light and studied its color, that of a pale rosé. "Good juice," he said, and drank down the whole glass, his adam's apple jogging, without a pause for a breath. He wiped his mouth on his sleeve.

"Orin," Ellen said, to fill a pause it seemed would never end, "this is Chris. We were just married."

"Ya, I figured. Ya, that's what I thought. The partner there—" He made a gesture toward Anna with his head. "She mentioned. Chris what?"

"Van Eenanam," Chris said.

"Are you Lutheran?"

"No."

"You could be, with that name, you know. Is your dad Lutheran?"

"No."

The vestiges of Orin's smile went, and his pale eyes narrowed. "You aren't Catholic?" His accent made it sound like cat-lick.

"No," Chris said.

"Ya, them Catlicks," Orin said, and now his tentative smile seemed a tic or a wince. "They got to have all the women and boose they can get, you know." He paused and thought this over. "Ruth Sanderson, now, a cousin to old Pete over by Boyne City, she married a Cat-lick—"

Chris waited through a long silence to hear the details, the disintegration of personalities, the apparently disastrous outcome.

"Ya," Orin said, "there's a Sanderson girl for you."

"Instead of going on about people they don't know and probably don't care about," the voice behind them said, "why don't you do something useful. Why don't you drive them up to the cottage? They've been locked out since they got here and most likely want to get inside and get things tidied up and get to bed. I'm sure they're worn out from the drive. Do you hear?"

"Ya, sure, I'll give them a ride on up. Right away, too."

This time Orin lifted the can itself to his lips and drank the whole thing down. "Them come in handy, too," he said, staring at the bent can. "You can't ever tell." He set it down on the steps and slowly rose. "Ya, well, I s'pose we better get you up there, then."

Chris and Ellen stood, turned and said goodbye to Anna, and started for the pickup.

Orin was urinating against the side of the house.

They turned and said goodbye to Anna, promised to come and visit her soon, and then a metal door slammed and they were lit by headlights. All the way to the pickup, Chris felt, like an extra garment covering him, Anna's eyes on his back. What was it? Why was she that way with Orin? And why had she been so weird with him at first? And then it came to him.

Anna didn't believe they were married.

Well, Chris thought, as he climbed into the smelly cab of the pickup and settled himself on the seat, straddling the floorshift, that wasn't such a strange thing to think.

He didn't believe it, either.

. . . 3

Orin, a brake-jammer, brought the pickup to a sudden halt at the head of the hill. He mumbled something to them, hinting that if he had a jacket he'd stay, or he'd have to check some hay, so they got out and as they were thanking him he popped the clutch and started across the meadow, the truck jerking ahead in the spasms of a badly accelerated first gear. They watched the headlights go up the meadow, turn off into some trees, and vanish. The sound of the racing motor faded and began to assume the shape of an orange O in the night.

"Strange," Chris said. "'Very strange."

"Oh, he's all right, he's nice. And Anna is, too, really. You'll get used to them."

"I didn't say they weren't nice. I said, strange. How long have you known them?"

"Since I was a child."

"He works for your grandfather?"

"Just odd jobs. Mostly, he farms his orchards."

"I bet he's loaded with dough."

"Why do you say that? That's what Grandpa says."

"He's the type."

They turned and started down the driveway toward the lodge, their way partially lit by the lights he'd left burning.

"I imagine Anna and your grandmother get along."

"Not at all. I visit her more than Grandma does. Anna likes me. When I was a child, I used to walk all the way to their place just for some of her applesauce."

"Her applesauce is all right but, holy god, can she be a demon, or what? I don't know how he takes being married to her."

"He isn't."

"What?" Chris stopped short.

"He isn't married to her."

"Aren't they the Clausens, plural?"

"Yes."

"They're sure as hell not related?"

"No. Orin's been a bachelor all his life, and Anna was married to his brother, Hans, who was in a partnership with Orin. Hans died quite a few years ago, but Anna's lived on in the house ever since. I think she owns half the farm."

"Ahh," Chris said, drawing out the word as though revelation had finally come. "Now I see. Now I understand." Jesus, he wondered, did he?

They came to the back door of the lodge.

"You did bring the key, I hope," he said.

"Yes, but it's to the front door. We'll have to go around."

"Oh, my Christ," he said, "I must be losing my mind!"

"What is it?"

"You have the key, right?"

"Right."

"It's to the front door, right?"

"Yes, I—"

"Keep it."

"What?"

"Here. Hold the flashlight, too."

"What is it?"

"Just stand right there," he said, and took off running.

"Chris! Where are you going?"

"Stay there! Don't move!"

He circled around to the front of the lodge in the darkness, reached up through the broken pane and located the hook, lifted it loose, swung the window out, hoisted himself inside, and went trotting through the building to the back porch. He unlatched the door and swung it open.

"Chris! What did you do? How did you get in?"

"That window that was broken? Through it. If I'd have used my head, we could have got in that way in the first place. We didn't have to go through all that. We didn't *need* their damn key."

For some reason, he was pleased with himself for the way he'd got in, and he grinned at her. She blushed, then stooped to pick up the twigs she'd left by the door. He took her by the wrist and held tight.

"Wait," she said. "We need these for the fire."

"To hell with it. And the chimney screens, too. To hell with it all."

He reached an arm behind her thighs and lifted her against his chest, a rush of blood dimming his vision and making the veins in his head swell, and though he was afraid he might stumble or drop her, he carried her through the door, kicked it shut behind him, carried her through the porch, kicked that door shut, carried her through the kitchen, holding his breath all the way, through the hall and through the main room, under the approving auspices of the moose, and into the bedroom. He dropped her onto the bed and, hoarsely, with his last reserve of strength and breath, said, "*Make it.*"

The sheets, which she'd found underneath some beach mattresses and buckskin rugs in a bottom drawer of the dresser, were damp and clinging and smelled of naphthalene. He'd fallen asleep to the smell and waked to it in the night, and now, as he looked out at the meadow overlaid with moonlight, the smell seemed responsible for the silver color of the grass and the silver color of the trees encircling it, and for their unnatural stillness. The meadow was higher at its far end and sloped down toward the lodge. Three brushpiles, black against the silver grass—the near one looking large as a haystack, the far one small as a bowl—stood in a straight row up the center of the meadow. There was a dark rectangular shape against the trees to the left. That would be the pumphouse.

What had caused him to wake? He usually slept a deep sleep sometimes for eighteen hours, until the clock in his head went off, and he had passed from loving her into oblivion without even setting it. Was the marriage, her grandparents, this place, all of it, affecting him that much, upsetting his sovereign province, Sleep, where he accomplished everything he couldn't in real life? Jesus, that would be the limit. But then he heard a sound, metallic as the scene outside, and knew he'd been waked by that sound. He stopped breathing and held himself in suspension to listen better. Whispering. And then another sound came, going right down to his marrow. *Pang.* A note was struck on the piano. Illusion? Then, *bong*, another one, in the bass register, followed by some tinkling in the treble keys. Without turning to look behind him, he recalled, yes, pregnant women did strange things at strange hours, and just as he was finding some solace in that recollection, the covers, pulled by somebody else, stretched taut. She was in the bed with him. Or better be. He swung around—she was there, asleep—and for a second he was relieved, and then realized how absurd it was to feel relief. That counted her out. And it would be up to him to go out there and investigate. Why hadn't he checked the attic?

He started cursing in a loud voice, using the dirtiest words he knew, and then jumped to the floor and walked all the way into the other room before he realized he was stark naked. It made no difference. No one was there; that is, no one visible. He approached the piano with caution and a sense of reverence. He believed in ghosts. The old trapper returned? The spirit of his wife as a music-hall matron? With a scrabbling, whispery noise some keys depressed and there was a dissonant chord.

He batted at the air, swinging to check behind him, crying, "Heigh! Heigh up out of there, you sonofabitch! Heigh!" Slowly, he calmed enough to go toward the piano for a closer look, and noticed sliding doors at its front. A player piano. Could the mechanism have been cranked up and chosen this moment to run down? He slid open the doors. No rolls of music inside.

He'd created such a disturbance that when he came back into the bedroom she was awake, half sitting up, the light from the lamp on the crossbar of the bed shining down on her. She was holding the covers close, either in modesty or in fright.

"What is it?" she asked.

"Nothing."

"Was somebody here? I thought I heard you talking to somebody."

"Right. Myself."

"Couldn't you find your way to the bathroom?"

"As if I were going to the john at this hour."

"Were you checking the doors? Did you stub your toe?"

"No!"

"What's the matter? Are you angry with me?"

"No!"

"Yes you are."

"I'm not, dammit!"

"What is it, then?"

He stretched out under the covers and stared at the ceiling, trying to decide whether the emptiness he felt was due to the scare he'd been through, to his impatience at her questions when what he needed was comfort, or to his sense of hurt at having to suffer so many indignities for her sake. He waited for his strength and equilibrium to return. Moths, with wings folded, clung to the beams and bare boards of the ceiling above him. He felt something dark, scrofulous, lop-winged, and destructive as a moth nudge at the back of his mind, testing wet wings. The sensation made him sick. His equilibrium wouldn't return, he grew weaker, and then his sense of humor, whatever that was and wherever it was held, in his chest it felt, gave way and bled from him as he lay there. From such a small thing? After the unrelenting gamut of the past weeks, from such a small thing?

She put her hand on his chest. "You feel quaky," she said. "What is it. Tell me."

"Oh, El, I . . ."

"What?"

What, yes, what?

"Chris?"

"Oh, El," he began, but the immediacy, the indignity of it caught him up, and he cried, "There are *mice* in your piano!"

"Oh, I'm sorry. I keep thinking you've been here, and know everything. Did they make noise? I should have told you. I'm sorry. They've lived there for years. You didn't disturb their nest or hurt them, I hope."

"No!" he shouted, and snapped off the lamp. "No, I didn't hurt them!"

He turned away from her and was taken by surprise when the meadow silvered even more and began sparkling as he watched, sending out tines and shafts of splintered light. He hadn't imagined that the events of the past few weeks had upset him that much. He held himself still so Ellen wouldn't know he'd been overtaken by emotion, and tried to purge himself as he had in childhood, but there was no relief now in tears. Springing from a source he was unable to locate or comprehend, they only made him feel more broken.

FIVE

THE NEXT DAY, after waking late, they drove seven miles to the village for supplies. Ellen sat behind the wheel and, with an enthusiasm and thoroughness that were almost proprietary, took him on a tour of the dirt streets of the village, pointing out everything of interest: a squat hexagonal lighthouse, one of the first in the area, that had been constructed in the late 1800's out of massive fieldstone, and another structure dating from the same time, tiny, wooden, white, with a foundation of similar stone, that was originally the home of the lightkeeper and now housed a small library. There was a Western-style hotel with a high false front and a wooden porch running along its length, but it no longer kept guests, she explained, unless they couldn't make it home. *HOTEL LIQUOR*, its sign read. There was a drugstore that sold Indian souvenirs (sheathed with a shingle material that simulated gray stone), a general store, a restaurant (sheathed with the same material but of a sandstone color), and two other bars—all of it within the space of a block and a half. Main Street. Farther down, a Lutheran church with a high white spire.

The frame houses of the village encircled a small bay which had once been a busy fishing port, but the fishing trade had fallen off during the Second World War and never picked up again, and now a new cherry factory, built of brick, sat next to the old docks, spilling its vermilion waste into the bay. A low modern hospital, also built of brick, stood on a hill overlooking it all. At present the village was supported by farmers and a growing tide of tourism; a ski lodge was under construction nearby, a site for a trailer camp was being bulldozed in a growth of virgin cedar, and the forested land that surrounded the village had been bought up by speculators from Detroit and was being subdivided for summer cabins, a few samples of which were already standing as lures, all of them pre-fab A-frame or flat-roof bungalows that were sleek, style-conscious, pristine, and looked as if they might stand up to the weather for ten years. On a county road of macadam leading out of the village, some tourist cabins, tiny as toolsheds, were clustered around the newest improvement to the area, a laundromat, or, as its hand-painted sign proclaimed: *THE LAUNDRYMAT.*

She turned back into town and stopped at the docks. "Come on!" she said. "Let's look at the boats!"

She ran ahead on the heavy planking of the old docks. He followed after her with reluctance, giving sidelong glances at the tourist craft, the yachts, the cabin cruisers, and the highly varnished sloops flying triangular flags from tall masts.

"Aren't they beautiful!" she said.

"Nice."

"Don't you like them?"

"Sure."

"I love to sail. I've been only once. Oh! Look at this." She leaped onto the deck of a forty-foot sailboat. "Wouldn't you like to sail this? Wouldn't you like to sail together around the Lakes, out the St. Lawrence, and down the coast?"

"What are you doing?" he said.

"What do you mean?"

"What are you *doing?* Get down from there."

"Why?"

"Get down from there!"

She jumped onto the planking and came to him and touched his shirt front. "What's wrong? I thought you liked boats. I thought you liked to sail."

"I do, you know that," he said, and looked away. Should she be jumping around like that in her condition? He stared over the water, squinting against the reflected sunlight, and saw that the docks were enclosed by a breakwater of big wooden spiles, whose ends, standing above water level, were sharpened to points a man could impale himself on.

"Chris, what is it?"

"That boat's not yours."

"So?"

"So you shouldn't be on it."

"Oh, they don't care!"

"How do you know? Do you know them? Are they old friends, old sailing buddies of yours or something?"

"No." She flushed and lowered her eyes.

"Then how can you say they don't care?"

She shrugged her shoulders. "They just don't."

Behind her back, a tanned and unshaven face poked out of one of the portholes of the boat. A middle-aged man. Red baseball cap and steel-rimmed glasses. He studied Chris's face and Ellen's backside with interest, the inquisitive bastard.

"Come on," Chris said. "Let's get the groceries."

They walked to the car and drove in silence to the main street. She parked close to the general store, across the street from the library.

"Where can I call the watchman?" he asked. "I still have to do that." He sighed.

"There's a phone in the store. I'm going to the library first. Do you want to come with me?"

From the way her voice brightened, he could tell she was trying to draw him out of his dark mood. He stared at the only other vehicle on the street, an old blue Ford with a veil of heat waves hovering above its discolored hood.

"The librarian, the same lady, has worked here ever since I can remember. She's large, hearty and gray-haired, and every summer when I walk in, she says, 'Oh. You,' as though she's put out, but she's not that way at all. It's just an attitude she adopts the first time I come in. Then she goes to the shelves, gets out their books on birds, flowers, fossils, and trees, a whole armload, even for her, and checks them out to me without looking up or asking my name. She remembers it, and she knows what I've come for. This year, when she's all through, I'm going to say, 'I'm sorry, but I believe you've made a mistake. My name's Van Eenanam.' I can't wait to see her reaction. Do you want to come?"

"No."

"Probably, without batting an eye, she'll say, 'It's about time.' You'd like her, the way she affects being stern, and is so knowledgeable and kind, and the—" She gripped the top of the steering wheel and leaned forward. "I'm morbidly afraid as strangely never before, or perhaps oftentimes before. Discontinuous. Transparent as light. Whole patterns of thought and reality escape before I can articulate them, and lately I can only say what *isn't* and not what *is*. Or is that sophistry?" She looked at him. Her large eyes were troubled and anxious, and she seemed ready to apologize for what she'd said, or for falling into one of her verbal states. Then her eyes altered. "Oh, hell, I'm going to see Edna. That's her name." She stepped outside and slammed the door. "You make the phone call. I'll be right in," she said, and went running across the street to the library, while he stared after her, uncomprehending, afraid.

He started out of the car and stopped. Four or five Indians were sitting on the wooden steps that led to the entrance of the general store, and he was positive their eyes had followed her. Now they were all staring at the ground. A couple of them, teenagers with thick black hair slicked back, had on sleeveless T-shirts and blue jeans, and another man, old and toothless, was wearing a plaid lumberman's jacket and a plaid cap turned off to one side. His tongue hung from his open mouth. In front of the steps, an empty wine bottle lay on the ground, flies and gnats orbiting it. As Chris came even with the Indians, he said hello, but they remained motionless, elbows on their knees, studying the ground. He went up the steps and opened the screen door and turned. They were all staring at him.

He stepped inside. Six-packs of beer, stacked in chest-high piles, divided the long room into two sections. There was a meat freezer at the front of the store, and a paint and hardware department at its rear. Storage shelves lined the walls, but most of the merchandise was displayed on the staggered stacks of beer; orange workman's gloves, overalls, and children's toys in plastic bags were piled together with bananas and celery. The clerk, an Indian in a long-sleeved flannel shirt and a bow tie, got up from a chair behind the check-out counter and came over to Chris and offered his assistance. Chris introduced himself and shook hands, and the Indian, who seemed baffled and surprised at this gesture, finally gave Chris his last name.

"Attawhisky," Chris repeated. "That sounds stiffer to take than mine."

The Indian's reaction was instantaneous and almost surreal. Spokes of wrinkles appeared around his eyes and his long upper lip jerked as if on strings, giving Chris a glimpse of short teeth and a wide band of glistening gums, and then, as suddenly as it had flown up, the Indian's upper lip fell, his inch-long eyebrows drew down, and he stared at the floor and rubbed his chin (where a triangle of stubble grew, his only sign of a beard) as though he were deep in introspection. He lifted his eyes to Chris; there was hesitance and fear in them. "Hey," he said. "You drink?"

"Love to," Chris said.

This time the Indian laughed aloud, throwing back his head, showing a greater amount of light-brown gums, and Chris caught the smell of sweet wine on his breath and understood why the man was switching, without transition, from dead earnestness to such hilarity. The Indian's eyes made a furtive search of the store, he moved closer, so close they were almost touching, nudged Chris, and said, "When the boss ain't around, we'll sneak some once." His words came out as spasmodically as his face worked. "Hey," he said, using the word more as a friendly salutation than as a command for attention. "Hey, you're a good kid. Good white. New, huh?"

"Yes."

"Cause nobody talks to us Indians." He nodded with solemnity. "Yeah. That's right. Nobody. Not even the Indians." He looked over Chris's shoulder, bent closer to him, and whispered, "Hey, you got a buck?"

"Sure."

"I just got six bits is all. If I had me a buck I could get us a bottle, see? Just you and me. None of my friends. You see my friends out there?"

Chris nodded.

The Indian, copying Chris to an extreme, did big dipping nods. "Yeah, that's right. They want some, too." He nudged Chris. "Hey, I'll pay you back and give you half too, okay? I get my check the end of this week."

Chris gave him a dollar and told him to keep it, and the Indian became expansive, profuse in his thanks, and offered to show Chris around the store and carry everything he purchased back to the check-out counter. That wouldn't be necessary, Chris said, and anyway he was waiting for his wife.

The Indian winked.

"But there's a phone booth here, isn't there?" Chris said. "I'd like to make a call."

The Indian became solemn, walked over to the check-out counter, turned around, swayed once, and with his forefinger beckoned to Chris. Chris went over

to him and the Indian reached behind the counter and
set down a Princess phone.

"Oh, no," Chris said. "Thanks. I'd just as soon use
the booth."

"No booth."

"There's no phone booth here?"

"No." The Indian shook his head. About this he was
serious.

"Just this?"

"Just it." Very serious; his lips pursed tight. "Not a
long-distance call, no?"

"No," Chris said.

The Indian pointed to the phone, lining it up in his
vision. "That's it."

Chris took the list of instructions out of his pocket
(V. Weeks, 843-7448) and dialed the number while the
Indian, with a gleam of curiosity in his eyes, stood in
front of him and watched.

"Virgil Weeks here," said the miniature voice in the
receiver.

"Mr. Weeks, I'm unknown to you. My name's Chris
Van Eenanam. I've just married Mr. Strohe's
granddaughter, Ellen, and Mr. Strohe said for me to
call you and say we'd be up at the lodge for about a
month. Okay?"

"Mr. Strohe?"

"From Milwaukee. In the beer business."

"Strohe, you say?"

"He owns the lodge on the lake. You know. I believe
it originally belonged to a trapper."

"Oh! Oh, you mean the old *Nicholson* place! Old
honeymoon house, huh? Sure, sure, out there on the
bluffs there, right?"

"Right. Aren't—"

"You spending a honeymoon there?"

"Sort of."

"Give her hell, boy!"

"Listen, aren't you the watchman there?"

"Yes I am, that I am, I am that."

"Oh," Chris said, and looked up and received a big grin from the Indian. He stared down his nose into the receiver. "Oh. Well, I was just wondering if you knew what happened."

"What's that?"

"That window."

"Which window?"

"The lodge. Front one's broken."

"Really? Damn! I bet it was a nishnob did it."

"A what?"

"One of the nishnobs!" There were some short metallic barks of laughter, and the voice said, "Little injuns from the reservation over by the county line. Yeah, well, in my business, you know, you got your names for different types—your crooks, your petty offenders, your swindlers and whatnot, and I didn't have none for Indians so I made that up myself. Nishnobs. Ha! You see, they're always the ones getting into the summer people's places and snitchin' stuff so I thought the name fit perfect, right? You got anything missing?"

"No."

"Lucky boy!"

"You didn't know about it?"

"What's that?"

"Window."

"The window? No, no, it's news to me. I haven't been up there, oh, I don't know, since the first of winter, I'd say. Are the roads still so bad?"

"I thought Mr. Strohe paid you to keep an eye on the place."

"He does, yes, that he does, and every time I'm out that way, believe me, I drop in and have a look. Except if the roads are so bad. And then it's no use, because you couldn't even get a fool nishnob to go up. They won't walk, you know. Gotta have wheels. The reason I understand them so good, see, is I'm a half-breed myself. Also, I'm depitty sheriff in this here county—your Mr. Strohe knows that—and what with car wrecks, gun accidents, people getting lost in the woods (a bad year for people getting lost), oh, and all that, I'm kept on the go most of the time, usually further south, where more people are."

"Then why take a watchman's job? If Mr. Strohe's paying you to do a job it seems to me you should be doing it. I'll call later. And I'm sure Mr. Strohe will be getting in touch with you, too, because he's going to hear about this," Chris concluded, as emphatically as he could with the Indian there, and hung up. His hands were trembling. He turned away from the Indian, whom he couldn't look in the eye now, walked over to a Pepsi machine, and with a dime sent a bottle rumbling into the trough. He snapped off the cap, and stood sipping the Pepsi until Ellen came in. He followed her around the store as she shopped, carrying the bottle of soda. He had shopped enough for himself to know what a bore it was, and how futile, too, when you thought of where it ended up, but she went at the task in an absorbed and pleasurable manner, reading labels, checking prices, testing vegetables and fruit, studying different cuts of meat. Whenever she had hesitations, or when there was a question of quality over price, she would turn to him and say, "Will this be all right?"

"Sure. Go ahead. Whatever you want." He noticed that she always selected the best. He was surprised to see that there was as much available as in a good supermarket, if you looked long enough and in the right places. Besides the liquor. Besides the dry goods. Besides a complete stock of hardware.

Once, when Ellen's back was to the check-out counter, the Indian held up a half-empty bottle of wine. And as Chris and Ellen moved around the store, the Indian kept beckoning to Chris, but Chris shook his head and tried to indicate with his eyebrows, Not now, later. So the Indian winked and gave him the O.K. sign, and every time Chris faced the check-out counter he received a wave or a big grin. It began to make him uneasy. Finally, Ellen sensed this silent communication, and turned and caught the Indian with his hand in the air.

"Do you know him?" she asked.

"We made friends."

"Oh."

She went back to her shopping. Chris felt more and more uneasy and the Indian kept gesticulating. Some townspeople had come into the store and as they shopped they gave Chris and Ellen surreptitious looks. Two Indians walked in from the front steps and stood at the Pepsi machine. Chris's hands were still trembling from the phone call, but there was something more. Was this the first time since they were married that he'd been with her in public? That was the way it seemed, and worse. He felt that a facet of himself he couldn't account for, a double-backed Janus vulnerable from all sides, had detached itself from him and was wandering loose. And he kept turning in circles, glancing over his shoulder, glancing behind, trying to keep this detached part of him, this female Janus, within his field of vision.

. . . 2

Go up on roof and check screens on chimneys.

He got out the ladder and leaned it against the eave. He stepped onto its bottom rung and with bent knees bounced his weight, driving its legs deep into the loose dirt. He climbed the ladder and stepped onto the roof of the dining wing. It had a low pitch, and was covered with wide-tab shingles that looked like hundreds of E's turned on their backs and arranged in neat rows. The shingles, of asphalt composition, red in color, were littered with bits of twig and pine needles. Sand had blown into the spaces between the tabs and lay there in drifts. The dining wing was low and small, like a miniature copy of the lodge, and it formed an L at the side of the building. He walked its peak to the juncture of the L. The roof of the main building ran perpendicular to the roof of the wing, slanting down past the wing, and it was pitched as steep as the roof of a barn. From where he stood on the peak of the dining wing, its slanting overhang passed him just above the groin.

He hoisted himself onto the main roof, turned toward its peak, and started moving toward the chimney in a bent position, using his hands, like an ape, to help him forward. Sand gritted under his leather soles and he started slipping backward. He threw his body flat to get more resistance and grabbed at the tabs of shingles as he slid along. No handles. It was a ten- or twelve-foot fall, a fall he could take if he was prepared for it and didn't panic, but he didn't care to try. He flung out his elbows and pressed down hard. His shirt ripped at the elbows and finally he came to a stop, flat on his stomach, far below the point he'd started from. His cheek was resting on his hands. Should he call for her? He tested with his foot. Extending his leg and toes as far as possible, he still couldn't feel the edge of the roof. Lifting his head, he saw that he had bruised some of the shingles black. Damn.

Gripping two of the tabs, he got to his knees, splayed his lower legs out in a V, and, using the flats of his calves and the flats of his forearms, he edged up toward the chimney. It was near the peak. He passed the dining wing and when he was close to the chimney he lay down to rest.

The chimney, a small brick one, vented the cookstove. It emerged through the overhang and rose five feet above the roof. He would have to stand to see the screen, which was wired over its top. He got hold of the chimney, pulled himself around so that he was on the area of roof above it, and stood up and leaned against it at an angle. He picked the twigs, dead leaves, seed sheaths, and leaf stems off the screen. It was windowscreen and its mesh was clogged with soot. He slapped it with the flat of his hand. The soot stayed. He picked up a twig and scraped it back and forth across the screen, then slapped it again. Still it stayed clogged. Hell with it. It would be easier to hose it down, or just leave it off until they were ready to go. The heat and smoke of the stove would keep animals away. He unwired the screen and tossed it to the ground.

With the help of the chimney it was easy to make it to the peak of the roof and he sat there for a moment, straddling the peak, until his breathing and heartbeat slowed. The fireplace chimney was at the other end of the lodge. He stood, keeping one foot on either side of the peak, and walked over to the chimney. It was made of stone, was six feet in breadth at its top, as big as a door, and most of its mass extended beyond the over-hang. He looked over the edge of the roof toward its base. It was built up along the outside wall of the lodge, its large stones exposed to the weather, and it stood exactly at the center of the building, so that the peak of the roof, meeting at its middle, was like a pointer indicating how well it had been placed. Its screen was of inch-square mesh and didn't need clean-ing. He picked off the few twigs that were lying on it and threw them to the ground. This end of the lodge was near the woods and the roof was darkened by leaf shadow. Moss grew on the shingles. He sat on the peak near the chimney, in the coolness of the shade, and stared at the lake.

There was a slight breeze. He could see small white-caps catching the sun. The air was damp and smelled of pine and water. He made himself more comfortable, and began rubbing his skinned elbows. Sitting like this in the kitchen. The brightness of the room, the cool shadow lying over his arms, over hers. A smell of water. Some spools on the floor, the thread gone from them. Standing the spools in a tower. Her at the stove. Water being poured, always the sound of water when she was present, water for the drinking pail, water to cook with, water to rinse the milk from the separator parts, water for dishes, water for baths and washing—the smell of water pumped from the well and the sound of it being poured. A sturdy woman. Short and well-built, with a broad forehead and eyes that he watched, so light blue. Shy and wary of him even then, though he was only five. At ease only doing chores or at the stove, her dark hair pinned up for chores and down in the house, strands of it down her back. Her hands, broad and strong, moving from vessel to vessel as she worked. Tipping her head back and shaking her hair. Then her eyes on him, then away quick. Rolling a spool toward her.

A nuthatch flew from the woods and landed close to

the chimney on the log of the eave and clung there, hanging at an angle, studying him with cocked head, then walked around the eave and started tapping at the shingles with its beak, making soft buzzing chirrs of content.

She never spoke to him in a raised voice. Seldom spoke to him. His father, large and silent, his brow forever furrowed, spoke only to Grandpa or gave commands: Get away before you get hurt. Don't do that. Don't ask. There's no use trying to tell you, just watch how I do it. Button up your shirt. Stay away from there. And one summer, when Chris fell out of a tree, fell off the drawbar of a moving tractor, and wandered so close to a pile of burning trash that his pants leg caught on fire and he had to be taken to the hospital, his father said, What I'm going to do, I think, is get a new kid.

The farm was near the edge of town, and his father told him to keep from underfoot, mix with the town kids, but he liked being alone. Or in the kitchen here.

Outside, there was a series of footpaths worn in the grass. One led to the barn and one to the toolshed. Another one, bordered with lilac bushes that spotted it with blossoms, led to the outdoor toilet. Another path led to the chicken coop, and another to his rabbit hutch. Off to the side of the hutch the ground was covered with planks and there were bushes around the planks. A sewery smell rose from the planks. The cesspool. Stay away from there.

Standing on the planks one day, he and a boy from town turned a baby rabbit loose and were watching it hop, feeble and trembling, over the rough boards. It stopped and turned scared eyes on them, and the sunlight made its ears so incandescent Chris could see the delicate veins in them.

—Oh, look, he said, A halo. Oh. It came from God.

—No, siree, the boy said. It came from his mother's cut.

—Cut?

—Just like you.

—What do you mean?

—Your mother's cut. You came out of it.

—She doesn't have a cut.

—She does too. Every mother has a cut. They got to have one. That's the way you get borned.

—I wasn't born from one.

—You were too.

—My mother doesn't have a cut.

—Yes she does.

—She does not!

—You want to bet? It's right between her legs.

—She doesn't have a cut there.

—Every mother has a cut there. Girls too. Even my little sister does.

—My mother doesn't!

—She does too, you dumb hick.

—No she doesn't, I know she doesn't!

—How do you know?

—I looked once.

A lie. But, oh, what a hell of a place to hear about it, on those boards. And with all the beauty, all the essence and mystery of it missing. The softening n.

The nuthatch came pecking past him, busy, businesslike, unafraid, and climbed onto the chimney and started circling it, its quick beak searching the spaces in the mortar.

Rolling the spool toward her. Moving up to it. Rolling it closer. Her at the stove. Rolling it closer. Stopping at her heels. Then his cheek to the floor. ... Bare legs, the calves, knees. Moving closer to see thighs. Higher, it would have to be higher. There. A dark line on the white between her legs. A tiny fissure. A hair? Finally rising up inside her skirt to see.

Her scream.

Then getting him disentangled, and the blow that sent him skidding across the linoleum.

"What's the matter with you! Don't you know how terrible that is! Don't you know it's the worst sin!"

Though he hadn't moved, the nuthatch took off with the nosy *yank-yanks* of fear.

He stood. The altitude and sudden change in position made him feel faint and displaced. He made his way slowly along the peak, eased himself into a sitting position, scooted down the roof feet first, lowered himself onto the dining wing, and came down the ladder and went into the lodge. He was pale and introverted the rest of the afternoon, and Ellen's questions and concern irritated him, confused him, and eventually made him angry. He himself wasn't sure what was wrong, and he paced around the rooms as though searching for a clue. Finally, he took the key to the pumphouse from a hook on the kitchen wall and went out the back door. He had only taken a few steps toward the meadow when he saw something that made him stop with such suddenness it was as if one of his parents had materialized.

He had left the ladder standing.

He went back into the lodge, hung up the key, and walked into the bedroom and lay down.

. . . 3

By dinner time he was in better spirits. When the meal
was finished, he uncovered the furniture in the main
room and, under her supervision, began to scoot it back
and forth over the board floor, from one corner of the
enormous room to the other, arranging and rearranging
it to suit her whims. There were several large pieces:
three or four stuffed chairs, a plank banquet table, a
daybed, a couch. The furniture rumbled and thundered
over the floor, and it gave him a strange feeling to make
so much noise, with no one present but her, in this big
building so far from other human life. At last she was
satisfied. He decided to add a touch of his own, and
went to the piano and took the bearskin rug off its top.
He carried it across the room and placed it where he
felt it properly belonged, on the floor in front of the
fireplace.

"Oh," she said. "We never put that down."

"Why's that?"

"Grandpa says we'd wear all the hair off. He wants
everything preserved the way it was. He's very fastidi-
ous."

"Oh."

"Leave it if you want."

"No."

"I like it there," she said.

132

"No. Better not."

He carried the unwieldy thing back to the piano. She stretched out on the couch in front of the fireplace, turned on a floor lamp, and started leafing through one of the books from the library. He stared at her for a while, juggling the bearskin, then walked back with it and spread it on the floor. She gave him a curious look, and said, "I thought you decided not to put it there."

"I did. But we must, absolutely must, have it down for tonight."

"Why?"

"To use it," he said, and grinned.

She blushed and turned back to her book.

"It's in all the movies," he said.

He went to a wicker hamper next to the fireplace and picked out the thinnest twigs, pencil-size and smaller, snapped them into even lengths, and laid them across the andirons. He broke up more twigs of the same size. and placed them in a crosshatch over the first layer. He repeated this procedure once more. He broke up larger, dowel-sized branches and laid them in a row over the little ones, and of these he also made a three-layer crosshatch. He put down a row of larger limbs that were sawed to length. He took up kindling the size of his wrist, nine pieces of it (an odd number being the best for a fire), and laid down five sticks, then laid the remaining four over the gaps he'd left between the first pieces. He took up a scroll of birch bark, tore it into strips, and made a pyramid of the strips on the floor of the fireplace, beneath the wood on the andirons. He lit a piece of newspaper, held it as flat as he could at the top of the fireplace, near the flue, and let it burn down until he had to release it. The orange and black papery ash hovered for a while above the wood, dipping down, winging up, and in a sudden swirl was sucked up the chimney. A good draft. He put a match to the birch bark and when the twigs, the branches, the limbs, and the sticks of kindling were lit and burning, reporting and spouting sparks, and the flames had begun to climb the chimney, he laid on three logs.

He sat on the bearskin rug and watched the flames, feeling his cheeks grow warm and his pants legs heat up over his shins. She rose from the couch and came and sat beside him. He lit a cigarette and smoked it slow, handing it to her for drags, and when it was smoked down he flipped it into the fire. She took him by the arm and they stared at the flames.

"What books did you check out?" he asked.

"The usual ones. Birds. Trees. Plants."

"No others?"

"No. Why?"

"I thought—" He shrugged his shoulders. "Birds, trees, bees"—he made a face and altered his voice to cover his uneasiness—"uh, duh, you know. Babies."

"Oh." She swung her legs around and lay down and put her head on his lap, placing her hands, clasped as in prayer, under her cheek. "I don't think about that."

"Why not? Shouldn't you?"

She lifted her shoulders and snuggled closer; she obviously didn't want to talk about it.

"What did the doctor say?"

"What doctor?"

" 'What doctor?' The one I sent you to."

"Oh, him. Nothing much."

"He didn't give you any instructions?"

"About what?"

"*You* know." He was getting irritated.

"No. Nothing."

"Well, what did he say? He must have said something."

"Just that I should be myself, but go easy. Drink a lot of milk. No horseback riding. And that if nothing came up, I wouldn't have to see another doctor for about two months."

"That's it? It's that simple?"

"He did mention that most women aren't in the shape I'm in. He said I was very muscular."

"What did he mean?"

"Inside."

"Inside!"

"He said I have strong walls."

"He said *that?*"

"Yes."

"The bastard!"

Her mellow self-satisfied laughter matched the play of the flames. He lit another cigarette and smoked it down. He tossed it into the fireplace. He looked at her face and ran his hand over her hair, which was hot from the fire, and drew gold strands of it back from her cheek. He laid the back of his fingertips on her cheek and it seemed more hot (*her* temperature?) than her hair. Then he turned, easing her head onto the rug, and lay beside her. She moved against him. He kissed her, and for the first time he felt that he was married, that he was with a married woman, his wife, and he savored and prolonged each stage to fill himself with experience, feeling the familiar shape of her mouth, teeth behind lips, the tongue, the curve of her rib cage and firm stomach, her hip, the strength of her legs, the cords in her inner thighs, and then the same curves with no clothes, the closer curves, the aroma of her skin, the feel and texture of it when she was ready, the taste, savoring that, her breasts aroused, one cool and one hot from the fire and both tipped up to him, their texture, tips, stretching out her arms to feel them taut against him, and he would enter for the first time, now, his wife, wet, the strong legs, walls, and then in a blossoming in his upper consciousness knowing she held his child, a life inside her, there, the nudge of muscle, that kiss, the light of the fire over her hair, her eyes, thighs rising, the points of her hair like stars, like Orion, Oh, love, love, Oh, El, Oh, love, "Oh, El."

"Yes, Chris, yes."

Holding him tight inside, she whispered, "That's the first time you've talked to me like that since we've been back together."

They lay together for a long time in silence. He felt her arms grow heavy and lifted his head and saw that she was asleep. He drew gently out and away from her and got a blanket from the couch and covered her, watching the light from the fire waver over her face.

He lifted his head quick, his hands still on her, and held himself tense. There was some sound. Someone knocking? No, it was too faint for that. A woodpecker? Too metallic. And it didn't move from tree to tree. He strained himself to hear. Nothing now. He went to a front window (why didn't any of these windows have curtains?) and looked out. If there was a moon tonight, it was buried in a cloud bank. The yard was dark. Only the trunks of the birches gave off a pale glow. He went to a back window and looked: a square of light on the ground from the window, a pine seedling standing in a corner of the square. Then the sound came again. It was measured and regular, like the tapping he imagined for himself when a watchman in a Russian story tapped the hour.

Or like the tapping of a blind man.

It stopped.

He felt there was someone watching him as he stared out the window, waiting for him in the dark. It was someone he knew. Suddenly he was afraid.

Or had he imagined it?

He went toward Ellen to wake her, knelt at her side, reached out his hand, hesitated, then slowly drew away. No.

The tapping started again.

He pulled on his pants, put on his shoes and a shirt, and went through the kitchen and out the back door. He stood still in the night air, listening, feeling the breeze cool his face. The sound was coming from the woods ahead of him. He walked across the driveway to the edge of the trees. It was too dark to see. He cupped his hands around his mouth.

"Hey!"

The echo of his shout carried and carried like a stone

skipping over water, growing smaller and smaller with distance, then sank. Silence.

And then once more the tapping began.

He started through the woods, heading in the direction of the sound. Dead leaves, twigs, and mulch crushed underfoot, making so much noise he wasn't certain he heard the tapping. Surely not at the moment. He stopped. Was he losing his faculties? No. There it was again, farther ahead and to his left. He waded through a stand of waist-high underbrush and suddenly was slapped and jumped back. In the darkness, he felt around for the branch that had slapped him, found it, held it out of the way, and went ahead faster, bearing toward the left, feeling his way, one arm raised to shield his eyes.

He stopped. It had to be close now. It seemed to originate in front of his face. He held out both hands, took a few steps forward, and bumped into something. A small tree. Then, on the ground in front of him, he saw it. The dim bulk of something big. Motionless. He feinted toward it and made a noise. It didn't move. He edged forward and prodded it with his toe. Hard. He went down on a knee and touched it. A steel barrel rusted thin, holes eroded in it, a fallen limb lying at its side. He squinted his eyes to see better. A wind sprang up, lifting his hair from his forehead, and the tapping began again. He bent his face close. A branch of the dead limb was springing in the wind, wavering tautly and striking the barrel in regular taps.

He reached out and grabbed the branch with one hand. It wouldn't break. He scrambled over on his knees and crouched above the branch and used the force of both hands. It broke with a sound like a gunshot in the still woods. He threw it from him as if it were alive and wiped his hands on his pants. Then he stood and looked around on all sides. He must have wandered into a valley without noticing it. In every direction for as far as he could see there was nothing but darkness and trees.

SIX

HE WOKE THE NEXT morning to the sound of crows *caw, haw, hawing.* He lifted himself up in bed and saw the birds, three of them, maneuvering around in a tree at the edge of the bluff, and at that moment, as if they sensed his eyes on them, they flapped off in silence. She was already up. He could hear, through the board wall between the two rooms, her footsteps and some clattering of utensils as she moved around the kitchen. He lay back, pitched his baritone in a high childlike treble, and sang on the same note, "Break—fast—in—behhhhh—ed," letting the last syllable drop down the scale a third, as in a liturgical chant.

"What was that?" she asked from the other side of the wall.

He sang again, "Break—fast—in—behhh—ed."

"Oh," she said. "You ruined it."

A few seconds later she came into the room carrying a tin tray and he scrambled up into a sitting position. On the tray was a plate of buttered toast, orange juice, a grapefruit half, sprinkled with brown sugar and broiled, two soft-poached eggs, still steaming, and a steaming cup of coffee.

"I was going to surprise you," she said. "Here, anyway." She placed the tray on the covers across his lap.

"How'd you know I'd feel like an invalid?"

"I didn't. You're my husband and I want to please you."

"A glass of water would have taken care of that."

"You have to eat every bit!"

"I will."

"And you have to do it without moving."

"Even my mouth?"

"From bed."

"God, it's beautiful. It reminds me of the mornings you used to come to my room and wake me. Remember?"

"Of course."

"Will you do this every day?"

"No. Once in a while. Eat, before it gets cold."

He, who had a bad morning stomach, and usually could tolerate no more than a glass of milk, ate everything on the tray. She sat on the edge of the bed and watched with satisfaction, with contentment even, it seemed, which was a rare emotion to see in her. When he was finished, she took the tray into the kitchen and he got out of bed and started dressing. Sunlight glowed like new gold on the top of the dresser and lay in bright squares on the wood floor, but a night chill was still in the building. It was so big and barny. He stepped into the main room and stopped at the sight of the bearskin. Should he tell her about the tapping? Last night he'd carried her, dead asleep, in to the bed. So why bother her with it now? He took up the bearskin and put it in place on top of the piano. The glass eyes and open mouth made him uneasy. He shoved its face toward the wall. He went into the hallway that led to the kitchen and tried the bathroom door. It held as though locked. He jerked on it.

"It's me," her voice said.

He leaned his cheek against the door and raised his eyebrows. "May I visit you?"

"No! I'm changing."

He shrugged his shoulders and wandered into the kitchen. The breakfast dishes were soaking in a metal dishpan on the cookstove (which was still radiating heat), and coffee grounds had boiled over onto the stovetop and lay there in splotches, shriveled and burned black. The water in the dishpan was steaming, and the pan rocked gently as streamers of bubbles swayed toward the surface, breaking through a film of oil there. He lifted a lid from the cookstove and held a cigarette close to the glowing coals, feeling their heat as icy pain against his fingernails. He jerked his hand out and drew on the cigarette; it was going. He turned and leaned his rump against the stove and crossed his arms.

In a few minutes she came out of the bathroom in the same Levi's and sweatshirt she was wearing when she served him breakfast. He brought the cigarette close to his lips and looked her up and down. "What did you change into?" he asked. "A vampire?"

"My swimsuit. It's underneath."

"Oh."

"We're going to the beach."

"It's too damn cold!" he said, and rubbed his upper arms, which turned nubbly at the thought.

"You at least have to come and see the trail. We can sunbathe."

"You can," he said.

From a closet in the hall she got out an army blanket, riddled with moth holes, and handed it to him. She stuffed some books and bottles of cream into a terrycloth beach bag, drew its drawstrings tight, and started toward the front door. She stopped and surveyed the main room. "Unbelievable!" she said.

"What?"

"Cleaning up. I hate even the thought of it."

"It's a chore?"

"That, yes, but just *doing* it."

"We should at least sweep up that glass," he said. "And I'll have to fix the window somehow before more sand blows in. Also, I have to mow the damn lawn."

"Oh, God, that can wait," she said. "It can all wait. Come on."

He slung the blanket over his shoulder and followed her out the door and through the tall grass of the front yard, which was wet with dew and dampened his pants legs to the knee. The sun was brilliant and the sky above them and the sky above the lake, all the way to the horizon, was banded with ribs of cirrus. A mist enveloped Manitou Island. "This is it," she said, and started down the trail. It traveled across the face of the bluff, descending at a gentle angle, passing through ground hemlock and trees, then cut back in the opposite direction and descended again in a switchback pattern. It was a narrow path, just wide enough for one person, and was slashed deeply into the clay of the bluff, so deeply that at certain points (where the terrain was especially precipitous and she was on a switchback beneath him) her head was moving just below his feet. It grew steeper. They entered a thicket of evergreen, where pale ferns grew against a bank of dark moss, and for a while they were walking on a level. Dried tufts of grass, fine as cornsilk, drooped from the face of the bluff. Dead branches had dropped onto the trail over the winter, and as he went along he picked them up and tossed them to the side.

"Oh, come on!" she cried, and took off running and got several switchbacks ahead of him and started grabbing tree trunks and swinging herself around corners. She disappeared into a thicket. He continued at the same pace, clearing up the branches as he went, and came to a large birch log, part of a dead tree, that lay directly over the trail. On the downhill side of the log he could see the print of her foot where she had leaped it. He couldn't budge it with his hands. He put down the blanket and braced his back against the bluff and shoved with his legs. The log started rolling, slowly at first, but picked up speed, went crashing through underbrush, then one end flipped up high and there was a *WHOMP* and splintering as it struck a tree. On the next switchback, he moved half of it off the trail again.

The face of the bluff grew more and more gravelly,

the trees thinned, and he came to an area that was absolutely barren. The trail cut back at the edge of the wash. He eased himself forward and looked over the edge; a long fall, a Niagara fall, with the regular creases of erosion streaming downward like water. He glanced over at the island of cedar, which was above him now. No sign of Mr. Woodchuck. He turned away, went shuttling back and forth in a slow descent, and came to more trees, mostly spruce with a few oaks growing among them, and then the trail led across a wooden footbridge that spanned the wash where it was narrow and sliced into a deep ravine. Now the ground was soft, sandy, and he could hear waves and smell water—the fresh smell and the other smell underlying it, always present if the body of water was large enough, and which gulls'cries, to him, embodied: a smell of decay. At the base of the bluff the trail branched to his left over a plateau of clay and gravel washed from above, to his right over a manmade ramp of piled stones, and straight ahead down a sandy cliff covered with small aspens. He took the branch to the right, over the stones, and when he came through the last of the trees the sun on the sand blinded him.

He blinked rapidly, trying to get his eyes to adjust, and looked up and down the beach. The water was breaking in small waves, scudding evenly up the beach except straight out from him. There, four or five pointed rocks, large and black, stood above the level of the water and the low waves exploded and foamed around them. There was an undulation of dunes in all directions and the dunes nearest the woods were covered with grass. He didn't see her anywhere. He went toward the rocks ahead. At first the sand was packed, but soon he was moving through it with the effort it took to move through the sand of his dreams. He stopped and looked around. Behind him, in a flat area enclosed by trees on three sides, he saw her lying on her back.

"Holy Christ!"

She sat up, startled, propping herself on an elbow. He walked over and dropped the blanket and started to circle around her, making sounds that bordered on astonishment and the obscene.

"What is it?" she asked. "What's wrong?"

"Where did you get *that?*"

"What?"

"The fig leaf and bottle caps." It was an orange bikini, not that scant.

"Oh," she said, and lay back again, positioning the beach bag under her head. "Is that all. I don't know. I've had it for a while."

"I've never seen you in it."

She lay silent, eyes closed against the sun, her skin glistening with lotion, her palms turned up. He walked around her once more, trying to see her with a detached eye. "I bet you got it in New York."

"The sun's great," she said. "Come lie beside me. Take off your clothes."

"I don't want to take my clothes off."

"There's nobody around."

"As if I gave a diddly shit."

"Just your shirt, then. I love to see you tan."

"You got that thing in New York, didn't you?"

"I don't remember."

"Why can't you just come out and say it? What is it with you? Why do you have to be so goddamn evasive?"

"I don't remember. Really."

"There's been a hell of a lot lately you don't remember," he said. "A hell of a lot." He turned away and started down the beach, heading toward the cove where he'd seen the wreck. Detritus. Weathered boards, driftwood, ship's timbers, cans and bottles, a cardboard ice-cream container, a scattering of bleached paper and bits of colored plastic, pieces of rusted tin, feathers, a dead gull—a collage of sea wash, a gallimaufry of it. He went down close to the waterline and walked on sand that was wet and firm and printed with sandpiper tracks. There was a maroon chair cushion snagged on a rock, slogging in the water, the cotton wadding coming out of it like sheep fat. Then the beach turned rocky— gravel and stones stretching from the treeline to the water—and he came over a slight rise and scared up a group of gulls; they wheeled off on creaking wings, crying.

His left boot sank as if in quicksand. He tugged at it, startled, and it came loose with a sucking sound. He stepped up on a stone. A small stream was trickling through the rocks. He followed the stream up to the edge of the trees and saw that a bowl-like pool had been scooped out in the smooth stones. He went down on his knee and put his hand in the water and jerked it out as though shocked. It was so icy it felt electric. Could you drink from it, he wondered, and looked up the beach in her direction. He had come a long way, and she was no longer in sight.

He walked another quarter of a mile to the cove and stared out at the wreck. It didn't look as tempting as it had from a distance; just a dark area, about fifty feet out—an oblong of water stained pinkish-orange. Hell. Maybe the edge was taken off his interest because of his mood. He looked back in her direction, and then walked toward the trees, up a slight rise, in order to see it better. No difference. Just a meaningless blur. Damn. *God*damn. Goddamn it, goddamn her, goddamn everything.

He sat on a boulder and covered his face with his hands and listened for a long while to the sound of waves near him and the sound of gulls in the distance. Then he rose and walked back up the beach to the sheltered area where she'd been sunbathing. She had spread out the blanket and was lying in the center of it, still in the suit, still on her back

"Saint Lawrence," he said.

"What's that?"

"A martyr They put him in a fire, were roasting him

to get him to renounce, and he said, 'Turn me over. I think I'm done on this side.' Sound advice."

"Oh," she said.

"What's the matter?"

"Nothing."

"Why the small voice?"

"It's how I feel in the sun, I guess. Mutable."

"What's that got to do with a voice?"

"I don't know."

"You feel like shit, don't you, about what I said."

"No. Just exhausted. Drained."

"Oh," he said, and the anger went out of him. "It's probably because of the way you came down the trail. Maybe you shouldn't do that any more."

"No, it's good exercise. I think it's just that the sun's getting to me."

"Then you're ready to go up?"

"Soon. Not yet."

"I am."

"Don't you like the beach?"

"Yes."

"It's almost always this deserted. Once in a while somebody wanders past."

"I looked at the wreck."

"What did you think of it?"

He shrugged his shoulders. "It's a wreck. When it's warmer, I want to dive around it and see what it's like. I can't tell from shore." He lingered beside her. A conversation like this, he realized, could only take place outdoors, under an afternoon sun.

"Well," he said, "I guess I'll go up now."

"Go ahead."

"Don't you want to come?"

"Soon."

With the toe of his boot he moved a rock around beside the blanket, then pressed it into the sand. "El."

"Yes?"

"Do you love me?"

"Of course!" She shielded her eyes to see him. "Why ask such a thing?"

"You haven't said it since we've been married. You used to."

"I didn't think I had to. I thought it was assumed."

"It's not bad to hear now and then."

He stood a long time in silence to give her a chance to say it.

"Well, hell," he said. "I'm going up. Is there anything I can carry?"

"No. Thanks."

"The blanket? The bag?"

"No, I'll get it."

"Fine," he said. "You do that." He stalked over to the plateau of clay and gravel and started up the trail. It was steeper than he anticipated, the switchbacks longer, more formidable and tortuous, and before he got to the footbridge he put his hands on his thighs and started pushing down on them to get more leverage. Even so, he soon had to stop and lean against a tree. Out of shape. Too many smokes. No physical work. Not for years. Unless you counted sex. Might as well count it. Hey, where were the lungs? It was like sucking air into a cistern. Come on, alveoli, get hold of it. Do your stuff. He wiped his forehead with his sleeve, shoved off from the tree, and continued climbing upward, slower now, feeling the exertion in his calves, a cramp and flutter of muscle. Think good things. Exploring wilderness. Lewis and Clark. Come on, troops, this last hill and we'll have it made. Oh, ho, Onward Christian so—o—ol—diers, marching as to—ooo war! . . . Forging new trails. Daniel Boone, Davy Crockett. A coonskin cap with the tail flying. Another frontier. Hold those flags high, lads, it's for the land you love. O beautiful for spacious skies, for amber waves of grain, for purple mountains majesty . . . Majesty, *majesty,* hear that? March to those drums. A *rum* ta-ta tum. A, *rum* ta-tum. She's a grand old flag . . . Keep in step! . . . she's a high flyin' flag, and for—That's the way. Almost to the summit. Up Matterhorn with no sweat. Up Everest for the first time. Up— Oh, shit. He stopped and sat down on a rock, panting.

VAN EENANAM FOUND DEAD
AT ALTITUDE OF 60 FEET

. . . 2

He made it to the top, finally, after several more rest breaks, and stood at the edge of the bluff with his fists on his hips, looking over the lake. In the straight rays of the sun the water was pale turquoise and was now so calm he could see the sand bottom, the refracted light lying in ribbons along the sand, the submerged rocks and the places where there were pebbles instead of sand (which his mind recorded as no good for swimming), and the light-green areas where plant life grew. It was worth the climb, once the climb was made, just to look down on it. The air was sweeter here, less cloying and dense, and it was tranquilizing to stand at ease and breathe it. His heaving chest gradually quieted. His calf muscles, however, which were badly overworked, kept fluttering, and he felt as exhausted as if he'd done a day's hard labor in a half hour.

Then, to his left, he caught movement in the corner of his eye and turned just in time to see the woodchuck disappear into the island of cedar. The fatigue left him. He hurried over in that direction. Starting where the yard ended and the meadow began, a strip of thick brush grew along the edge of the bluff. He followed the brush until he felt he was in line with the high dorsal of clay that curved down to the island of cedar. He turned and pushed through the brush, scratching his forearms,

148

and came to the edge. He'd misjudged. A little more to his left. He sidestepped over toward the dorsal of clay, and saw that it did not, as it seemed to, extend all the way up to the lip of the bluff. There was a drop of at least six feet down to it, and the peak of the dorsal was pointed, as sharp as the mountain peaks on dimensional maps.

He tramped on the sod at the lip of the bluff. It seemed well anchored and secure. He looked over the edge and saw roots, the size of big grapevines, hanging loose. There were no toeholds on the dorsal of clay, though, just small streaks of erosion as fine as the lines of valleys on those maps. A popple sapling grew a few feet back from the edge of the bluff. Getting a good grip around its trunk, he lowered his legs over the bluff, then let himself slide down until he was hanging by one hand, and pedaled his feet around to find footing. Concave under there. He could just touch the face of the bluff with his boot. He tucked his head to look below. Not much of a drop, but it would be hell to straddle it. He searched out a big root with his free hand, tugged on it as hard as he could, then grabbed it with both hands and slid down quick to solid ground. Keeping hold of the root, he turned and put an arm over the dorsal of clay, gripping it with his elbow as though it were a timber adrift in water, a life preserver (which it might well be so long as it kept him from rolling down the side of the dorsal and into the big wash), and started moving ahead, stomping footholds into the steep slant of the dorsal's side.

The island of cedar was about seventy feet away and after a while, as the base of the dorsal began widening to meet the island, the going was easier, and finally he let go with his elbow and went in a dead run down to the flat sandy area in front of the cedars. A fire had been built there. Scorched and half-burned logs were lying around. On the other side of the island of trees, to the left of the big wash, there was a smaller wash, less eroded and precipitous, with a healthy stand of trees growing in it, and he imagined that was the approach people used to get here to build a fire. Or whatever.

He climbed onto the island of cedar. It was virgin land. Dead skeletons of cedar, standing at rakish angles, were nearly as profuse as the live ones, which grew so thickly it was difficult to move through them. In the places where sunlight pierced the maze of trunks and interlocking boughs, moss grew; not in flat patches, but in high, bulbous mounds, and on the trunks of the trees and on the moss, too, were spots of fungus the color of copper oxide. There was no grass, just the moss and a layer of needles three inches thick. It would be impossible, he decided, to find a parked automobile in this tangle of growth, much less a wary animal, and then he saw, through a gap in the branches ahead, a mound of dirt. It looked freshly grubbed up. Twisting around, shouldering his way through the scratchy boughs, he worked his way down to it. A cavity large enough to be the entrance to a den had been dug into the earth, but if the woodchuck had originally planned a den here, he must have abandoned the idea. The cavity dead-ended after a foot. He stuck his boot into the hole and kicked around to make sure this wasn't a false bottom of dirt hurriedly pushed into place to deceive him. No. Then, with his foot, he tested the ground in the vicinity of the digging but it, too, was solid. Elusive Mr. Woodchuck.

He sat down in the open, mossy area next to the mound of dirt and lit a cigarette. A small birch trunk that lay in front of him, half buried in the needles, had split so regularly with age as it settled into the earth that it seemed someone had sawed it in sections. He kicked it and pieces went flying like splashed liquid. It was just a roll of bark rotted to sawdust inside. He looked at the sky. The cirrus clouds were gone, replaced by mounds of cumulus moving in from the lake. He put the cigarette between his lips and lay back with his hands behind his head. He liked feeling hidden.

He watched the cumulus clouds move ponderously in

his direction, massing, billowing out, overtaking and enfolding one another. From where he lay, isolated, it seemed a performance staged especially for him. He listened for the woodchuck, for any unnatural noise, but heard none. There was only birdsong, birdsong, the kyriology of it, and the sound of wind in the boughs. Like dresses rustling. Crinolined skirts of crepe and silk. Bustles. A gathering of women at a costume ball holding their voices to a whisper. Their full-length and expensive skirts brushing against other skirts. Crinolines. Satin and taffeta. Perfumed breath.

He wanted to stay here.

He stood up and ground out the cigarette.

Why should that thought terrify him?

He worked his way through the trees and jumped onto the area of sand. Who'd built this goddamn fire? He kicked the logs into the wash. He started up the dorsal of clay, and then stopped, remembering the easy way up, the wooded wash on the other side of the island of cedar. A flat shalelike rock was imbedded in the clay in front of him, and he noticed that its surface was covered with fossils shaped almost like snails. He tried to lift it loose and the top layer snapped off like wood shingle. There were fossils beneath the layer that had snapped off. He dug all around the rock, driving clay under his nails, and saw that there were about ten seams, ten layers in all, and most likely each of them was covered with similar fossils. She would want to see it. He looked toward the lodge and the trail. No sign of her. He lifted the rock loose, then set it back in place.

A boulder the size of a tub, up in the wash close to the bank swallow holes, had caught his attention. Most of the boulder's surface was exposed, and it clung precariously to the face of clay, ready to roll. He started climbing, stomping footholes and grabbing hold of occasional roots for safety, and by slow process made his way up to the boulder. He kicked and dug above it to fashion a place to sit, a wide ledge with a deep seat, and settled himself into it and shoved at the boulder with his feet. It began to give, a wet rim showing around its base, and he pushed with all his strength, his leg and back muscles trembling, and at last it broke loose.

It started slow, thumping the ground—a stream of sand and gravel trailing behind in a small landslide—and picked up speed, taking longer leaps, thudding with each one, crashed through a silver maple as if it were sage, struck a rock, chips flying, went high in the air and came down with a shock he could feel, and rumbled down a gorge out of sight. He listened to the retreating noise of it, and then heard a loud report, like muffled thunder, and wondered what it had hit. Not the bridge, he hoped. Loose clay and pebbles were still sliding in its path, shifting down the face of the bluff. He heard chattering and looked up; bank swallows were poking their heads out of their holes, curious, nervous, and withdrawing them quick.

He spotted another boulder, a smaller one, farther away near the center of the wash, and it also looked ready to take the trip down. He started toward it. The face of the wash grew steeper, almost vertical it seemed, and the clay beneath his footholes slipped away several times and he had to throw himself flat and grab at rocks to keep from sliding. He began kicking holes straight into the face of clay with his toes and taking sidesteps to each new one. He kicked several times. *Ze gods are angry at me because they knew.* He stepped over to it. *Ze gods are angry at me because they knew.* The driving rhythm of the song wouldn't leave him. He kicked again. *Ze gods are angry at me because they knew.* What the hell came next? He could remember hearing it only once. It must have been a popular song at the time. It came over the radio. *Ze gods are angry at me because they knew.* His father and uncle sat in the front seat, singing along with the radio in the car. His mother and aunt were in the back, and he stood between them with his elbows on the front seat so he could see out the windshield. It was spring. A gravel road. The green fields going past. *Ze gods are angry at me because they knew.* "Stop," his mother said. "Here! Stop!" The car slowed and swayed in the loose gravel of the road, pressing him against the front seat, and the adults got out, leaving the doors open, the radio playing, and ran into the ditch, where a high yellow spray was growing, and picked handfuls of it, all that was in sight, until the ditch was green. Then they came back to the car, laughing, and loaded it in his lap. It was mustardseed. Then what? What was said? What? The car took off and the men began singing again, loudly now, as if intoxicated. *Ze gods are angry at me because they knew.* The mustardseed in his lap, the smell and color of it.

He stopped. At this slow rate, picking his way along, it would take another five minutes to get to the boulder. And where would he be then? In the middle of the wash, at its steepest point, with nowhere to rest and his energy gone. He sent some rocks near his hand rolling down. He looked up and judged he was near the intersection of the meadow and yard. To his left, a small birch with trembling leaves jutted over the edge of the bluff, looking frail as a fern, delicate as a web against the sky, a thing to be photographed. The erosion would take it next, he thought, and just then Ellen appeared beside it and put her hand on its trunk.

"Hey!" he called. "Get back from there!"

She looked over the edge and located him, about fifty feet below her. "What?" she said.

"Get back from there! It's all eroded underneath. I can see roots hanging down!"

"It's safe," she called. "I always stand here. It's my thinking place."

"Maybe it was safe before, but it's not now."

"What are you doing down there?"

Good question. "Looking around. Exercising. Trying to get back in shape. Have you ever climbed along here?"

"Once. When I was young."

"It's a gas."

"Are you going all the way across?"

"Not now. I have to go back and pick something up. I found something for you."

"What?"

"Wait and see." He was tired of shouting up to her. He took a few sidesteps, then stopped and looked up. "Really, El, I don't think you should be there. The thing you're standing on is just an overhang of sod. I can tell from here. Why don't you move back?"

Her head disappeared.

With footholes already dug, the return trip was speedy and effortless, and he picked up the fossilized rock, crossed over the dorsal of clay, and walked up the easy slope of the other wash. When he came around to the yard, she was sitting cross-legged close to the birch, several feet back from the edge of the bluff, the beach bag and the blanket beside her. He handed her the rock.

"Oh, yes," she said, turning it in her hands.

"You've seen that kind before?"

"Yes. I have lots in the attic."

"What is it?"

"I forget the name. It's very common here."

"But look." He sat down and took it from her. "It's all in layers. There are fossils along every layer."

"I know. It always comes that way."

"Oh." He was disappointed; things like this usually interested her no matter how many times she'd seen them. He gave it a toss and it went clattering down the wash.

"Don't do that!" she said. "Why did you do that?"

"You said you have lots of it."

"Keep it for yourself."

"Sure." He took out a cigarette and smoked in silence, staring down at the lake. The sight of the water, the clear air, and the taste of tobacco interwove in a way that, for some reason, aroused him sexually.

"I've lost all time sense," she said.

"What's that?"

"I've lost all time sense. Just yesterday we were in the minister's office, but this morning is months distant. It's as if the accident just happened and I'm alone again."

"What do you mean? This morning was great. Breakfast in bed."

"That's miles away. I can't remember the last time I was happy."

"This morning! And last night. And when we first got here."

"When we got here was nice. That's closer. The plants and flowers."

"You were happy."

"Yes. But now I'm alone."

"Why, when I'm here?"

"It's an inborn thing I don't think anybody can change, and it's been with me all the time, even before the accident. It's as if I grew up alone, in a room by myself. The first time my life isn't solitary or bottomless is when I met you, and even though that was three years ago, it's as if you just walked into the room and touched my hair."

"Then you aren't alone."

"I feel I am. It's impossible to explain a feeling so basic. And now that my time sense is gone, everything is confused. I guess it's time for lunch. Do you want lunch?"

"If you do."

"Also, I miss Winston. He's been here every summer, and I keep looking everywhere, expecting to see him. Whenever I go outside, I'm surprised he's not there. I want to call him. I want to see him come through the trees."

"It'd probably help if you talked more. You probably wouldn't feel so bad."

"Haven't we been talking?"

"You've been quiet."

"Then that must be confused with something else,

too," she said, and picked up the beach bag and the blanket. "Because I feel as if I've been talking every minute since I got here."

She turned away and walked toward the lodge, trailing the blanket behind her like a lost child.

. . . 3

Noodle soup from a package, sandwiches, tea, and a
total silence between the two of them as they lunched in
the sunlit dining wing. When he was done, he got out
the power mower and saw that it was not self-
propelled. He undid the rope from the handlebar. It
was hard to start. Winter was still in its piston. *Ka-slog,
Ka-slog, slog-slog-slog*, it went, then *screak, screak*, as
the flywheel slowed and *pok!* kicked back. Finally he
got it started, got the carburetor adjusted—for density
of smoke it seemed, in the case of this machine—and
wheeled the noisy thing around to the front of the
lodge, feeling already the flat sense of deafness that
would remain with him as long as the motor was going,
making his mind feel insulated and insular, a satellite
gliding above the grass, following the orbit the lawn
mower made. By the time he cut a swath out to the
bluff, staying a distance from its edge, and cut another
swath back to the lodge, describing a long rectangle, he
was able to gauge the speed at which the grass demanded he travel—the cautious plod—and his mind was
freed.

How's the weather in the head?

Bad.

What's the matter up there?

Her.

What's the matter with her?

Who knows?

With a tinny sound the blade sent a branch flying through the air.

Second thoughts about him, sure as hell, about the marriage and all its complications. At first she'd even considered an abortion, without letting him know, but then sent the telegram. Van Eenanam flying North to play white knight, her still undecided about what to do, and who wouldn't be with the grandparents, the accident, and him, the disaster, around her in legion. "It's up to you. Do whatever you think is right. I love you, you know that, but I refuse to pressure or trap you." Quoth knight to fair maid. Now abortions were fine in the abstract, when granted to mothers whose lives were in danger, to victims of rape, disease, and so forth. But when the life was inside the woman you loved, and a part of you . . . Nevertheless: "I have money if you need it. I'll go along with whatever you say." Finally, after three days of lying in silence in the motel room, she turned to him (he was on the floor, drinking from a bottle of gin), and said, "I've decided. We're going to be married."

Who knows what went through her head in those three days?

He worked to keep his blank.

He walked along the end of the rectangle, turned, and started back.

How could he say that marriage was right for him? Where did the pressure really fall? She knew that he loved her and would marry her if she asked him to. And now he was responsible for her, and a child besides, before he'd learned how to take care of himself. And what was marriage? A sculpture? Hell, if it was what he'd felt for the past weeks, this alternation between terror and rage, could he take it?

Better let that one go.

She came back from New York quiet and reserved, in a way more sure of herself, in other ways more uncertain, and he could never see her as the person he had known, perhaps because she wasn't. Even the color of her eyes had changed from light blue to blue-green. "Guile," he said, when he saw it. He'd been East to visit her once, just once, and that was a disaster (let that go, too), and since her return they'd been skimming along the surface of the present, which was so damn thin, enjoying themselves most of the time, true— those beautiful days at the Blackstone—but shying from any topic that was painful or touchy. Evading everything of importance.

What was important?

Her.

Why was it that when you cared for a person it sometimes moved you further apart? He felt closer to her, much closer in many ways, that first morning they talked in his room. Was it the year, that whole space of a year between them—was that it? The unknowns that were possible in that length of time, in that city, tended to make her more mysterious and desirable, if one cared to be frank, but in direct proportion to the relationship growing between him and this new Ellen, he was beginning to miss her, in retrospect, during the time she was away, and starting to hate that year. And from the hour of their marriage it seemed every conversation caused further uncertainty and confusion, until he sometimes felt he was with a stranger. And he'd been a bit subdued and weird himself. Had she changed that much? She was changed, of course, and changed even more by being pregnant, more than she might know or admit—the way she carried herself, and looked at him, the way her eyes were growing larger and more round—but the same persons they were when they met still resided in each of them, didn't they? So where were those people now?

He skirted the trunk of a birch.

And what about their love? His love, he should say, because, after all, it was only an emotion he carried in him and had nothing to do with her feelings. Why, when he loved her, did he act the way he did? Like that girl on the bus. He'd almost forgotten about that. Jesus, look at that. She didn't even know about that. That was desecration of both of them, of three of them, for God's sake. And what would the beast in him do turned loose in the city again? When he was alone in Madison, he'd run through so many women he realized he was on a new one every third week. He never used the word love to get through to them, or the emotion, just sex, unabashed sex, sex as a club, the women whipping posts of his despair. He remembered them as short, tall, plump, dark, skinny, nice, or as those thighs, this mouth, her mound of Venus, that action, with pity or shame or disgust with himself, but with no malice, and little personal attraction.

What the hell was he thinking of?

What a hell of a thing to be thinking of.

Soon they would have a child of their own, a *child*, and he would be responsible for doctor bills, hospital bills, food, clothes, a home, security for him. Love. Seeing it as *him*, he grinned, then turned solemn. He had the fellowship, he'd have to work hard to keep that, and he'd have to put in more hours at his job. But would that be enough? She was Spartan by nature, hoarding even, but, as her grandfather pointed out, the luxuries were there when she wanted them. Like this lodge. He couldn't allow her to work, his pride wouldn't permit it. Maybe he should just chuck school and go into business, what the hell, he knew he could get a good job. But could he stand permanent work?

Better let that one go, too. Play it by ear, as they said back home. Maybe he'd been doing that too much? Like the way he eased into marriage, his mind a blank (except for that minister's thing about lust, the bastard), without going into this before. But did you need to if you were in love?

He'd never thought much about an actual child and, hell, when you came right down to it, there was no way of really knowing whether it was his child or not. No, if he doubted that, even suspected it, he never would have married her. Still, dammit, there was no way, no absolute—

He killed the motor. Its last sounds went ringing through the trees. He lifted his eyes toward the woods, as if to see the sound go, and saw a sight as remarkable as that would have been. She was sitting beside the small birch, her head bowed, her legs hanging out of sight over the edge of the bluff. He hurried out and came up behind her. "El," he said softly, letting her know he was close. "Should you be sitting there? I told you it's all eroded underneath."

He took a couple stiff sidesteps and looked over the edge. It was steeper here, a sheer drop for sixty feet, and then the tan face of sandy clay fell away in a sharp slant, and he could see, far below, the trail the tumbling boulder had left, growing fainter and fainter toward the bottom until it was no longer visible. Far below that was the border of trees and the faint line of the beach. He stepped back.

"Hey, look," he said, and ran his toe along a line behind her, where the sod had parted and dropped down, putting the overhang she sat on a few inches below the rest of the lawn. "El, look. The damn thing could give way."

She wouldn't turn to him.

"El? What's the matter?"

There was no sign of response. He moved closer.

"Don't go into your catatonic thing. Tell me."

Not even a movement.

"You're worried about your grandparents, aren't you?"

There was a slight movement of her head that to him, an experienced observer of her, signified that she was shaking it no.

"Uncertain about the future?"

Again she indicated no.

"Me?"

He squatted beside her and reached over her shoulder and turned her face toward him. She averted her eyes, and the tears that had been gathering in them spilled over her lashes and slid down her cheeks.

"That's what it is, isn't it? It's me, isn't it?"

"I want to fall off and roll all the way down and kill it!"

He threw an arm around her and pulled her onto the lawn and pinned her by the arms. She struggled against him, arching her body up, and cried, "I don't want to be pregnant! I want to destroy it!"

"*Ellen!*"

"I don't want it, I don't want it! I'm oppressed by it, smothered, trapped! I'm not ready!"

"You are too. You're the most capable person I know. You can—"

"I don't want to waste my life! I don't want to turn into a do-nothing housewife like every other housewife in the world!"

"You won't!"

"How can I help it? It's starting already and it'll get worse! I'm not *doing* anything."

"What do you mean? You're making me happy."

"Oh, Christ, I'm ugly and miserable!"

"You're not. You're not even showing it, you know that. You're prettier than you've ever—"

"*Inside!* I'm miserable inside!"

"You're not."

"I've been miserable for weeks!"

"See, you should have talked."

"What could I say? *What*? It's growing inside me, a living thing—I can feel it!—and there's nothing I can do! It's ruling my life. That's not fair, it's not right. I want to destroy it!"

"You have no right to want to destroy it! It's a part of you!"

"If it's a part of me, it's a part I don't want!"

Her eyes altered, the color of her flesh changed, and she started choking. He released her wrists and she covered her face with her hands and rolled on her stomach. All his arguments, justifications, platitudes, and sanctimonious advice fell from him. It was the life inside her that bound them together, he was responsible for that life; and she didn't want it. There was nothing he could say.

He ran his hand over her hair and onto her back, feeling, through the thick opposing ribs of her sweater, the strong ribs of her back heaving against his hand, falling, and again heaving up, demanding comfort. He started patting her. "Don't," he said. "Don't. I'll make it all right. Don't. Please." He still had the money. He would get an abortion.

Why fight it? Why not acknowledge his fears, and admit that her grandparents were right, that she was right; that they had done the wrong thing. That he was not meant to be her husband. After the abortion, he would let her divorce him, and leave. Few people knew they were married, and nobody else ever had to.

But how let her go?

He sat for a long time, subduing his emotion, resigning himself to the decision. Then he said, "Ellen, here's what we have to do. First—" He was unsettled to see that his hand was still lying on her back and patting her, like a life in itself. He moved it away. "Ellen, here's what we have to do. Are you listening?" He turned her over so he could see her face.

She was asleep.

He lifted her in his arms and her eyelids fluttered and she murmured, "I'm cold, I'm cold, I'm cold." He carried her to an elm halfway to the lodge and laid her down on a wooden bench beneath its overhanging branches. Then he ran into the lodge and came back with the army blanket and covered her with it and tucked it around her feet, along her sides, and, more carefully, around her neck, staring at her parted lips and pale face, where lozenges and diamonds of sunlight were sliding from side to side. He sat on the ground next to her and lit a cigarette, staring at her face.

How let her go?

Dear El, I can't stand to see you in torment, and I don't know what I'd do if you ever hurt yourself . . .

Mentally, he erased that.

El, my wife, I want to call you wife once more . . .

No.

Dear El, we've been through so much and . . .

How?

He had to. He couldn't stand to see her spirit broken.

Oh, El, I . . .

His mind gave out. He smoked down the cigarette and watched her face become composed and flood with color, and her serenity in this state of sleep, from which he was excluded, made him absolute about his decision.

He put out the cigarette.

Since there was nothing more he could do at the moment, other than keep an eye on her, he started up the mower and began again around the rectangle. When he came to the part of the yard where the bench was resting, he hesitated, then thought, Well, what's the difference now, and mowed around the bench, behind it, and under it. She slept undisturbed. It was turning dark when he finished. He walked the mower around to the back porch and, using the toe of his boot, a semicircular collage of slick mulch and wet seeds, he pressed the metal strip against the spark plug. When the motor was slowed down to half speed, the metal slipped off to one side and a shock leaped up his leg. He hopped away, shaking his foot as though it would come out his pants leg. Jesus! Couldn't a thing like that ruin you? He pulled out the choke and with his hands on his hips watched with satisfaction as the mower died in a profusion of its own blue smoke. Then he remembered her alone out front and took off running.

She was awake, sitting up, the blanket wrapped close around her. He went toward the bench, exhausted, depressed, partially deaf, the nerves of his hands still vibrating at the frequency of the mower, and when he placed his palms on the edge of the bench to ease himself beside her, he discovered they were spongy and numb, as though deadened with novocaine. He lowered his body with careful slowness onto the bench, feeling broken as an old man. He rubbed his palms on his thighs.

She was staring straight ahead, her profile showing against the background of the lake, which was darkening as the sun went down. Night insects were filling the woods with song. He was about to put his arm around her when her lips compressed and a tear started down her cheek. That was it.

"Ellen," he said, "I've come to a decision. What I'm going to do, I think, is—"

"The flowers! You mowed down all the flowers!" she cried, and let her head fall against his chest, sealing his words inside him.

SEVEN

XENOPTERYGII. *What*? Billiards being racked, cracked into with a cue. The apex of a triangle blasted to bits. A row of bombs erupting below. No, a taxi trying to park on the roof of a skyscraper, backing around to the retaining wall (black lines scratched on air, not brick, look), backing through it without feeling the bumper touch and starting down, making a single, slow, end to end revolution in the air as ... Copernicus. Apples added up. + what? Rumbling down a trough into the bin. A smell of smoke, stuttering light, sirens, ladders, and four or five firemen in slickers and hats falling past his open window. Archaeopteryx. Broadside from a battleship. The flash and shock of it followed by silence like a ... Check trajectory. + what?—whom? The flash and boom again and a piece of it, a circle of force hitting flat. Across him. A piece. Ah! Anent: *Every even number is the sum of two odd primes*. Peace! Peace!

He lifted himself on his elbow and a flash of light at the bedroom windows blinded him. Blackness. Gradually a faint sign of motion (from his retinas?) began to show in the blackness, as though it were composed of fluttering particles, and suddenly the air of the room went compact as a clap of thunder hit, then the whole of it came rolling over the lodge and the bedsprings trembled. He'd never felt anything like it. Close, it must have been close. Was that ozone he smelled? Again the yard was lit, with a light so brilliant every color bleached blue-gray, so that it seemed he was staring at the birches and elms and grass and bushes on a television screen—all blue-gray, all of it—instead of seeing the real thing, then blackness, a blackness he'd known only at the back of closets, impenetrable. He waited. There was a dim arc of light far out on the lake. Finally, the shattering eruption of thunder.

Then a blinding cat-o'-nine-tails was strung along the edge of the bluff, and it felt like the impact would bring in the front windows.

"Are you awake?" she asked.

"Does this happen often?"

"No. Never this bad. I keep trying to focus on something when the lightning comes, but I can't. Everything jumps toward me and is one-dimensional."

"Are you scared?"

"A little."

He felt around in the darkness, found her hand, and took it in his.

"I don't really mind, though," she said, "as long as we're safe. I've never seen such violence."

"You sound as if you like it."

"I do. It's beautiful to watch."

"We're not that safe without lightning rods."

"Oh."

"No, not really. I hope the rain comes soon."

"Why?"

"This part of the storm will probably let up."

"But I love it."

"You wouldn't if one of those bolts came through the window."

"Is that possible?"

"Of course. But there's nothing we can do except wait it out. If one's coming my way I want to see it."

They moved up and sat with their backs against the log framework at the head of the bed.

"Is it really that dangerous with no lightning rods?"

"Oh, I guess it's not so bad with all these trees around, as long as—"

A fine tracery of light vermiculated the woods, illuminating her face, her wide eyes, and along with the thunder that came instantaneously there was a sharper crack, a splintering, then a groan of split wood, a sound of branches crashing against leafy branches, a long series of crashes—a large tree—then the wallop as it hit earth.

"As I was saying, it's not so bad with all these trees around, as long as none of them fall on the lodge. That one, for instance, could have brought in the roof."

"In Milwaukee, one fell on my bedroom."

"While you were in it?"

"Yes. I was asleep."

"You weren't hurt?"

Her face was lit as if by arc light, her skin stained ashy-green, her lips violet, and in the ensuing blackness her profile clung to his retina. Thunder.

"No," she said. "It didn't even wake me. The gutter was torn off and the roof was damaged."

"When was this?" he asked, curious, but also trying to keep her mind off the afternoon, and the evening, too, when she'd cried herself to sleep.

"Just before I left for New York. I saw it as an augury. I almost didn't go."

"Why did you?"

"I can't answer that."

He watched the storm, the alternation between the blinding flashes, when the lawn and the trees framed in the window were bleached of color, and the blindness of the dark. After a long silence, he said, "It's impossible for me to imagine you during that year. Once in a while a scene comes to me, and I see you happy, a free spirit, doing everything with total interest—running down streets, going through those shops in the Village, hurrying toward a restaurant or a movie house, always toward light, and I always see a smile on your face and

your coat open and flying. Or I see terrible things." He
tried to isolate one that wouldn't shock her. "Like the
time I came out."

"Don't think of that. Please. And don't think of that
year in those terms. It wasn't that liberating or romantic. I was in torment most of the time."

"You think I wasn't?"

There was no response, naturally, and he was furious
with himself for bringing her back to the point he
wanted to lead her from. Well, hell, since they were
here now he might as well go on; he might as well tell
her about the decision he'd reached that afternoon and
get it over with. But where should he begin? And what
if she agreed?

"There it is," she said.

"What's that?"

"Your rain."

Random drops, like paws pattering over the shingles
above them, the drops growing larger, their sound slowly moving across the roof, and then, as though impatient, the rain came in full force, driving down, and the
whole building filled with its roar.

"God," she said. "It's like under a waterfall!"

"Barrels of it," he said.

"Cats and dogs."

"Pitchforks and hammer handles."

She laughed. "Where did you get that?"

"On the form."

The lightning, which struck with less frequency and
farther in the distance, was too faint to illuminate the
yard or the room, but the room itself seemed to be
taking on brightness, or else his vision, now that it
wasn't being assaulted every few seconds, was beginning to adjust; he could make out the humps of their
toes under the quilt.

Suddenly she screamed and started struggling under
the covers.

"El! What is it?"

"Something's crawling on me! *Ahh!* Get it off!"

He fumbled around at the center of the bed, found the switch to the lamp, and snapped it on. "What *is* it?"

"I don't know. It was on my hair. Ah! There it is!" She turned and slapped at her back, and he saw the shiny dust from a moth on her shoulder. He picked the insect off the sheet by its wings and held it up.

"Awk!" she said. "A moth!"

"What's the matter with moths?"

"I don't know. I can't stand them. Look! There's another one! Get rid of it!"

He batted it off the bedcovers. "For God's sake," he said, "you scared hell out of me. Why can't you stand them?"

"I don't know. They've never bothered me before. But now I feel the same way about them that those stupid women do about mice. There's something unwholesome about them. They give me gooseflesh. There's some more. Get them!"

There was a flyswatter hanging from a nail on the wall, behind the lamp. He took it down and stood up in bed, and slapped at the moths as they wobbled in clumsy orbits around the room. She covered her head with the quilt, and kept crying in a muffled voice, "Get them out of here! I can't stand them!" He killed all the ones in the air, then slapped dead several more that were clinging to the boards of the ceiling, and flipped them off the quilt onto the floor. They kept appearing and wobbling toward the lamp, apparently coming from other parts of the lodge. He continued swinging at them, and after a while it became ludicrous. "There's one," he said, and slapped the quilt across her buttocks. "Oooo!" she cried under the covers. He slapped the quilt some more, saying, "There's one. There's another. There's one coming under the covers. Watch it!"

Highly excited, trying to entertain her, he slapped all over the ceiling and bed. "There's another. Awk! And another. Ooo! God, El, you should see!" he cried, and his dramatics, to him, were so convincing that he began to scare himself. Then he remembered the night he'd felt a scrofulous, mothlike thing opening inside his head, and in his stimulated state of mind he imagined larvae and eggs encased under his skin, and started itching all over, scratching at his arms and stomach and head and scrotum, and slapped in a fury at the new moths that came flapping into the room as if drawn to him. Finally he threw down the swatter, shut off the lamp, and jumped between the sheets and covered his head like her.

"Jesus," he whispered. "There's a squadron of them out there. Where the hell do they come from?"

"I don't know, and I don't want to know."

"The storm must have stirred them up."

"Did you kill them all?"

"Just about. With the light off, the rest will leave."

"I'm staying under here all night."

"You'll get aspix—afsix—" He couldn't say the word.

"Asphyxiated."

"That's right."

"I don't care. I'd rather go that way."

"Moths can't hurt you, for God's sake," he said. Then, in a lower tone, as much for his own edification: "What makes you afraid of them?"

"I don't know. It must have something to do with being pregnant."

"Oh."

"Hold me."

He moved over and took her in his arms, and she positioned her head under his chin, cheek against his chest, and put her hands on his shoulders. The rain was still falling in a torrent on the roof. She moved her body closer and murmured, "I love rain. I love to hear it."

And in a few moments she was asleep.

Her regular breathing against his chest.

Dear El, love, my wife . . .

. . . 2

Just as the sun was rising, he woke. He dressed and went outside. The air was rinsed clean and there was a pleasant smell to it somewhat akin to the smell of laundry bleach. The lake was calm, placid, glasslike, but it showed the signs of a storm; it was murky with sediment, and for a hundred yards out the water was stained beige from clay that had washed down. The yard was littered with fallen limbs. He gathered up armloads of them, carried them around back, broke them into even lengths for the cookstove, and put them in a woodbox in the back porch. He found a Swede saw and went into the woods and located the tree felled by lightning. It was an ash, splintered and truncated ten feet from its big base, too large a tree to cut up without a power saw. He pruned off some of its smaller branches and dragged them through the weeds and underbrush to the back of the lodge. He looked around for something, couldn't see it anywhere, and went into the kitchen. She had just risen and was sleepy-eyed.

"Where's the sawing trestle?" he asked.

"The what?"

"The sawing trestle, log cradle, whatever you want to call it. It has another name, too, I think."

"You mean a saw?"

"No, no, no. It's about the size of a sawhorse. Two

big X's at each end." He crossed his forefingers to illustrate. "You lay a log in the crotch of the X's and it's held solid while you saw it."

"I don't know what you're talking about."

"You mean your grandfather doesn't have one?"

"I've never seen anything like it."

"How does he saw wood, for God's sake?"

"On a stump or somewhere. Orin cuts all the big trees."

He shook his head in disapprobation and clucked his tongue. "I can't understand how a man can own a place like this, where nothing but wood is burned, and not have a sawing trestle."

So he went out in the woods, found a small straight maple about the diameter of his bicep, sawed it down, dragged it to the lodge, sawed it into four posts of uniform length, a little over three feet, sawed notches into the center of each post, and bolted two of them together in the shape of an X; then the other two. He nailed board braces across the bottom of the X's, and had a sawing trestle, which he used to cup up the branches of the felled tree. He stacked the pieces of wood pyramidically in the sun to dry, and when she called him, for the third time, to come in for breakfast, he went in for breakfast.

After breakfast he straightened up the workbench in the back porch, which he'd noticed was in bad disorder when he searched for the bolts, and as he was arranging the cigar boxes, mason jars, and tin cans, and sorting their contents, he came across a box of glazier's points. He cleaned up the rest of the back porch, rearranging things to suit his conception of orderliness, and on a high shelf above the workbench discovered several panes of glass and a can of glazing compound. He opened the can; the gray compound was still oily and pliable. He took a pane of glass around to the front of the lodge and saw, as he suspected, that it would fit in the empty sash without cutting. Standard size. He pulled out the old glazier's points with a pair of pliers, scraped out the hardened putty with a bradawl, and installed the new pane of glass, wedging it firm against the sash with the points, and then sealed it evenly with the glazing compound.

He started gathering up the tools and material he'd set on the ground and noticed, next to the foundation of the lodge, a dead bird, its skull bare and white, the bones of its skeleton showing through damp, matted feathers. It must have been diving toward the light on the other side of the lodge. Ants were threading in and out of its empty eye sockets. He looked through the window and saw her lying on the couch in the main room, paging through a book. He picked up the bird by a claw, ran toward the woods, and gave it a toss, and it went spinning into the brush. He came back, picked up his equipment, and put it all in its proper place in the back porch.

He went through the kitchen into the main room. She wasn't on the couch. He knocked at the bathroom door and, when there was no response, pulled it open. Empty. He ran around to the bedroom. Empty. He swung open the front door and saw nothing but the lawn, the bluff, the lake.

"*Ellen!*"

"Here."

Her voice came from the attic. He went up the steps on weak legs, deciding that now, in addition to everything else, he'd have to keep a close eye on her. He found her in a storeroom. Its low ceiling took the steep pitch of the roof, and unless he stood in the center of the room he had to stoop. The air was stifling near the board sheathing and the ends of shingle nails showed through the boards. She was sitting on the floor next to a large box, picking rocks out of it one by one and studying them with interest. He squatted down beside her.

"This is my rock collection," she said, without looking up. "I didn't realize I had so many. I came up to get the binoculars, but I suppose we better clean the downstairs before I start watching birds. Here." She handed him the binoculars and started shuffling through a pile of dusty books. "These are mine," she said. There were old Zane Grey's, adventures of girl campers, adventures of twins, adventures of teenage detectives, and paperbacks about nurses. She picked one out and handed it to him. "This is my favorite of these."

He looked at the cover. *Black Beauty*.

"I read it the year after the accident. It's the saddest story I know. At home, before they built the country club, a neighbor lady who owned that land had a horse. She was too old to care for it herself, and her children lost interest in him after a couple years, so she let me handle him. I exercised him every day and fed him vegetables from the house. He was an old pinto with front legs close together—sign of a bad heart— and high withers, a mean, ugly thing, and his name was Sam. But I loved him and thought of him as Black Beauty. That's when I was in the sixth grade. I hated myself. I hated other girls. My hair was short and curly, I was flat-chested, and I had big feet. I only had one friend, a girl friend, and once when I was at her place and we were squishing barefoot in some mud— we never played dolls, she hated them, too—she said, 'Oh, Ellen, look! You have such big feet.' I never talked to her again."

She took back the book. Her expression and voice had altered, as though she'd returned to her speech patterns and appearance at that age. She showed him inflatable beach toys that were hers at one time, gull feathers she collected one summer to make an Indian headdress, some paintings she had done (one of the birch at the edge of the bluff), a piece of plywood with the Lord's Prayer glued in place, letter by letter, with alphabet macaroni, a plastic boat and old clothes, and with each object there was a story. It was humid and close in the room, but he began to feel another kind of closeness, internal and claustrophobic, as though these effects were closing around his soul, smothering and constricting its substance. He found it hard to breathe and swallow, a cold sensation of sweat broke over him, and he began to edge away from her, staring from her face to the effects with wide eyes, trying to get her attention.

". . . and about the same time, when I was in the eighth grade, a new boy started attending our school. He was good-looking, a show-off, and his family was so rich they sent him to school in a limousine. Naturally, every girl wanted to go with him. At that time people looked on me as the silent, aloof scholar, but it was only a façade to cover my fear and self-importance. Anyway, for a while—I'll never be able to fathom this—the boy went with me. I don't even know if I liked him, but he was in such demand he was status. Once when I was at a football game with him, he said, for no reason, 'I don't like you.' 'Why?' I asked. 'I don't know. I just don't.' Then he got up, moved one bleacher above me, and sat beside a girl he knew I despised, and put his arm around her. 'What are you doing!' I said. 'Turn around,' he said. 'I don't like your looks.' I had a paper cup of soda in my hand. I threw it in his face. He was mostly worried about his new jacket, but everybody else was shocked that I, the quiet—"

"Don't!" he said.

"What?"

"Stop!"

"What's wrong?"

"Don't talk any more."

"Why not?"

"I can't stand to hear that stuff."

"Why?"

"Because I wasn't there! I wasn't with you then!"

. . . 3

Over the fall and the winter, the time of the big winds, fine sand and powdery clay had blown under doors, through cracks in sashes, along sills, and through the broken window, and now lay undisturbed over every surface in the lodge. Life had gone on in the deserted building. Mice had discovered the shelves where the food was stored and had, as a reminder of their feasts, deposited an array of commas; potatoes had sprouted through a gunnysack in the back porch, the moths had multiplied, webs had been spun, eggs laid, red ants had found a hole in a log through which they entered in a single file, following an established route, and went toward a box of brown sugar; and the honeycombs of wasps, that frail architecture, had been fashioned in the eaves. Now it was their duty to clean it away. They wrapped rags around brooms and knocked down the cobwebs, standing on stepladders and tables to reach them. He swept up the glass and most of the sand in the main room, and she got out a vacuum cleaner and started to vacuum with a passion, vacuuming even the logs and the chinks between them, vacuuming the moose, vacuuming the possum. Keeping her in sight, he began to swab the windowsills and wipe off the furniture that had not been covered. Near the end of the day she turned to him with weary eyes, her hair tied up like a peasant's to keep it clean, wisps of it drooping over her brow, and said, "It's never been done this thorough."

They were half finished with the main room. They went to bed early, overwhelmed by the work they'd done and, worse, by the work that was yet to be done, too exhausted to eat dinner. She immediately fell asleep. He was tired, but each time his mind started going below the border of sleep, a surge of energy, like electric current, swept up his spinal column and jarred him awake. Several times he heard himself crying out. He thought of the lodge standing unoccupied and the life that had continued inside it. The tenacious insects. The mice. Now his body lay in its blackness. And his living self, his flesh and reflexes and brain, lay inside the sack of his body. Was his spirit deeper inside that? Some humming point of light at his center kept the outer layers from closing around him in sleep.

And what was sleep? Who was here to observe for eleven months the minute movement of insects and animals in the lodge (how complex the patterns they were erasing with a broom!), but, more important, who was there to observe what happened when the mind, overtaken by sleep, went empty? Scientists could record and report on the life in the lodge, but no scientist, no researcher, not even the REM men knew what happened in sleep. Who could say? Not them. Not you, the sleeper. You especially, taken under by the sea of it, what did you know? What happened in that blackness other than dreams? And what were they? Caravans of the past trying to cross the present into the future? An adjustment of daily perceptions of the external world (unreality?) in order to fit it within the unique world (reality?) of the mind? Neither of those? Dialogues with God? Incremental charges of electricity, stored during the day in the roots of the hair, held in check by the power of logic, and then going wild at night in a miniature version of electric shock to keep you sane? Delirium caused from sleeping on the left side? Active

particles of energy you were too lazy to release? Dissoci-
ation? Orgasm of the gray matter? New ideas strangling
memory to make room for themselves? A crossing
down into the realm of death? Dissonant harmony of
the blood vessels, unheard during the day, setting up
sympathetic vibrations in the brain which were trans-
lated into pictures, like that birch glade seen while
listening to Shostakovich? Instant psychotherapy? Or-
ders beeped down from superior creatures in UFO's?
What? And what could happen while you were unconscious, vulnerable, impotent, without a mind to respond? Couldn't something unknown enter that dark
place? And what if it did? Who would you wake as?

Jesus, wasn't he responsible, now especially when he
had dependents, to bring himself through sleep with his
mind intact? How did you do that without knowing, for
the past eight hours, what went on there? What if some
morning you rose out of sleep and didn't know whether
you were a blade of grass, bug, dew, circle around the
moon, man, or a molecule of air? With that thought he
lay awake until the sun began to glow gold on the
surface of the lake, and then he got out of bed and
went into the kitchen and made breakfast for them
both.

They worked again cleaning the lodge, but at a slower, more resigned, and reasonable pace, napping in the
afternoons or going to the beach to sun themselves. In
the evenings they read. They drove to the village often
for supplies and always stopped at the post office, a
frame building that had once been a Catholic mission,
to see if any mail had come for them in care of General
Delivery. But who would they hear from except her
grandparents? He wanted to hear from somebody.

They cleaned the lodge from the gable end that was
presided over by the moose to the corners of the dining
wing, and it took three days. Then they mopped all the
floors. He plugged the hole in the log (entry and exit of
the ants) with plastic wood. He wirebrushed the chimney screen he had thrown down, and put it on a shelf

in the back porch. He replaced the soap dish that had come loose in the shower. He went around to each window, working from the inside where he could watch her, and checked the hooks that held the sashes firm, and tightened or replaced the screw eyes on some of them.

"Why are you always singing?"

He turned quick, taken by surprise, and found her standing behind him. "I'm singing?" he said.

"Lately you've been humming or singing, even whistling sometimes, no matter what you're doing."

"Oh."

"Don't look that way. I love it. I've never heard you do it before."

He stared at the floor. He wasn't aware that he'd been singing. He looked at her.

"Why are you?" she asked.

"To keep the spirits away."

"What?"

Her eyes widened, and he saw in their depths the familiar terror start rising. Her parents. She thought he meant her parents.

"No, no, no," he said, "I'm just joking. You know. Deep woods, primitive life, evil spirits. All that." He put his tools on the windowsill and took her in his arms. "Why does anybody sing?"

"Yes," she said. "Why?"

"Because they're happy."

"Are you?"

"Of course. I have what I always wanted."

"And that's why you sing?"

"*You* make me sing."

"That's what I wanted you to say in the first place!"

"It's true. And if I'm doing it all the time, and not even aware of it, I must be happier than I realize."

"That's even better," she said, and put her arms around his neck. "Now growl for me."

It was a thing she had heard him do in the mornings,

unconsciously, when he lay half asleep, and she liked the animality of it.

He growled.

"Now carry me," she said.

"What's this?"

"Carry me."

"Where?"

"You know."

He lifted her in his arms and carried her into the bedroom, and afterward, when their bodies and hairlines were wet with sweat, she took him by the wrists, and said, "No, you can't move," and lay on top of him. They slept together the rest of the afternoon.

When he awoke, he finished fixing the windows.

He became more particular and concerned about the condition of the lodge. He bought a new latch for the back door and installed it so that the door was no longer self-locking. He put a new screen in the lower panel of the front screen door, and planed down the door at a point where it was binding with the jamb. There was a metal shelf in the kitchen, which accommodated the detergent, the cleanser, the Brillo pads, and dishrags, and it was beginning to rust and sag down. He undid the screws that held it in place, wirebrushed it clean in the back porch, gave it a new coat of enamel, and reinstalled it, inserting shims of tin under its bracket so it rested level. As he was tightening the last screw, surveying his handiwork with satisfaction, he noticed a piercing acid smell and turned around and saw her at the stove, cleaning the oven.

"Jesus," he said, and went to her and took the jar of oven cleaner away. "Jesus, you shouldn't be doing that."

"Why?"

"The fumes. Look. It says use only in well-ventilated places, and that's for people who aren't in your condition. You better go in the other room. I'll do this."

She went into the main room, and he began wiping the jellied layer of grease and cleanser off the walls of the oven. The smell was so toxic that when he held his face close to the stove, his eyes began to water, his nose and lungs burned, and he felt lightheaded. Why in the hell was she doing something like this? When he first turned toward her, her head was inside the oven. Jesus God. He opened the windows and the back door, and went to work again, trying to keep back from the smell, but he got whiffs of it, and every time it stung his nasal membranes he remembered her at the oven, and suddenly he felt feverish and so weak he couldn't grip well with his fingers. He finished the job and went into the main room, pale and drawn, and lay down on the couch.

"What is it?" she asked. "What's the matter?"

"Rank smell."

Again that evening he had trouble getting to sleep. What had he decided about dreams? About his spirit? Where was his soul? At his center—in his mind, his medulla, his marrow? In his right auricle? Or was it square, resting behind his lungs like an X-ray plate, as the nuns used to depict it on the blackboard? They made an outline in white chalk. With delicate strokes of colored chalk they drew twining vines and flowers inside to show purity and innocence. The state of grace. Then sin. They erased the flowers. They made gashes with drops of blood dripping. *Sin.* They slashed in ugly asterisks. Then they stomped it with a chalk eraser, chalk dust smoking, drying your throat, until the square was a solid slab of gray. Mortal sin. The death of the soul. Then they erased it. Ah. Now it was fluttering like paper above the flames of Hell, burning eternally but never burning up, constantly reviving to feel the fire. Eternal rest grant unto them, O Lord, and let the perpetual light shine upon them. Eternal rest grant unto . . . Oh, are you there, lilies and roses of my soul?

With each succeeding day, it seemed that his dreams, more and more, were chasing him, pursuing him to his last point of consciousness; when at last, with difficulty, he fell asleep, and then woke, the dreams mingled with his thoughts, tainting the reality around him, and finally overtook him so completely he went unconscious against his will. He began waking in the warm forenoons with a painful headache.

"Are you all right?" she would ask, watching him pick at his lunch with a glazed, abstract look in his eyes.

"Yeah. I think I'm on the trail of a solution to that four-color thing I told you about. Ideas come to me best when I sleep like this."

"Oh, that's great."

"Yeah."

Every time they went to the village he bought something new for the lodge: an extension cord, nails and bolts, ash trays, safety goggles, a caulking gun to use for sealing the cracks around the fireplace chimney, a towel bar, utensils and trinkets that he gave her as gifts—small articles for the most part. But one day he walked up to her while she was shopping, showed her a double-bitted ax, and gave a big grin.

"What do you want with that?" she said. "We have an ax."

"A little one. Not one like this. To do real timber work you need an ax like this. That three-pound thing back there is only good for kindling. *This* is what we need."

He bought it. He bought articles, most of them for Ellen or for the lodge, but one day he bought himself a twenty-five-cent balsa airplane, a dogfighter, and flew it in curves and loops in the meadow all that afternoon. She was outside watching birds. She had found a field guide in the attic, along with the binoculars, and now she spent whole afternoons in the meadow or in the woods surrounding it, watching birds, and he was at his wit's end to keep her under surveillance and at the same time (since once in jealousy he told her that birds bored him) to be unobtrusive about it. When it grew dark she studied the field guide, foxed and dog-eared from an adolescent phase when her love for birds had begun. All her interest centered on birds. She talked about their coloring, their songs and calls, the way they flew and perched, and how their bodies were shaped—"Like long slender ovals," she said. "And their legs stick out of their bellies. No wonder they lay eggs." Her eyebrows drew down and her brow furrowed. "Don't you see the logic in that?"

The birds seemed to sense her interest. They were drawn to her. Once she wondered aloud if she would ever see a cedar waxwing, and that afternoon seven of them flew into a fir beside the lodge and perched there in a cluster, so close to a window that there was no need for binoculars. Then she said she would like to see a flicker close up and find out whether its speckles were really speckles or just the way its feathers were fitted together. A few mornings later, when she lifted a lid off the cookstove, a flicker stared up at her from the grate, and stood still long enough for her to study it. Then it flew up into the kitchen, fluttered against the windows of the dining wing, and finally she called to him and he came into the room, and together they gave the bird exit by way of the back porch.

He went up to the roof and put the screen back on the chimney.

She became quiet and meditative, drawing more and more into herself, and seemed content to read and add birds to her growing life list. He was greatly relieved, believing she had purged herself and somehow found peace, but then he noticed, almost hidden in the passiveness of her face, an alert secretive quality, as though she were listening to instructions—intricately detailed, seductive, wise, and irrefutable—on what she was to do. He became more watchful and disturbed. Or was it a look all pregnant women wore, that hint of the Mona Lisa? How should he know when he'd never lived with a pregnant woman? Unless she was aroused, she was shy of her body, he noticed, more shy than before they were married, and she wouldn't let him watch while she undressed. Almost every night, lying under the covers, he held her at bay, teasing her about her shyness (his was as bad; he couldn't go to the john if he thought she could hear), and suddenly became the gentleman and turned his back on her, the voyeur in him thrilling at the sight of the miniature woman, framed in a pane of glass, who, nervously, as quickly as she could, stripped naked, held crossed arms over her breasts (why there?), and did a stiff-legged scurry across the room and flipped off the light.

When the next storm came in from the lake, turning the outdoors black, then blinding, then black, then splitting the sky with thunder, rain falling, branches falling, she went up to the attic and came down with an armload of games—Parcheesi, Chinese checkers, Bridge-It, chess, Monopoly, Yahtzee, all of them—and placed the pile in front of him and asked him to take his pick. Trying to be kind after his outburst in the attic, he asked her if these, too, were a part of her childhood. "Oh, no," she said. "I never really cared for things like this. Grandpa got most of them. He loves games." He looked up quick but her face registered nothing. A fact. "Oh," he said. They lay down in front of the fireplace, where a high blaze was burning, and played each game once, except Monopoly. He claimed it took too long, but he knew it would make him think of money and he was trying desperately not to think of that.

Since it was still too cold for swimming and since the lodge was cleaned and repaired, there was little to do, other than sunbathe on warm days, so they spent most of their evenings and many afternoons playing games. She had remarkable luck, uncanny luck, and he lost so many times he became a bad sport. He refused to play Yahtzee with her, he ruled it out, because it was based on throws of dice. The same with Parcheesi. Chinese checkers bored him, and Bridge-It, where you constructed a bridge of interlocking blocks from your side of the board to your opponent's side, was almost the same game, but it went much faster, and since it depended less on luck than the other games (and since Monopoly was out), they played it most often. He tried to plan far ahead to block her bridge, using math to gauge probability, and got so out of touch with the immediate game that she invariably made one practical move and ruined his calculations.

They started playing chess. He considered himself a good amateur but soon discovered that they were almost evenly matched; she played intuitively and there was no pattern he could depend upon. If she beat him, he insisted that they play for two out of three games. If she won two, they played for three out of five. This went on for several days. They played everywhere. On the beach, or on a broad stump in the front yard. In the dining wing after meals. His insomnia was growing worse, so they also played in bed every night. She began to notice the patterns in his attack and defense, and after that they were no longer evenly matched. And when he tried to play intuitively, like her, he was lost. One night, when they were lying in bed, she checkmated him in five moves. He slapped the men off the board. They stared at one another, the expressions on their faces strained, and then both of them began to laugh at the theatrics of it. Chuckling, he gathered up all the men and said, "All right. One last game. This is the championship." She was tired, but she consented, finally, and when in exactly the same number of moves he was checkmated again, he picked up the board with most of the men still on it and with a roar threw it into the main room.

That was the end of the games.

They went to the beach. They sunned themselves. She watched birds. He cut wood, gradually stripping the felled ash down to a branchless log. He flew his dogfighter in loops and ovals in the meadow, watching its red-tipped wings scroll the air in patterns he tried to repeat. She cooked meals. They ate them in silence. The feeling between them, however, remained close, perhaps because of a drive neither could control; their sexual appetites were insatiable, as though it were necessary to counterbalance the year apart, and they made love several times a day, several times in succession, wherever the desire overtook them, on the couch, in bed, in the meadow, on the kitchen floor, on the banquet table, and after these apostrophes of tenderness (with an underlying violence that gave the tenderness an edge) he would usually have to carry her, dead asleep, into the bedroom.

She needed to sleep more and more. She napped every afternoon, and some days slept for eighteen hours. They lay in bed until early evening and watched the sky, streaked with violet, go crimson and orange behind the long line of Manitou. He couldn't nap, and now that there were no more games, he was alone at night with his insomnia. He found it more comfortable to sleep facing away from her.

One evening as she was preparing dinner, simmering sauerbraten on the stove, he burst into the kitchen.

"What's the matter?" she said. "You look like you've seen a ghost."

"Well there's a goddamn porcupine right out by my sawing trestle."

"Porcupines won't hurt you. They're so bashful around people—shy and bumbling and harmless."

"Who's worried about it hurting *me*? The next one I see I'm going to pick up a stick and beat it to death!"

"That sounds just like you," she said, without a trace of irony, and turned back to the sauerbraten. Her reaction fascinated him; he wanted to learn as much about himself as he could.

"What's like me? That I would want to kill it?"

"No. The way you said that. About picking up a stick."

EIGHT

UNKNOWN AND OMINOUS, sending out waves of warning that grew stronger and stronger, washing at his consciousness, some dark thing was overtaking him. What was its shape? He was helpless against it. He grasped at details of the dream—a wall of glass, a desktop covered with light, a profile—but they were sensitive to examination and vanished. He was staring at an empty bed. Lifting up on his elbow, he saw a woman's body silhouetted against a blended background of water and sky, her long hair streaming off to the left, rippling, caught up in a wind.

She was at the edge of the bluff.

He threw back the covers and jumped out of bed and his knees gave out. Why hadn't he told her he'd let her go? He made it to the front door, wide awake now, and flung it open. She was running toward him over the lawn, leaving a trail of green footprints in the silver covering of dew.

"I thought you'd never wake to see it!" she cried. "Look at the sky! Look at the water! They're transparent."

His eyes flew up, blinded by the bright sun, by the brilliant reflection of light on water, and he said, "Sky. Oh."

"But look at it!"

She came up the steps onto the cement landing and put her arms around his neck, unabashed by their nakedness. "It's as if I've seen through to everything," she said. "I'm lucid as the day. Can't you tell? Can't you feel? Isn't it great!"

"Yes," he said, squinting over her shoulder, the tops of his eyes and his forehead hurting from the light.

"No, no, no. I mean— You know what I mean. *Everything*."

"What? What's that?" This was it. She'd divined his thoughts about the abortion and parting, and believed it was the best thing to do.

"You know," she murmured.

"*What*?"

She held him close, laughing, her breath passing over his neck, the faint sensation of it repulsing him, causing a slow trail of gooseflesh to travel along his nape. Excited, laughing, she finally admitted, "I can't say it!"

"Come on," he cried, at his limit. "*Come on, what is it?*"

She raised her lips to his ear and whispered, "Being pregnant."

"What's this!"

"Yes, yes, being pregnant! It's the most natural way to be. It's the ultimate I can do as a woman. It's the greatest gift I can give you. And now I can't imagine just being married to you, just being your wife, and *not* being pregnant. Isn't that great?"

He couldn't speak. He reached up and pressed her head against his chest. He wanted to respond, but until he understood what had him in its possession he didn't want her to see his face. Pale, with cold staring eyes, it had a stony set to it, as though he hadn't heard what she'd said. And then the corners of his mouth lifted in a detached, ironic smile.

. . . 2

Very early in the afternoon, when she lay down to take
her nap, he drove to town by himself and came back
with a Winchester Model 250 lever action .22 caliber
carbine and three boxes of shells. He looked in the
bedroom. She was still asleep. He laid the long red and
black carton on the banquet table in the main room,
opened it, and took out the new rifle. He lifted it up
and down to feel its balance again, ran his hand over
the length of it, over the walnut stock, the smooth
blued ejecting mechanism, the walnut handgrip, the
barrel, and then sighted out a front window. He took
up the booklet of manufacturer's instructions and
studied it. He wasn't familiar with the workings of this
rifle, it was a new model, but the minute he saw it he
knew it had to be his. Its design appealed to him that
much. The instruction booklet and the pictures on the
carton—black silhouettes of African beasts—were unequivocal: this rifle was patterned after big-game guns.

Following the manufacturer's instructions, which
he'd memorized, he untwisted the magazine tube underneath the barrel, pulled it out until the end of it
cleared the loading port, and slipped several shells into
the slot with care, wondering if they could explode
dropping on top of one another, and pressed the
springy cylinder back into the magazine, twisting it to
lock it. He snapped down the cocking lever, hearing its

metallic echo come off the log walls, glanced at the safety button again, and slammed the lever back into place, seating a shell in the breach. He went into the bedroom. She was curled up under the quilt, half asleep, her drowsy, pink-rimmed eyes turned toward him.

"Hey," he said, and held it up. "Surprise."

"A gun!" She struggled into a sitting position, and the startled expression on her face satisfied something in him; he was a bit afraid of it, too.

"Where did you get that?" she asked.

"In town. At the store."

"*Why* did you get it?"

Avoiding her eyes, he examined the windage screw; then turned the knurled knob for adjusting elevation.

"How much did it cost?"

"About sixty bucks."

"Sixty dollars!"

"Why? What's the difference?" Compared to what her grandfather had, his money meant nothing; it was something to get rid of.

"You had sixty dollars?"

"I wrote out a check on my account."

"I thought we were saving that."

"We need this," he said, patting the stock.

"What for?"

Suddenly he was confused and indignant, and a fever spread through his cheeks. He thought it was obvious why they needed it, that the reason should be absolutely clear, but when he tried to tell her no words came.

"Why?" she asked.

He shrugged his shoulders. "We just need it. That's all. In a place as wild as this, you need one."

"Can we afford it?"

"I still have a couple of hundred dollars in my checking account, and that's for this summer. There's my savings account, too."

"But you're so funny." She was smiling and shaking her head from side to side. "Why buy a gun?"

"Because I wanted it. Can't I spend my money the way I want?"

"Of course," she said. "You know what you're doing."

His eyes traveled over her face nervously, with suspicion, but she stared back at him with an open look, having meant no more and no less than she said.

"Are you worried about money, or something?" he asked.

"Sometimes I wonder how much we have. That's natural, isn't it? You've never really told me, and you've been buying so many things. We'll need a lot of money in a few months."

He went to the closet and took a bankbook from the inner pocket of a suit jacket, where he kept it hidden.

"There's this," he said. "My savings." He tossed the book on the bed. "That should be enough to get you started."

She opened the book, and he watched her eyes widen as she studied the amount, which he knew to be $3,768 and some odd cents.

"Where did you get this!"

"Where do you think? Working. Saving. The year you were away. Last year in Chicago."

"You've been so frugal and considerate."

"And there's my fellowship," he said.

"You're fantastic!"

"Hell."

"Are you sure you don't have anything more in abeyance?"

"The part-time job. I can put in as many hours as I want."

With a big smile on her face, she got out of bed and put her arms around him. He swung the rifle barrel off to one side.

"You're so kind," she said. "You've thought of everything. You're so *good*!"

"Come on outside," he said, stepping back from her and jogging the rifle in his hand. "I'm going to show you how to use this."

Keeping the rifle pointed toward the lake, he fixed a matchbook cover to the bark of a broad-based maple about a hundred feet from the front door. He returned to the lodge and sat down on the steps beside her, in the shade, holding the rifle upright.

"Now," he said. "Have you ever fired a .22?"

"I've never shot any kind of gun."

"Rifle, I keep telling you."

"Rifle."

He then explained what drill sergeants in the Army sometimes made trainees do if they referred to their rifle as a gun.

"But that would hardly apply to me," she said. "I mean, anatomically."

He gave her a weary look of long-suffering.

"Rifle," she said.

"Well," he began, "in the hierarchy of firearms, not just small bores, but rifles and shotguns both, the .22 is the smallest and least powerful of all, next in rank to a pellet rifle or BB gun. But you should never, never underestimate its fire power or potential. It has a range of one mile, that's a straight line from here to Orin's, and its bullet—these long rifles especially—can pierce a 2x4 like it's butter. I've seen a .22, in the hands of an expert, drop a horse in one shot, and it can maim a man for life, or"—he snapped his fingers—"kill him like that. Ruby shot Oswald with a pistol that was a toy next to this piece."

"I'm already afraid of it."

"There's no need to be afraid. It's not that dangerous if it's handled right. It's a deadly weapon, true, but it's as safe as the person whose hands it's in," he said, a trifle sententiously, and realized he loved the superiority he felt when he gave lectures. Maybe he should be a teacher? First, before you fire, you should always make sure there's a solid background just beyond your target to stop the bullet in case you miss—trees, an embankment, a hill, anything like that. Now. Let me show you how it works, and how to handle it so you won't have to be afraid."

He explained in detail every part of the mechanism; he showed her how to load and eject shells, how to aim and fire; he demonstrated the proper way to carry the rifle when she walked in open fields or through woods, or with anybody close. It was cool in the shade, and a breeze came from the woods behind them and set into gentle stirring and susurrus the leaves at the tops of the trees. As he was nearing the end of his lecture, he broke off in midsentence; he thought he'd noticed, mingled with the smell of pine and leaf from the woods, a smell of carrion, of flesh in advanced stages of decay. He turned in the direction of the dining wing, and said, "What's that?"

"The safety button."

"No, no, no. That smell. Don't you smell it?"

She tested the breeze, her nostrils flaring. "A bad smell?"

"Like something rotting. Have you thrown out some meat we didn't finish?"

"Never. I use everything up."

"You smell it too, then, right?"

"Sometimes. Faintly."

"Good. For a minute, I thought I was imagining it.

Anyway, here, let me get the elevation adjusted for this distance."

He braced his elbows on his knees so that the barrel wouldn't sway or dip, snapped off the safety, and fired.

"Ah!" she cried. "It's so loud!"

"That's just an echo you get from the lodge. If you shot over the wash it'd sound like a popgun."

He went out to the matchbook cover, saw where he had pierced it, and reckoned the elevation was too high. He adjusted the screw, fired several more times, and then handed the rifle to her, barrel pointing up, but kept a firm grip on it. "You know how to use it now," he said. "But before you start firing, just let me say this once more: it's a deadly weapon."

He let her take it. She followed his instructions, confusing none of the procedures, raised the rifle, blinking her eyes in anticipation, and jerked back the trigger. She missed the tree. Which delighted him.

"Don't be afraid of the sound," he said, trying to suppress his amusement. "It can't hurt you."

"But it's so loud!"

"You'll get used to it. And squeeze the trigger like I told you, otherwise you'll always fire to the right and every whichway."

After she had fired several more times, she began to overcome her fear of its report, and learned to hold the stock close against her shoulder and cheek and squeeze off each round. She hit the matchbook cover a couple of times. He told her to eject the shell quicker, because it could freeze in the chamber, and suggested she was taking too long to aim. "Once you've got it in your sights, squeeze off. Otherwise you start getting wobbly and insecure. If you're holding the rifle right, the same way each time, you can trust your aim. Here," he said, and took the rifle from her. He tore the cover off another matchbook, fastened it to the tree, and came back to the steps. From a standing position, ejecting as quickly as he could, he fired off five rapid shots, and went out and got the matchbook cover and handed it to her. Three bullets had ripped through the center of the cover in nearly the same spot, making a small clover-leaf, and two others had pierced its right edge.

"God!" she said. "Where'd you learn to shoot like that?"

"My father."

He walked out to the tree and put the matchbook cover back in place. He unscrewed the magazine tube below the barrel, loaded the rifle again, and passed it to her. She fired slowly and deliberately, taking careful aim each time, and began to improve and grow more confident. Placing his locked hands behind his head, he lay back on the steps and watched her face. She was enjoying this. He smiled. Dark leaf-shadow rocked across his face in a cooling motion. The leaves of the small birch at the edge of the bluff started trembling in the breeze, their light undersides catching the sun, and then the smell of carrion came, stronger this time, and Chris turned toward the dining wing.

Orin was standing next to the steps.

Chris sat up and made an inarticulate noise that was meant to be a greeting.

Orin's pale blue eyes were squinted as if in humor, and the gold fillings in his front teeth kept flashing as a tentative smile played over his face. He nodded hello to Chris.

Chris touched Ellen on the shoulder, and said, "Uh ... We have company."

"Oh?" She turned. "Oh, Orin. Oh, hi! How are you?"

"Ya," Orin said, and turned his gaze toward the tree and squinted even more, so that his weathered cheeks drew up. "Ya, I thought I heard one of them hammering away up here." He broke into a breathy, almost soundless chuckle of "Ya ha ha ha ha ha," and then shook his head to one side as though to break it off. "Ya."

Chris took the rifle from her. "I just got it," he said. "It's a new model. Would you like to see it?"

"No," Orin said. "No, ho ho ho, no, I got plenty of them down home."

"Did the sound bother you?"

Orin raised the bill of his striped cap, revealing the full length of his long, amused face, and made a thumb toward the meadow. "Oh," he said, "I was driving this way, just over the hayfield down the hill. Good first cutting, too, I tell you! Till that rain come." He lowered his head and shook it once. "Some rain that!" His brow furrowed with a look of perplexity, as though there were something incomprehensible about the rain, and he lifted his face to them. Again, he shook his head. "Then the other rain come right on top." He hooked his thumbs under his suspenders and stared at the ground for a long time in silence, and Chris began to feel he was missing the import of this whole conversation.

"Ya, well," Orin went on, "we turned the windrows again, oh, here a few days back, a side delivery, Hank Olsen's, you know, and it'll be dry soon, I'd say. Maybe now even." He squinted at them. "Still good hay!" he said, as though they'd claimed that it wasn't.

"Would you like to come inside, Orin?" Ellen asked. "And have something to drink?"

He gave her a critical squint. "Not boose?"

"Oh, no. We have lemonade or orange juice or soda. Or milk if you like."

"Sure," Orin said. "I think soda maybe."

She opened the screen door and Orin followed her into the lodge, going across the main room with his stooped, slow-moving shuffle. Chris ejected the live ammunition from the magazine, put the shells back in the box, and brought the shells and the rifle inside and laid them on top of the piano. He went into the kitchen. Ellen was telling Orin, apologetically, with a flush of embarrassment, that she realized the only soda they had on hand was bitter lemon. Why embarrassment, Chris wondered. Because it was a mixer, and she knew Orin would have nothing to do with booze? Or because she had developed an uncommon taste, a constant craving, for the bitter acidy liquid, and always kept a stock of it in the refrigerator? Women. They looked on everything, even external objects, as personal exposure. From Orin's circumlocutious answer, it was impossible for Chris to tell whether or not he'd drink the stuff. Ellen apparently understood him better, however, because she said, "Oh, good, we'll all have some then."

She got out the soda, took down two tumblers for her and Orin, knowing that Chris preferred to drink from the bottle, and Chris got out an opener and snapped off the caps. It gave him such pleasure opening bottles, he should have been a bartender, he thought. Orin made it understood, somewhat more clearly this time, that he didn't care to drink from a glass either, and he took the bottle Chris offered him. Chris tossed the three caps into the wastebasket. Their clatter against metal made the silence in the kitchen more marked. Ellen suggested that they move to the dining wing and sit.

"Oh, no," Orin said, and leaned with one elbow on the refrigerator top. "No, the partner, she'll have supper." He stood in silence, staring at the floor, his lips twitching back in the hesitant half-smile. He tilted the soda bottle at an angle, studying the sediment at its bottom.

Chris couldn't wait to see his expression when he tasted it.

"Sardines," Orin said.

A simile of the sediment? His talk constantly baffled Chris, who never knew what to say to him and thought it best to just listen until he came to his point. If he had one.

"You're having them for supper?" Ellen asked.

Orin looked up. He seemed startled by such a direct question, so contrary to his manner of talk. He broke into a long series of the breathy chuckles, which he finally cut short with a shake of his head. He stared at the bottle again, swirling it a little to see the sediment. "Ya," he said. "Sardines." He sighed. "Well, you know, you got to eat them fish now and then they say, Catlick or not. I got me this case, oh, back here in the winter months, from this fella over by Sutton's Bay, and he said they were the best. Ya, ha ha, he *said*." Orin shook his head. "You can't ever tell about what these fellas say." In the pause that followed, his expression turned solemn. "They're the best sardines I ate. Ya, I'll probably have some with my meal tonight maybe." He stared a while at the floor, and then his brow furrowed deeply. "That Hank Olsen now, there's a good fella you got to admit. He goes to our church, you know, and he's been there every Sunday I been, and I don't miss. That new preacher though!" Orin clucked his tongue and his silent ruminations about the new preacher made his half-smile start working again. "Olsen," he said, and tipped his head in the direction Olsen must live, "he's the fella turned my hay, his side delivery, and he's got him a new baler. Good rig too." He closed one eye in an auspicious way, and declared, his voice rising into a high whine with emphasis, "I tell you there's money in that, that baling business, there's good money in it!" He looked at the bottle of soda. "Ya, well." He swirled the soda around, put the bottle to his lips, and started chugging without pause, without change of expression, and then set the bottle down, empty, on the refrigerator top.

"Ya," he said, "you should see that baler go. Deering, I think. I think they changed that to a new company, too, in some deal, like those Co-op tractors you see around. Well, my partner, she has the supper there, so I got to get."

He readjusted his cap and stood motionless. Then a broad grin appeared on his face, and he turned to Chris. "Say," he said. "What would you think about playing farmer?"

"What do you mean?"

"When that baler gets going, that Olsen, he don't stop, I'll say that for that fella."

"You mean you need help?"

"Well, you got to think of rain with the lake so close. It could rain again hard as before, and they say if you pile your bales two together and one on top it'll keep the moisture out of the sides, and the sides, open like that, are the worst for spoilage, you know." He did his skeptical shake. "I don't know how much truth there is in it, but that's what they say. Olsen, now, he says it too, so I do it, and I can't say I've had any spoilage yet to speak of. Ya, then I haul them in the barn."

"And you want help?"

"It'll probably be a nice sunny day tomorrow, that's what the weatherman says, and you probably wouldn't mind being out in that sun, huh?"

"If you need help, I'd be glad to."

"That is, if you don't mind the working part of it."

"Oh, no. I've done it before."

Orin went to the door and opened it; when he felt he'd terminated a conversation, the conversation was over. He walked out the door, saying, "Well, I don't expect you to work for nothing, you know. I pay, too."

Chris followed him outside, and said, "That's not necessary. Really."

Orin stopped and stared at his pickup at the head of the drive, once more clasping his hands under the bib of his overalls. "No," he said. "No, I always pay." The admission seemed to cause him immense pain.

"It's up to you. I'd as soon do it just for the exercise."

Orin laughed aloud. "It's more than that, I tell you!"

"I know. I used to live on a farm."

"Can you get up at seven?"

"Sure."

"Then I'll come up the hill about then, seven or eight, and give a honk and we'll go down there and see what's doing."

"Okay."

"These are big bales. This Olsen, he makes them big and tight." He squinted at Chris, and the smile starting playing over his face. "You say you handled bales?"

"Yes."

"It's going to be heavy hay and this baler cuts them off slick as a whistle, I better tell you that."

"You mean I should wear gloves?" Chris had seen the sharp stubble at the side of a bale, with the weight of the bale behind it, take the flesh off a man's hand.

"Ya," Orin said, heading toward the pickup. "Ya, I think you might as well bring some, if you like, if you got a pair." And with his hands clasped over his chest, Orin proceeded toward the pickup with the slow even shuffle that made it seem his overalls were standing still —while he glided ahead inside them.

NINE

CHRIS GOT UP AT SIX, as the sun was rising, and built a
fire in the cookstove to drive the chill from the kitchen.
He made his own breakfast, cleared away the dishes,
washed them, put them in the cupboard, and sat down
at the table in the dining wing and began to read a
paperback Western, feeling the sun warm his back as it
climbed higher above the trees. At eight o'clock, Ellen
wandered in from the bedroom, wearing a full-length
nightgown she never wore at night, her hair stringy and
tousled, her eyelids swollen, her hands hanging limp at
her sides.

"Did you eat?" she asked.

"Yes."

"*I* was supposed to make breakfast!" she said in a
belligerent pout, an early-morning mood.

"I didn't want to disturb you. You looked so peace-
ful."

"Don't stare at me like that. I'm ugly!"

"I love the way you are in the morning. Absolutely—"

"Don't even look at me!"

She went into the bathroom, and he heard running
water and the sound of her brushing her teeth, a morning ritual that had to be performed before she could

turn human, and soon she appeared with her hair
combed and her face shining from washing. She made
herself a bowl of cereal, sat across from him, and began
to eat in isolated irritation.

"Put more milk on it," he said.

"Why?"

"It's good for you."

She poured on more milk. He was growing restless;
even the Indian battle he'd reached in the book
couldn't hold his attention. He looked at the clock
again. It was close to nine and he still hadn't heard the
honk of a horn. He wondered if Orin had dismissed
him as being inexperienced, an incompetent, and the
thought infuriated him. It also disappointed him. He
wanted to work, he wanted the pure physicality of it,
the mindlessness, he wanted to test his animal self, to
sweat in the sun. He closed the paperback and laid it
on the tabletop. He looked at the clock. Past nine. He
turned to her and saw that she was emerging, at last,
from her morning mood.

"Maybe he won't show up," she said, and smiled.
"Then we can go back to bed."

"Do you need more sleep?"

"Mmmm," she hummed, and her large eyes became
bright green. "Not sleep."

There was the buzzing drone of a weak horn.

"Oh, hell," she said.

She hurried to the door with him and they kissed.

"I feel you're going off to war," she said.

"It's only a few bales."

"I don't want you to leave me."

"You'll have to get used to it. It'll be like this every
morning, once we get back."

"No, it won't, I won't allow it."

"What can you do? I'll have to work."

"But you're my husband."

"That's why I'll have to work."

The horn sounded again.

"El, let *go* of me. He'll think I couldn't get up at

seven—pardon, nine—and that's already one count against me."

"Show them how to do it."

"If I remember."

"Your muscles do. They're beautiful."

They kissed again, a more prolonged kiss.

"Go," she said. "You have to go now if you're ever going."

"I don't want to."

"I know."

"Goodbye."

"Goodbye."

He ran up the slope of the driveway to the waiting pickup and got into the cab, redolent of manure and more personal smells, and slammed the door. Two shiny baling hooks lay on the cracked vinyl of the seat.

"I was wondering if maybe you forgot," Orin said.

"I've been up since seven."

"My pigs," Orin said. He popped the clutch, jerked ahead for a few yards, and then evened out in second gear and drove along the woods at the edge of the meadow, past the first, the second, the third brushpile, past the pumphouse, and went down a sand road through a strip of trees, climbed a low hill, and came onto an open rolling field where low windrows of hay, spaced at regular intervals in a closing concentric pattern, described over and over, as though it were a thing to be memorized, the shape of the field. A red baler, pulled by a John Deere, was moving slowly down an outer windrow, the fast arm of its packer slamming down hard, and a new bale dropped from the chute at its back. Orin drove through the field, and hearing the sound of high stubble under the tires Chris cranked down his window in order to smell hay. When Orin was close behind the baler, driving down the space between two windrows, he buzzed his horn. The man on the tractor turned and waved and hit the clutch, and Orin switched off the ignition and coasted to a stop behind the tractor.

Chris and Orin each picked a baling hook off the seat and stepped outside, and the man on the tractor, who was dressed in a gray cotton work suit and a gray cap, shut off the engine and placed his hand on a fender and vaulted to the ground. He was a stocky, middle-aged wrestler-type with small eyes, a broad nose with nostrils the size of dimes, and pale eyebrows that were almost invisible on his wide pink face, and he came toward them in a flat-footed step, rocking from side to side. He put a hand to the bill of his cap, and said in a raspy baritone, "Yo there."

"How's it seem?" Orin asked.

"Not so perfect, not so perfect, she's pretty damp in some of them low spots yet, but she'll go, the sun's gettin' to her. I been keepin' them old bales short as the machine'll do 'em, but some um 'll still weigh in mighty heavy—ninety pound or more by guess." He glanced at Chris. "Also, there at the first, the right-side twine wasn't tyin' so good so some of them bales where I started, well, you'll see they're loose on one side, and that there twine on that side ain't liable to hold. So you're goin' to have to watch it for them buggers on that side."

He glanced at Chris again, and then went back to the tractor, took a grease gun out of its toolbox, and started greasing the baler. Orin showed Chris how he wanted the bales stacked; two standing on end, their tops tilted toward one another so they touched, forming an inverted V; and then a third bale laid, twines up, across the tops of the other two.

"Yup," the man said behind them. "That's the only way to do it. Otherwise you get damp and rain in them open sides and they rot out to holy hell."

"Oh, ya," Orin said, turning to Chris. "Hank, this here is— Well, you better tell him. This here is Hank Olsen."

Chris hung his baling hook over his shoulder, went up to Hank Olsen, introduced himself, and shook the man's hand. Olsen's big hand was pudgy and damp, and Chris didn't receive the vise grip he expected. Olsen gave Chris a quick survey from head to foot. "Say, boy," he said, "it don't look like this work is right up your alley." His laugh made a loud racket.

Right up yours, Chris thought, and walked over to a bale, slammed the hook into it, let the bale drag behind him as he walked toward another, which he grabbed by the twine, dragging the two of them, one in each hand, over to a third. He raised the bales in his hands upright, leaned their ends together, then hefted up the third and slammed it flat on top. He proceeded around the edge of the field, leaving a pyramid every few yards. The tractor started up again, and soon the packer on the baler was battering at the hay. Chris estimated that the field was at least ten acres in size, and he made a complete circuit of it, stacking the bales as he went, while Orin made a few neat pyramids along one edge. The bales began to grow heavier for Chris. Sweat came out on his forehead, and now, as he went to lift the third bale into place, he had to give it a helping boost with his knee. When he'd worked his way around to the pickup the second time, he took off his shirt and threw it into the cab.

With each circuit he made of the field, two more, three more, he moved closer and closer to its center, so there was less walking to wear him down, but the weight of the bales grew so bad he felt he couldn't lift another one. He stopped and stood at the top of a small hill, breathing hard, his T-shirt soaked, the hook hanging at his side, and saw that Orin was sitting on the running board of the pickup, in the shade of its cab, fanning himself with his cap. Chris judged they had worked for about an hour. They were half done. He started off again, hooked a bale, dragged it with effort to the next bale, and used what felt like the last of his strength to lift the third bale on top. He hated the regular metallic tamping of the baler, the sight of its feeder teeth picking up a windrow and conveying it into the machine, and he willed it to break down. He began to see it as an enraged beast resurrected from prehistoric time by a man as bestial and mad, gobbling hay up its maw, banging at it in a frenzy of sex and letting it drop, egglike, out its ass, banging continually, destroying everything in sight, an insatiable devouring thing out to do him in—and his hate for it grew to such a pitch it became a positive force to work with. He slammed his hook into the bales of the beast, killing them, and made form, made pyramids of its disorder. *Ze gods are angry at me because they knew.* He hooked a bale. *Ze gods are angry at me because of you.* He piled two together. *Ze gods are angry at me because they knew.* He stacked a third on top. *I stood at heaven's portals but that was too high for any mortal such as I* . . . That was it. That was the rest of the song. But what had been said that afternoon? Oh, hell, did it make any difference now? He'd only remembered it because of the smell of mustardseed in the hay.

He worked faster, in a fury, for another half hour, and then had to go over and sit in the shade of the pickup, where Orin was again fanning himself. The baler was finishing up the field. Good. Good riddance. There were only about fifty bales left to stack. Olsen switched off the power take-off, shifted the tractor into a higher gear, and drove over to the pickup and stopped. "Hey!" he called to Chris over the low chug of the two-cylinder John Deere. "I thought you was going to catch us there all by yourself!" Another rackety laugh. To Orin he called, "Hokay! I'm goin' now and catch that corner six."

Six broken bales, pray God.

He drove to the corner of the field and disappeared in a strip of trees, and soon Chris heard the baler hammering again. Continuing to hammer. Without letup.

Six acres.

"It's no good, you know, with no cap like that," Orin said, and gave Chris a furrowed look of concern. "A fella could get sunstroke." He pointed with his hook toward the unstacked bales in the center of the field. "We'll pile what we can of those there in the pickup now and haul them in, and what few are left we better stack them up."

They got approximately half of the unstacked bales into the pickup. Then Orin sat behind the wheel and followed Chris around with the pickup while he stacked up the remaining bales. Chris climbed into the cab, exhausted, and they drove out of the field and up the meadow, from which vantage point Chris got a longing glimpse of the lodge, but no Ellen, and then they turned and went down the rutted hill to the first crossroads and drove up to Orin's farm. Orin pulled around to the back side of a large gray barn and parked at the bottom of a dirt ramp, with retaining walls of stone, that led up to the second story of the building. "If them doors are slid back," Orin said, nodding toward a pair of big doors at the head of the ramp, "them on the rollers there, a fella can drive this rig here right inside." Chris got out and rolled back the doors.

Inside the loft it was cool and dark, and the darkness seemed intensified by the smell of dust, the fine dust from hay, dust that had gathered for ages. One half of the loft, to the right of the alleyway Orin had parked in, was piled high with bright straw, and the floor of the other half was covered with a single layer of gray, decaying bales of hay. Orin was staring at these, as though contemplating whether or not to remove them. "Ya, well," he said, "we'll want to put those on the pickup here on these, and it'd be best, I s'pose, if we started our pile way there at the back." He walked out of the hayloft. Chris unloaded the bales from the pickup and carried them, one by one, to the far end of the loft, walking thirty feet each time over the layer of broken and decaying bales, stumbling and getting his feet hung up. When he was done, he went outside, into bright sunlight, and started looking for Orin, wondering if they were finshed for the day.

He found Orin on the opposite side of the barn, on

his knees, pulling up weeds from along a fence line. "These ragweed sure are some nuisance," Orin said, without looking up. "You can't stop the buggers growing. No, ho ho, I pull them up and scythe them out but they still come up every spring here just like wildfire. Well, you can use them, too. Your pigs, you know, they like their greens, and they ain't so particular, not like your stock are." He was putting the weeds he pulled up into a five-gallon bucket. Chris got down on his knees and started to help. Orin settled back on his haunches to watch, and then, in a rare sudden movement, lifted his chin high and turned his head to one side as though attempting to catch a faint sound. "Ya," he said. "There's that crittur again." He gave his skeptical shake. "No, I don't know about that stock, whether it's worth the monkeying to keep it or not. And then the hay you got to have. I think maybe pigs are better. I'm trying them once, and come fall I might get rid of this few stock I got. Just a while back here, oh, a few weeks I guess, I come out and found this crittur keeled over in the back of the barn, bloated up big as a bathtub. Must have been something he ate. Now pigs, you know, they ain't so sensitive that way." He gave another shake. "Good crittur, too! Healthy all along and then just dead like that. No, you can't tell."

"Did you have the vet out?"

"Now pigs, there's going to be a market change on them they say, and then they're something a fella can haul himself from place to place in a pickup if he wants. That crittur! He was a real corker, a fat one, a nice steer all right, would have made good beef, but you can't sell them or butcher them up when they go like that, that's for sure. I drug him off behind the tractor. He's up at the edge of your woods there, this side of the property line. That's him now, I s'pose. Ya, ha ha ha, I wouldn't doubt but what you get a sample of him too when the wind's switched your way. Well, the crows, they'll have a feast this summer, I'll say that." He laughed and shook his head. "Them crows!"

When the bucket was packed with weeds, Orin picked it up and went toward the barn, and Chris trailed hesitantly after, wondering for the first time about the man's sanity. Orin, stooping down, entered a low door next to the silo, and Chris, stooping also, found himself in a dim room filled with milking machines and coolers and cream cans covered with dust. He went through the room and came into the cow barn, which had been divided into two sections by two long rows of square wooden pens. One set of pens stood higher than the other on the milking platform above the gutter, and there was a narrow walkway leading up the center. A sow lay in each of the pens and many of the sows had farrowed. The sound of piglets, their persistent bicker and squeal, echoed in the concrete area of the barn, and now and then there came, undercutting this sound, the great low grunting huff of a big sow. The baby pigs, front legs bent back, snouts against the bellies of sows, were busy feeding, butting and tossing their heads, switching tits, nudging and pawing at one another, squealing—continually squealing and scrambling over the backs of siblings in a senseless pushiness that Chris had never liked. Orin moved slowly up the walkway, distributing with parsimony into each pen, as though they were plated with gold, a few of the ragweeds. There was a larger pen of good-sized gilts and barrows, and Orin tossed the biggest share of the weeds in to them. He came to a pen where a sow lay flat on her side, her flank heaving, her breath escaping in a belabored wheeze that ended in a whine of pain.

"Ya," Orin said, "I suppose I should have somebody take a look at her if she don't come through pretty soon. She's way past due and I'd hate like the dickens to lose them pigs. This is her first and sometimes on their first they—"

A prolonged squeal, like the shriek of a rabbit, pierced the underlying sound, and Chris ran down a few pens and saw a baby pig under the split hoof of a sow, his pink gums and tiny teeth bared in pain, his legs pawing the air.

"Jesus," Chris said, and slapped the snout of the sow. "Hey! Suey! Get up out of there! Heigh!"

He kept slapping her snout, and she tossed her head up and down but wouldn't budge. He punched the front of her neck with his fist. He jumped inside the pen, landing on spongy straw, and kicked her hind leg. She lifted it as if in irritation, and the small pig went scrambling away, limping, whimpering with pain. Chris turned and saw that Orin was watching, leaning his elbows on the upper board of the pen.

"Jesus," Chris said, out of breath. "Jesus, did you see that?"

"A fella should watch his tongue," Orin said, and then stared at the sow for a long time in silence. "Oh, ya," he said. "They'll do that. Pigs, you know."

He picked up the bucket and walked out of the barn. Chris climbed from the pen, feeling weak all the way to his marrow, and followed Orin around the stone silo, around the barn, and up the ramp into the hayloft. Orin set down the bucket.

"Good," he said. "You got them bales."

He took a pocket watch out of his overalls bib. "Ya," he said, and glanced out the big door toward the sun. "Eleven forty-five. Fast day."

Oh, God, no, Chris thought. No more work, not now?

Orin got into the pickup, Chris climbed in beside him, and they backed out of the barn and drove up the hill to the lodge. Chris hopped out, feeling lighthearted and relieved, and was about to thank Orin for the exercise.

"Eleven forty-five," Orin said, squinting out the windshield. "About twelve. So I guess I better wait till one. Then I'll come by and give a honk and maybe we can stack up a little of that other six."

... 2

"Eat slower," Ellen said. Though he was ravenous, he ate slower, but not because of her admonitions; when he came into the lodge, he'd drunk a quart of water from the refrigerator and now its coldness was starting to cramp his stomach. She stood behind him and massaged the muscles of his neck.

"It's not there," he said. "It's everywhere. It's my arms and legs; it's my back. It's my hands from those damn bale strings."

"Didn't you wear gloves?"

"Of course. But I might as well be barehanded the way they cut into your fingers."

"Maybe you shouldn't go back. You're not used to it."

"Bull, too. I'm going back. It's a rural custom to break in a new man by seeing how far you can push him, even if you have to kill yourself doing it. Well, with Orin, there's no worry about him killing himself. Unless it's from overtaxing his brain figuring out how to get me to do something without actually saying I should do it. At home we worked hard too, but everybody worked together and there wasn't this god-awful feeling of being driven. We had lunch breaks between meals, and on some days, if it was real hot, we drank

212

ice-cold tomato juice spiked with beer and then napped under a hayrack out in the field. I don't mind the work. It was that damn pig. He didn't give a shit about it, just: 'A fella should watch his tongue.' God! And do you know what else that crazy bastard did? You know that rotten smell? That's a dead steer, for Christ's sake. He found it dead and just dragged it up to the woods. Didn't even have a vet out. Jesus! The thing could have died of anthrax for all he knows."

"What's that?"

"A disease that can spread like the plague. There's an inoculation for it, but I doubt if Orin's ever taken the trouble or the money to have it done. The stuff is deadly to stock. It can kill off a whole herd in days. And it can kill people, too, damn easy, if they come in contact with an animal that had it, or if it gets into drinking water. Thank God the pumphouse is where it is."

He shoved away his plate, still hungry, his stomach still cramped, and went into the bedroom, where it was cool, and lay down on his stomach, being of the persuasion that the best way to treat an ailment such as the cramps was to force the pain to its maximal limit and get it done with. She straddled his rear and massaged his back. Because of his anger, he was tense, unable to relax, and this compounded his discomfort and exhaustion, but after a while the action of her hands soothed him, he loosened up, and the gentle warmth he felt above his buttocks as she rocked forward and back began to arouse him. Just as he was about to turn over, unzip his fly, and let her mount him and do all the work, Orin's horn buzzed. He cursed and got out of bed and she followed him to the back door.

"Did I once say Anna was a demon?" he said. "He's the demon."

"I know. I feel guilty about not visiting her. She's so alone there."

"Right. With him. Which is worse."

Chris walked up to the pickup and got inside and

they drove over to the six-acre field, a triangular field on the slope of a hillside. Chris started around it, stacking the bales, going uphill and then downhill, while Orin worked back and forth along one end at his steady pace. There was no baler here for Chris to hate, no machine to drive him forward in fury, and the sun was hotter. His fatigue became so great he felt his bones were of lead, heavy improbable things to move, much less work with; he had shin splints, stomach cramps, and the exertion of lifting seemed to have worn his shoulder blades down to sharp points, because they were cutting into his back. When they were half finished with the field, Orin got in the pickup and drove off. Chris continued to stack the bales, dropping some of the top ones now, too weak to place them securely on the inverted V's.

After fifteen minutes had passed, Orin returned in the pickup, drove over to him and parked, and came out of the cab with a can of apple-cherry juice, one of the dented ones, and poured them each a coffee cup full. The juice was worse than nothing. It made Chris's parched mouth so full of fuming cottony stickiness he had to keep it open for a while, like a dog, to get his breath. He had only one desire: to finish this field and go back to the lodge and drink a gallon of water, even if it made his insides blow up. So while Orin sat on the running board of the pickup, drinking juice, Chris stacked the remaining bales.

He was done. He was too fatigued to appreciate it. He wanted to see Ellen, and be pampered and nursed by her. He wanted his gallon of water. He walked over to the pickup, hung his hook on its sideboard, and said, "Well. That's it."

"Ya," Orin said. "Well, now we'll go get the tractor and see if we can't bring some of them others in."

"What others?"

"Over to that ten we got this morning."

"What do you mean? It's all stacked."

"It's up now, ya, and it'll be pretty safe if worst

comes to worst, but that's just temp'ry, you know, just in case a big rain comes through again before it's in. No." He shook his head as though this was momentous. "No, I think maybe while it's still light we ought to try to get some of that in the barn where it wouldn't get wet, no matter what come."

First, since it was standing ready in the six-acre field, they loaded the pickup. They drove back to the farm and into the loft and, while Orin was hitching a hayrack behind the tractor, Chris unloaded the bales from the pickup. He went outside, got onto the waiting hayrack, and they started off, Orin's collie barking them all the way to the crossroads and then wheeling around and going in a dead run back to the farm. They drove to the field beyond the meadow. As Orin guided the tractor among the pyramids, Chris disassembled them and threw the bales onto the hayrack, a higher lift than the previous lift to place the third bale, and when the bales on the rack needed straightening, Orin stopped and they did it together. They loaded the hayrack seven layers high, and drove back to the farm. Orin backed the pickup out of the barn, he backed the loaded hayrack inside the loft, unhitched it, invited Chris to hop on the drawbar of the tractor, and drove around to a machine shed of corrugated metal. Waiting there was another empty hayrack. Chris hitched it up and they went back to the field and started loading again.

Chris was beyond second wind, exhausted to senselessness, his fingers numb, nerveless, curved like pawls to fit the twines, and sometimes now, when he tried to toss a bale up to Orin, it fell back down on him, and he grew furious as he calculated that was the third or fourth time that particular bale had been handled, not counting the rearranging that was done on the rack, and for what? The fury renewed his energy, and they got the rack loaded, and drove back to the farm.

Orin backed a two-ton truck with high sideboards out of the machine shed. They returned to the field and loaded the remainder of the bales onto the truck. The truck was half full. There were no more bales. Chris climbed up into the high cab, drowsy with relief, expecting to see Ellen in the next few minutes, but Orin, instead of taking him to the lodge, drove over to the six-acre field. Here, with Chris working from the ground again, they loaded the truck full. Once more Chris expected to be dropped off at the lodge, but Orin drove to the farm, backed the truck into the machine shed, and the two of them went out again in the pickup (the dog chasing them to the crossroads on each of these trips like a Keystone Cop) and loaded it. There were about five pyramids left in the field. "These few that are here now," Orin said, speaking for the first time in several hours, "I can get these by myself sometime."

So Chris was more than amazed when Orin drove back to the farm. "Ya, well, here we go," Orin said, and walked into the hayloft. They began to unload the bales from the rack. Chris stood on the load and threw down to Orin, and Orin carried the bales to the end of the loft and stacked them. Chris threw down fast, hoping to wear Orin out, but Orin continued to work at his steady pace, and the unstacked pile of bales grew large, he said, "Ya, I s'pose we better change now, don't you think? I know it's hard going, giving them bales a toss way over here." It was harder walking over the bales, floundering into gaps between them, carrying a ninety-pound bale as he walked. He rested most of their weight on his thighs, bouncing the bales forward with his legs, and that helped. Dust and pollen rose from the hay, filling the loft, and it became difficult to breathe. Chris spat up black. Dusk started to descend and, since the big door of the loft faced east, soon it was almost impossible to see. Now they would have to quit for sure, for good, Chris thought, and then Orin got off the rack and switched on a set of overhead lights. They finished unloading and stacking the bales. Then they went down to the pig barn and drank from a hose.

Orin backed the second hayrack into the loft and

they started unloading it. Orin kept working at his steady pace, silent, his weathered face set. Bales were dropping from Chris's hands and he had to stop and knock his knuckles together to get feeling back in his fingers. His legs were turning watery and he stumbled over the stacked bales often. Orin was doing twice as much work now as Chris; he would toss down a pile of bales, hop onto the stack and help Chris arrange them, and then return to the rack and toss down another pile. It was more than testing a new man, Chris realized, as he stared at the set of Orin's face. Orin hated haying as only farmers hate the particular tasks demanded year after year, over and over, by the cycle of Nature. He hated it with the same passion that Chris hated the baler. He hated it so much he wanted to finish in one day. Even taking into account all the times Orin had rested and copped out, Chris had to admit that the lean, elderly man must have muscles of steel; he kept up the same pace, not even breathing hard, all the while hating this goddamn hay.

Chris got another wind, the one that cross-country milers apparently get, and was able to keep up with Orin. He tried to calculate how many bales were left, so he could last until then, but that seemed self-defeating. What if there were thirty extra? Then there was the truck. And then the pickup. He said to himself, I'll carry five more bales, and when that was done, he said, I'll carry five more bales, and the incantation kept him going. Then he began to see the bales in terms of time, as the minutes consumed in handling each bale, each bale a solid slab of time, wasteful, useless, used-up time, a time when he could have had a beer, a smoke, listened to wind, walked the beach, fired the rifle, slept, a time he could have held Ellen, kissed her, and, as the stack grew, a time they could have made love, many times they could have made love, a day of it, smelling of one another, and suddenly he felt light-headed and dizzy, in vertigo, spiraling down through hours of time, time stilled forever and stored away in squares, time he should have spent with her, her, his love—but of what consolation was she, what was love, moreover, when everybody knew where this waste, this spiraling downward went?

"Orin," he called. "Orin, I think you're going to have to give me a hand."

One of his legs had plunged through a space between the bales and he was wedged in up to the crotch, too weak to lift himself.

... 3

Damp with sweat, they worked until eight o'clock. Orin
confirmed the time with his pocket watch. He sighed.
He went to the doorway, looked out at the gathering
darkness, and then squatted down with his back against
the doorjamb and tilted up the bill of his cap, exposing
one half of his face to the light from the loft. He sighed
again. He was finished with haying once more. He was
at his ease. He began to reminisce, giving long genealo-
gies ("Ya, that was Ralph's cousin, the son of Les, who
married the Loomis girl . . .") in which all of the people
named were strangers to Chris, but Orin spoke of them
as though they were familiars, and as universally
known as the *dramatis personae* of a Shakespeare play;
and Orin's talk became more maundering, reaching
back into the regions of the dead, exhuming names of
those who were related to him, those he respected or
didn't like, those who had temper or humor, beauty or
arrogance, all of them gone, "just the old bachelor left
now." And Chris realized, from his knowledge of farmers and what they divulged, that Orin liked him. Why?
Because he'd helped him through the ordeal of haying?
Because Orin needed to pass these people on to somebody he thought would be walking the earth when he
wasn't?

And so, although Chris was impatient to leave, to
wash off the nettles prickling him everywhere, and was
famished and exhausted and wanted above all to get

back to Ellen and eat a big meal and go to bed with her, he stood in respectful silence and listened to Orin for ten minutes, for twenty minutes, for a half hour, for longer, pinned like a fly by his desire not to offend. Finally there was a long silence from Orin. He took out his watch again. "Well," he said, "let's see if we can figure this time here."

"No, no, that's all right."

"Nine thirty to eleven forty-five—twelve, say. That's about two and a half—Now you tell me if you think I'm all wet on this. Then about one thirty to eight, that's six and a half more, so, ya, that makes nine, I guess. Does it?"

"Really. You don't have to pay me."

"No, ho ho ho, no, I always pay." Orin squinted and his smile started working. "Now what would you say is a fair price for you?"

"If you want to pay me, let's settle it some other time."

"Well, the least I pay, for cherry pickers or any of them, and aha ha, you can't tell what you're getting with that bunch, well, I s'pose it's not like wages in the city, either, but the least I pay a fella is a dollar a hour. Now doing this hard work like baling is, when a man knows—"

"Fine. A dollar an hour's fine."

"Well," Orin said, prolonging the word as he rose to his feet, "that's up to you. If that's what you want then, you come on inside, in the house here, and the partner, she's the one with the money, she'll give you a check." He shook his head. "Them Indians, they want cash. Boose." He turned and walked away. Chris followed him around to the house, through the clutter of the enclosed porch, and into the kitchen, where a place was set at the table. Orin, in passing through the porch, had somehow removed and hung up his cap without a pause in his gait, and now a white indentation was visible in his forehead; above that, his brow was ivory. He went directly to the stove and lifted the lid off a kettle. Chris could smell the odor of cooked meat and onions, and felt weak from hunger. "Nnnnn," Orin said. "Stew." He looked at Chris, as though contemplating how much Chris could eat, and then said, "Want some?"

"No," Chris said. "No, no thank you." He was salivating. "Ellen expects me back. I'm already late." He swallowed with difficulty. Did she know how hard he'd worked? Did she understand? She better have something filling and substantial ready for him when he got back.

Orin gave his head a toss in the direction of the living room. "The partner there, she'll make you out your check then." He lifted his voice into a higher pitch and called, "Make out a check for this boy for ten dollars!" He carried the stew to the table and set it down. He laid two pieces of homemade bread on a plate and started spooning stew over the bread, and Chris saw whole carrots, small onions cooked whole, large chunks of potato and big squares of beef, all in a thick steaming broth, and he started trembling from hunger and had to hurry into the living room. Anna was lying on a couch in her black dress and flannel shirt, on a layer of many blankets and quilts. Pillows of different shapes and colors were arranged under her upper body, and beneath her head was a silver-colored cushion that Chris recognized as the cover for a tractor seat. She stared at him with her large, watery eyes, looking frail and vulnerable.

"The doctor says I'm to lie down often," she explained. "At least five times a day, and today was hard. I guess I'm getting what they call set in my ways and old. I'm so used to seeing the lake from the bluffs, up high looking down on it, and this noon I visited a lady in town, she's ill, and her house was smack at the edge of the bay. Seeing the water straight out from me instead of from a height, the way I'm used to it, it looked right at the level of the house, higher than the house when you looked way out, and I got this close feeling I was going to be engulfed. My heart's weak, and it started beating so bad I had to get up and leave. I felt—" Her eyes grew wide as a child's and started moving from side to side as though searching the interior of her mind, and then, with a quick girlish gesture of her hands, she described a large shape in the air, and said, "I felt my heart was *that big*. Ten dollars?" she asked in a sudden, apprehensive manner.

"I guess that's what Mr. Clausen decided on."

Placing one hand on her forehead, she sat, paused for a while on the edge of the couch, and then slowly rose and walked across the room, her hand still pressed to her brow, and stopped in front of a rolltop desk. The pigeonholes of the desk were stuffed with letters, papers, electrical wires, tools, pens, and rolled doilies, and there were stacks of religious pamphlets and ledgers lying on its top. Anna took out a heavy black book the size of a spiral binder, a payroll checkbook, opened it, and asked Chris how to spell his name. She wrote a check in a bold, backward slant, and handed it to him. In the left-hand corner of the check, over an etching of a barn, he saw, in large black letters, CLAUSEN BROTHERS.

"Thank you," he said. "Thank you very much."

"I'm sure you earned every penny of it."

"I needed the exercise."

"That's something I *don't* need," she said, and went across the room to the foot of a stairway and placed her hand on the top of its newel-post. "You'll pardon me, but I have to go to bed now that he's had his meal. He'll give you a ride up."

"Thank you again."

She smiled her tight-lipped smile, in which there was kindness, and said, "You're probably the one that deserves to be thanked." She started up the steps, and then stopped and turned. "You and Ellen must come down some day and visit." There was a plea in her large eyes, and she seemed to be trying to communicate more. She disappeared up the steps.

Chris folded the check and put it in his shirt pocket and walked into the kitchen. Orin was sitting at the table reading a newspaper, stroking a tortoiseshell cat that lay in his lap. Chris was anxious to leave, to get the ride up, but he sat in a chair next to the table, giving Orin a chance to rest. Giving himself a chance to rest. Orin kept reading the paper, releasing an occasional sigh, and then he got up—the cat leaving him in a leap—and went out to the porch and came back with a chunk of wood and dropped it into the cookstove. For morning? He went to the sink in the corner, where two bare pipes came through the ceiling and traveled along the wall on either side of a mirror, and studied his eyes in the mirror, pulling down their lower lids, and then washed his hands, then his face, apparently caught up in a ritual that made him oblivious of Chris, and then reached up to the front of his mouth, took out the gold-filled teeth, and dropped them into a glass of water. He sprinkled some powder into the glass, took down a toothbrush, and stirred the teeth with the toothbrush. Chris sat in astonishment, unable to move, convinced that Orin didn't realize he was there. Orin ran the toothbrush through the space at the front of his mouth a few times and laid it down. He smoothed back his graying hair, sighed, and turned to Chris. "Ya," he said, "I guesth it'sth about that time." He went to the door of the living room. "You can let yourthelf out. I guesth you know the way up by now all right, aha ha. Maybe you want a ride up?" His brow furrowed, and he squinted out the window. "Well, there'th sthill sthome light to sthee by."

It was too preposterous. Chris covered his mouth, and the first spasm of laughter escaped in a blast of air at the back of his nose. Giddy from hunger and fatigue, his laughter grew. He covered his face, unable to stop, and turned sideways in the chair. He sat up straight, put a hand on his stomach, and tried to talk. "Brrah— HAW!" He turned sideways again. The laughter was getting painful. "No, now, no," he said, his diaphragm heaving, jarring the words out. Finally he said, "No, it's a great night!" He was convulsed again and doubled over. "I'll walk, I'll walk, let me walk!" And then, as suddenly as the laughter had overtaken him, it left. He wiped his face and stood up, pale and weak, and said to Orin, who was staring at him in bewilderment, "I'll be damned."

He turned and went out the porch, through the farmyard and orchard, through the meadow, and through the woods, so angry at being denied the token kindness of the ride that there was no effort to walking, and so hungry and exhausted he felt at the point of tears. He came down the driveway to the lodge, went into the back porch, and took off his shirt. He was removing his pants when Ellen opened the kitchen door.

"What are you *doing*?" she said.

"I'm all nettles and burrs and beards of hay and other shit. I have to wash it off. I have to eat. What are we having?"

"You look tired. Your eyes are terrible."

"I asked what we're having!"

"It's a surprise."

"Surprise, hell! What is it!"

"You'll see. I went into town. Mmm, you look strong. Kiss me."

"Don't touch me!" he cried, and threw down his boots and stomped past her, naked, his existence narrowed to two things, the shower and the dinner, the shower first (#1), and then (#2) the dinner, his mind fixed on #1, shower, his perceptions so narrowed that the only things he saw or comprehended on the way to the bathroom were boards of the floor.

He spent a long time under the shower, regulating the water so that it was cool, then warm, then cool again, and then he washed himself from hair to toenails, several times, working up a heavy lather each time and rinsing it off well. Still the sting of nettles stayed on some patches of his skin, mostly across his back. He rubbed his back against the wall of the shower. He soaped the wall and rubbed his back against it again. He rinsed his back. It didn't help; the nettles still stung and itched. Maybe they were scratches. He shut off the water.

While he was toweling himself down, the door opened and Ellen handed him clean clothes, and said, "Take your time. It's not quite ready yet."

"Not ready! You've had all day, for Christ's sake!"

"The food is ready but, you know——everything else——" Her voice was moving around the kitchen and he didn't catch all this. It moved closer to the bathroom door, and said, "Besides, it's just a little after nine. That's the fashionable hour."

"Fashion, hell, I want *food*!"

"Just a second. Take your time in there."

"I'll come out when I damn well please!"

He finished dressing. The clothes felt medicinal on him, like clean sheets when it was humid. He sat on the lowered lid of the toilet stool and pulled on his boots. Only now did he look in the mirror. His eyelids were red and swollen from the dust and chaff, and his corneas were pink, interlaced with a brilliant mesh of red traceries. He hated his face. He brushed the wet hair off his forehead and stepped out of the bathroom.

The kitchen was dark. There were candles going in the dining wing. She took him by the arm and led him to the table, which she had covered with a white cloth. In front of his place at the head of the table, on an oval platter, was his favorite dish, a large pork roast, its fat crisped brown, a ring of parsley surrounding it. On their plates were baked potatoes with butter melting into their white meat, mounds of creamed cauliflower, and fried apple rings. There was a bowl of salad with cucumber slices, quartered tomatoes, and whole green olives (another of his favorites) tossed in with crisp lettuce. Next to the salad bowl was a bottle of wine. She had arranged a centerpiece of wildflowers.

"El," he began. Then the candle flames parted, and there seemed to be more and more candles burning, all

of their flames arrayed around the dining wing, encircling him and Ellen, and finally the cause of the distor-
tion, the tears in his eyes, brimmed over and slipped
down his cheeks.

"Chris, what is it?"

"It's so beautiful, perfect—" He sat down in a chair
and covered his face.

"Don't," she said, touching his shoulder. "Don't. I'll
think you don't like it."

"You're so good to me! Why are you so good to me?"

"I love you."

"Oh, El."

She brought him some Kleenex and he blew his nose
hard, several good blasts. They laughed. She sat down
and he carved the roast, cutting it in thick slices, and
laid the meat on their plates. He poured a small
amount of wine in his glass, held it to the candlelight,
swirled it, smelled its bouquet, and lifted the glass to his
lips and let the wine rest on his tongue. It was a
mixture of sparkling Burgundy and champagne, the
perfect choice for his thirst and the meal. They looked
at one another and smiled shyly. He poured them each
a glass of wine and they reached for their forks.

"Wait," he said. "Do you—?"

She understood what he meant, and placed her hands
in her lap and bowed her head.

"Bless us, O Lord, and these thy gifts, which we are
about to receive from thy bounty, through Christ, our
Lord. Amen." He looked at her with hesitant eyes. "It's
the only one I know."

"I love it. It's perfect, too."

They began to eat. A great residue of grief remained
in him, and he felt as he had in childhood, when, after
a lecture or physical punishment, he'd been forced to
eat through tears. The feeling didn't hamper his appetite, however, as it had then, and the food was as
perfect and delicious as it looked. They made toasts.
They toasted themselves. They toasted their friends.
They toasted her grandparents for the gift of the lodge,

and they toasted Orin for the meal, which his ten dollars would nearly pay for. They toasted themselves again. They toasted the deer head above them and they toasted the moose.

He wanted to toast their child, but was afraid, so he waited for her to propose the toast. She didn't.

In spite of all he ate, three times the usual amount, the wine went to his head. He'd never dined this lavishly except in restaurants, and then only when he was entertaining Ellen. At home, with his parents, he had had plain serviceable meals like Anna and Orin.

On the fumes of the wine, images of his parents rose in his mind; his father's gravity and commands, his mother's dark hair, her eyes, her voice and her gestures, her cheeks, lips. Had they in their lives had a meal like this? Could his mother, skillful as she was in the kitchen, ever prepare such a meal? Could she prepare it so that each dish would complement the other dishes, as Ellen had, and could she do it with such confidence and taste? Would his parents ever see or understand even this much sophistication? Would they know, like Ellen, to pick only the best? Or would his mother watch the newspapers and TV spots for bargains? She always searched out the products on sale. Bargains. Cut-rate. Price slashed. Cheap. Christ, it depressed and shamed and humiliated him for his mother's sake that she would buy bargains, regardless of their quality, and then not have the knowledge or finesse to serve them up with taste.

He began to sense the pressure, the pain, the residue of grief rising, but this was a grief he felt Ellen should never see, so he excused himself and got up from the table and locked himself in the bathroom. After he'd sat for a long time on the closed-down lid, biting a towel to stifle the sound, Ellen tapped on the door.

"Chris? Are you all right?"

He removed the towel and steadied his voice. "Yes. I think. What I did, I think, was eat too much."

TEN

RISING EARLY the next morning, Chris drove in to the village alone and found that they'd received their first mail, a package about the size of a shoebox, with a first-class letter taped to its top. It was addressed: ELLEN STROHE [Van Eenanam,] THE STROHE LODGE, PYRAMID BLUFFS, MICH. The return address was given, simply, as One Toboggan Road, Milwaukee. Her grandparents. He picked up the groceries they needed, plus three boxes of shells, and brought it all back to the lodge and gave her the package. She tore the letter off the package, tore open the envelope, and read the letter through. "Oh, God," she said, and tossed it aside. It was less than a page long, written on a sheet of monogrammed stationery in cramped, spidery handwriting.

He picked it up. "Do you mind?" he asked.

"Of course not." She was busy opening the package.

Well, dear, how do you find connubial life? You certainly are in the ideal setting and your Grandpa and I hope that throughout your life you are mindful of the fact that you were fortunate enough to have a place to go to begin it. We continually thank our Creator for the gift He bestowed in leading us *There*—we can hardly wait to come up ourselves! It will be only two weeks! Write and tell us, dear, what is in bloom and how you found everything—no trouble I should imagine. I'm enclosing some clippings I think you should both read—also sending along some of your wedding announcements. I went to a printer and had them printed up myself, not some stationery shop where there's such little selection, and I picked out the paper and type face myself *and* composed it—quite some experience! I've already sent off several hundred myself—the names are in the box so we don't make repeats—and you'll find another two hundred enclosed you may send to whomever you like—to what relatives of his you care to and friends. I assume, Ellen, that you are familiar with the proper manner of addressing announcements. If not, you'll find instructions enclosed. It's a pity they couldn't be *invitations*. Love to you dear—and see you soon!

Grandma

P.S. Drop a line and let me know you got this. You know the shape the mails are in.

At the bottom of the page there was an additional postscript, in the slanting, energetic hand of her grandfather:

You're up in the woods there so watch it with those smokes.

Appended to *her* letter? Some balls. Chris picked up the newspaper clippings, which Ellen had glanced at and tossed aside; one was on birth control, one on the Kirtland's warbler, and the other on the increasing divorce rate among couples under twenty-five.

"Prophecies?" he said. "Or hints?"

"Put them away," she said. "Burn them."

"What about the bird one?"

"Keep it."

He laid them all down on the work counter, and watched as she stripped the last layer of paper (there were four or five) off the box and opened it. She took out an announcement. It was of heavy eggshell paper and the family crest was embossed on the overleaf. She opened the card and studied it, and a smile appeared

on her face. "Not so bad," she said, and handed it to
him.

*Mr. and Mrs. Aloysius James Strohe
wish to announce that their granddaughter
Ellen Dilone Anne
has been joined in matrimony
to
Mr. Christofer Van Eenanam
in a private ceremony in the chapel of
The First Presbyterian Church
Madison, Wisconsin
on Friday, the twenty-second of May
Nineteen hundred and sixty-four*

He was willing to bet there'd been a hassle with the
printer. Not all announcements were that detailed or
couched in such a cold, factual tone, were they? Didn't
they usually say, *are pleased to announce the marriage
of?*

"Well," he said. "I guess that makes it official."

"The license did. You signed away your freedom
then."

"The hell I did."

She turned to him with hurt eyes. "Didn't you want
to?"

"Oh, of course," he said. "Of course." He ran his
fingertip over the raised engraving. "Where'd she get all
the info?"

"Before we left, she had me write it down. Should we
make out a list now?"

"Why not? You start."

She took the box of announcements to the table in
the dining wing, took a tablet of paper off the window-

sill, took her fountain pen from her purse, and sat down. He pulled up a chair across from her. The sun was pleasantly warm. As her hand traveled across the tablet in her large and rapid handwriting, he watched the point where the shadow of her pen met the pen's nib, and the black shadow of the pen, darker than the shadow of her hand, began to take on the appearance of a reservoir from which she drew the lengthening list of names. In his mind he went over possible recipients. There were a few friends in Madison (she was most likely listing them), a couple of acquaintances in Chicago, a couple of professors there, his boss at the accounting firm (a bonus? a raise?), two uncles he'd lost touch with; his parents. He picked up an announcement and examined it again.

"Wait a minute," he said. "I'll be damned!" He looked up and found her studying him with puzzlement. "Your name's *Strohe*," he said. "Why Strohe?"

"It isn't. It's Van Eenanam."

"No, I mean, aren't they your mother's parents?"

"Yes."

"Then why Strohe?"

"Grandpa had it changed."

"Why?"

"I don't know. I guess he figured he and Grandma were my parents. Legally, they are."

"When did he change it?"

"Shortly after the accident, I guess. I've always thought of it as my real name."

"What was your father's?"

"Cutler."

He saw the terror start in her eyes and, though he wanted to learn more, he placed the announcement on the table and turned and looked out the window, making it understood that he would not pursue the subject. He listened to the nib of her pen moving over the bulk of the tablet. It stopped.

"I think my father's name was changed, too," she

said. "I think I remember an argument about it. I think originally it was Cotler."

He didn't turn to look at her, and soon he heard the sound of her pen moving once more. He felt, like a cloud shadow passing over him, a wash of the terror she must feel. He stared at a birch, at the meadow, at a stump close to the dining wing that had a heart-shaped hole in its center. Her pen continued to travel over the tablet, but with longer pauses between names. There was an extended silence.

"I have a few over fifty," she said. "Are you ready?"

He didn't know an uncle's address. Together they tried to recall any friends she might have overlooked. They wondered how many people would save their announcements and count backwards from the date the child arrived. "All of Grandma's cronies will," she said. "But the time from the marriage to the due date is close enough to nine months. The child could just be a few weeks premature. They'll never know for sure. They'll be frustrated as hell." She laughed her rich, cascading laugh. "Go on," she said. "Who else do you have?" He couldn't think of anybody else. He made up some ringers to tease her. He suggested sending one to the local grocer, to Reverend Nelson Hartis, to Orin and Anna, her grandparents, the Pope. In the end, when he was done amusing himself, she counted up the actual number of names he'd been able to add to the list. There were five.

"You should send one to your parents right away," she said. "And you should put a note in it."

"*Come on,*" he said. It was like the protest of a child told to do his homework.

"You must. You're right here now. Here's the tablet."

"Oh, come on. They don't care."

"Of course they do. Here's a pen."

He sat with the pen in his hand, staring at the tablet, twisting and pulling at the hair along his nape.

Dear Mom and Dad,
   I know it's been a long time, and perhaps I've been remiss in keeping in touch, but

He tore off the sheet of paper, wadded it in a ball, and held it in his free hand, squeezing and kneading it.

Dear Folks,
   Quite a while back when I was a junior there at Madison, I met a girl by the name of Ellen, and I might have

He'd never even mentioned her name. He ripped off that sheet and wadded it up and held it in his hand. He sat for a long time, staring at her as she addressed the announcements, and then wrote:

   Surprise! I've gone and done it. I bet by now you thought nobody would ever catch me, but this one did. You'd love to meet her. She's a beautiful girl, a great girl, and I know you'd like her. We plan to move to Chicago soon and hope to drop in at the place when we do.
                                                  See you then,
                                                      Chris

He folded the note, put it in the inner envelope of the announcement, sealed the envelope, put this in the outer envelope, sealed that envelope, and then addressed it to his parents.
   She looked up. "Did you finish?"
   "Yeah."
   "You didn't seal it?"
   "Yeah."
   "I wanted to read it."
   "It's nothing. Just a note. I said maybe we'd stop and see them on the way to Chicago. Explain things."
   "We'll have to. I'm really excited about meeting them."
   He felt uneasy. He picked up the balled pieces of paper, took them to the cookstove, dropped them inside, and set a match to them. When he was certain they were burning well, he replaced the iron lid. For a

long time he stood and looked toward the dining wing, staring at her head bowed over her address book and the announcements, at her hair shielding her face, and the golden streaks of sunlight arrayed over her hair. Then he started prowling around the kitchen, picking up cups, ash trays, an asbestos pad, the coffeepot— picking up objects and moving them aside as if he expected to find something under them. He came across the three newspaper articles. Mindlessly, he read them through. He read them through again, with as little comprehension as before. He turned them over. On the back of one he saw:

Recovers Wallet Lost in Sea 4 Years Ago

[From Tribune Wire Services]
BARROW-IN-FURNESS, England, March 15—Derek Jones, a truck driver, thought he had seen the last of his wallet when it fell into the sea here four years ago. But today the wallet was washed up at a spot only a mile away from where he had lost it. A fellow worker found it, remembered Jones had lost a wallet and returned it. Everything inside the wallet was intact.

. . . 2

"Hey," he said. "Let's go to town."

She looked up from the couch where she was lying on her stomach, under a circle of light from the floor lamp, paging through a book on birds of prey. "What do you mean? It's after eight o'clock."

"I know, I know, but it's Saturday night!"

"There's nothing to do there, even on Saturday."

"Let's go see."

"I'd rather spend the night with you, alone."

"Oh, come on," he said, and pulled the book from her hands and placed it, covers splayed out, across the arm of the couch, and dropped onto the cushion beside her. "We haven't been out since we came up."

"Are you bored with me?"

"No, no, for God's sake. I just want to get out. I want to take you out. Don't you want to come?" He stroked her hair, her forehead, her eyebrows, and then took her by the chin and kissed her. "Come on," he said. "We deserve a night out."

"You have to promise we'll be back early. I'm tired."

"Sure, sure, sure. We will. I just want a couple of beers."

She went into the bedroom and in a few moments reappeared wearing clean Levi's and a cotton jersey patterned with broad horizontal stripes of maroon and forest-green; it fit close at the neck, had three-quarter-length sleeves, was long and tubelike, and hung below her hips.

"Why are you wearing that thing?" he asked.

"I like it."

"You wear it all the time."

"It's perfect for up here."

"It makes you look—" With interlocked hands, he pantomimed a massive stomach. "You know."

"I am."

"But you're not even showing it. Why wear a thing like that? You look like you're trying to hide something."

"It's comfortable."

She went into the bathroom. He paced around the main room, flicking his forefinger against the varnished nose of the possum, flicking the coon, and paced through the hall and into the kitchen, around the kitchen, and around the dining wing, and back into the main room, slapping the backs of furniture, setting a rocker going, patting his palm along the split-log mantelshelf when he passed the fireplace, and then went into the hall and stopped at the bathroom door.

"What are you doing in there?"

Her voice was made flat-sounding by the small bathroom, and he heard a barely distinguishable phrase, as though her mouth were full or distorted, that sounded like, "Planning to make it."

"What? Talk louder."

"Putting on makeup."

"For that place!"

"I always wear it. Even here."

"*Here*? What the hell for?"

"You."

"Oh. Well, I never noticed it."

"I'm subtle."

" 'Subtle'? How about sneaky?"

"Oh, please."

"Hurry up!"

"I am."

He lit a cigarette, and paced around the kitchen, moving aside cups and other objects, and then began tapping the top of the cookstove with the handle for lifting lids. He saw the newspaper clippings on the work counter. He picked them up, dropped all three of them inside the cookstove, and made a fire of them. He lit another cigarette from the stub he was smoking, which had turned hot and weedy-tasting, and tossed the stub into the cookstove. She came out of the bathroom with her hair done up in a French roll, a style that emphasized her eyes, which had grown more and more round as the life inside her grew, and she had applied more eye liner and mascara than usual, which made her eyes look even larger.

"Nice," he said. "You look almost too nice to take out." He studied the front of her jersey, where she had also grown, and frowned. "Are you wearing a bra?"

"Yes."

"Good."

"I hate it. It's spoiled me, not having to wear one. They're unnatural."

"Why not just go nude?"

"Don't be extreme. You can't possibly know how terrible they feel."

"I've had on a jock."

"They're an imposition of society. They're worn for everyone but the wearer. They're . . ."

"Hey," he said, imperative now. "Let's go!"

They drove in and parked on the main street, a few automobiles down from a blue neon sign, with some of its tubes gone bad, that read:

T
 E
  L
Q U O R

Holding her by the elbow in a courtly, country manner, he led her up the sagging steps onto the wooden porch of the bar and opened the door. The smoke-filled room was big, like half a ballroom partitioned off, and they were struck by the odor of flat beer, beer breath, fish and wet wood, and the harsh metallic smell of cigarettes and cigars stubbed out in tin ash trays and lying there stale. As they stepped inside, everybody at the bar—a small U-shaped counter that jutted from the right wall of the room—looked up; they were mostly elderly men, one with a long vermiculate face and a baseball cap whose bill was tipped so far back that the gray of his crewcut was visible to the center of his head, one in a hunting vest and hunting cap with a cigar in his mouth, one wearing an engineer's striped cap and a plaid jacket, one old woman, and a few middle-aged men, interchangeable with the middle-aged men in any other small-town bar. There was a row of black-topped tables along the left-hand wall, and a family of Indians, including the grandfather, the parents, and three small children, sat around a table in a dark corner of the room.

"Do you want to sit at the bar?" he asked.

"Sure."

They mounted the high, plastic-topped stools, and he rubbed the toe of his boot back and forth across the underpart of the bar, which was paneled with small sticks of split pine and matched a wainscoting of split pine that lined the walls of the room. There was one small mirror, a round one, too high for anybody to see in it, mounted on the wall above the back bar, and above the mirror was a varnished bass on a wood plaque, with the tackle it had been hooked with still dangling from its lip. Some teenagers, drinking Cokes, were playing pool at a scaled-down pool table at the rear of the room. There was a bowling machine along one wall. The bartender, a squat, heavy-lidded man with fleshy lips and a high wave of black hair oiled in place, pushed himself off from the bar and wandered over to

them. Chris ordered two drafts. The bartender asked
for their I D's. They pulled out all the identification
they had on their persons (everything but passports)
and placed it on the counter. The bartender fiddled
around with the cards, comparing descriptions and pictures on different ones, checking their faces against each
card, and then went over and picked up a flashlight and
went through the same business again. Then the bartender let out a long rattling belch right in front of
Ellen, said, "Hunh," shoved the cards toward them,
and drew two drafts.

"Bring me a bottle of Auld Meister while you're at
it, if you've got it," Chris said, and turned to Ellen and
smiled. "And also a shot of V.O."

The bartender wandered off.

"You're not going to drink hard stuff, are you?" she
asked, imploring.

"One bracer."

"You know how you get."

"Bull." He downed his draft. He downed the shot,
and chased it with half a bottle of Auld Meister. He
looked at the Indians. The grandfather and the parents
were drinking draft beer in withdrawn silence, staring
at the tabletop, and the children, also silent, ate from a
bag of potato chips in the center of the table and drank
orange pop. Chris ordered another bottle of beer, feeling the thick taste of it crowding his mouth, and Ellen
continued to sip at her draft. The elderly men at the
bar were speaking to one another in subdued voices
and giving him and Ellen unguarded stares. He ordered
another beer, and drank half of it.

"It's time we faced this damn thing," he said.

"What?"

"What? What? That year apart, that whole wasted
year, what the hell do you think what?"

"It's a futile thing to talk about."

"It's a futile talk to think about."

"Don't be angry."

"Oh, hell, no. I'll just be a pleasant old hick like the rest here."

He ordered another bottle of Auld Meister. The alcohol was beginning to have its effect. He found himself staring at details for too long a time. At the blue label over the top of his cigarette pack. A crack in the polished wood of the bar. At a patch of porous skin beside her nose. A pin in her French roll. The bartender's high, oiled wave of hair. The stripes in her jersey.

His elbow slipped off the bar. He ordered another beer. The more he drank, the saltier and less satisfying his cigarettes tasted. So he smoked more. And the more he smoked, the better the beer tasted. He wanted another shot to wash the thickening saliva from his mouth. The teenagers had finished with the pool table and were playing the bowling machine; the crash of the pins, and then the clack clack clackclackclack as the counter racked up the score.

"Want to play some pool?" he asked.

"I don't know how."

"Come on. I'll show you."

He went to the table, put two dimes in the holes of its metal feeder, jammed the feeder forward, and sent the balls rumbling around to the back of the table. He piled the balls into the rack, placing the eight in the center, splitting up the stripes and solids, and scooted the rack forward and back several times, getting a tight one, and lifted it away.

"I'll break," he said.

He found a stick that was the right weight and had a tip he liked, but was slightly warped, and chalked it up. He went to the end of the table and positioned the cue ball with the end of his stick and shot, sending balls caroming off cushions, kissing, cracking into one another, and made two stripes and a solid. He sank two more stripes and blew a straight-in shot. He rubbed the sticky end of the cue in a fold of his shirt.

"Your shot," he said. "Try to make any of the solid-colored ones."

She stood erect, holding the end of the cue stick high, swung it from side to side, and punched the cloth.

"No, no, no," he said. "Here. Take another. This way."

He tried to show her how to use the cue, as he'd shown her how to use the rifle, but she couldn't learn to grip it so it slid free through her curled forefinger, and she persisted in swinging it from side to side. He had less patience than when he was teaching her to handle the rifle, and finally, to simplify things, he showed her how to use crow's feet. She improved, and when they finished the game she'd made two balls.

"I like it better now," she said. "Let's play again."

He got two dimes in change, got change for the cigarette machine, got a beer, and learned from the bartender that there was no talc. Piss. He set his beer down on a table, went over to the cigarette machine, put in the proper change, and jerked the plunger above his brand. How beautiful it would be to call somebody long-distance. He clawed around in the metal tray of the machine for his matches. Why didn't the assholes fasten the matches to the cigarette pack or have them fall on the floor where you could see them? At last he located them back in a corner, where they always were. The cover of the matchbook said, MAKE $100 A WEEK WEARING SHOES WE GIVE YOU! Jesus, why not? He went back to the table and racked the balls. She wouldn't break, so he broke again but nothing fell. Now, as he walked around the table, he found himself doing sudden sidesteps to catch his balance, and his eye was going bad; the stripes and the dots on the balls pulsed toward him, and every time he shot, even straight-in, the balls appeared to travel on parabolas. He shook his head to clear it. She made two balls while he made four. He watched her bending under the light, her lower lip bit in concentration, the stripes in her jersey moving as she moved.

Sweet Jim True's. The low lamp over the pool table. The room dark and the green cloth lit. Sitting in a booth staring at the table. How the players' thighs were in light. Then dipping their faces into the light for a shot, rising, and again their thighs lighted. Lynn, with long black hair, across from him in the booth, talking in anger, her high white teeth showing in the dark. Brown eyes. Only the third time they were together, but she was scolding and berating him as though he were an old lover. The first time they met, in this neighborhood bar, she gave him an animal stare so straightforward and open he could see down to her innards. He went to her and began talking about sex, the only subject after such a stare, and at one point he said that he thought women were untruthful about how often they wanted it. "Maybe some are," she said. "But I'm not. I know, for instance, that when I walk down the street and see certain men, you know, nice ones, I'd like to just go up to them and ask them for it. Maybe I'm different or childish that way, but that's how I am." Then she suddenly had to leave, saying she was already an hour late for dinner with her fiancé and her fiancé got nasty when she was late, and there was a flurry of address and telephone-number taking, and she set a date for Chris to come over for dinner. He arrived that night, and during the dinner she talked on and on about sex, as though it were a new fashion in clothes, and finally she said that her fiancé couldn't satisfy her, and nobody had, not even a thirty-year-old Frenchman she'd lived with for two weeks in Key West for precisely that purpose. She lowered her eyes. "I think I'm frigid." She talked another hour on the topic, and then said, "How old are you?" "Twenty-two," he answered. "You look like a boy. You aren't a virgin, are you?" His sudden laughter made him cover his mouth. He listened some more, and after another hour of it, and after a bottle and a half of wine, he said, "All right. I'm going to fix you up." She stood as though in fear, and he rose, a little clumsily, and realized again how tall she was, well over six feet, half a head taller than he, and he tried to calculate how long her black hair, which hung loose and unpinned and reached to her buttocks, would have to be. Two and a half feet? Three? Concentrate, you ass. He maneuvered her to a couch and began gently, holding back with effort because she was his first woman since he'd moved to Chicago. She was flat-chested and slow to arouse. He began to make her respond with no theatrics, of her own accord, when the telephone rang. It was her fiancé. She cooed into the phone and said suggestive things. He left the couch and went over to the table and finished off the wine. She talked for half an hour, and kept saying, "No, no, not tonight. I'm just exhausted. Well, *you* know why. What? You think I'd *lie* to you? Oh, hon, I just . . ." When she finally hung up, he said to her, "That was nice." She turned away. "I don't know what it is. He's no good for me, but he's a lawyer, and rich, to tell the truth, and, I don't know, maybe I need the security or something. In many ways, I'm a child. I'm funny that way." He went to the couch and began in earnest and was nearly there, her bra to her armpits, her Levi's unzipped, when she said, "No, I can't do this. I can't do this to him." She rearranged and refastened her clothes and lay on the couch biting her lower lip, and when he saw her nervousness and the look in her eyes, and realized how close he'd been, he grabbed her Levi's at the waist, unzipped them, and pulled them off while she kept kicking her long legs and saying, "No, no! No, I *can't*!" He didn't bother to take off the rest of her clothes or undress himself. She was small and close for her size, virginlike, ridgy, and this excited him so much he couldn't hold back. "Are you there?" he asked. "Are you there?" But he was done. Her eyes were squinted shut and she was biting her lower lip more rapidly and harder. "Oh, Christ, Jesus," she whispered. "Almost. I could feel it, it was so close. I've never felt it." Which revived him in an instant. And since she was already so high, he moved only a few times before her body stiffened, made a few weak convulsions against him, and then went limp as the whites of her eyes showed in a faint. He was frightened, he started for water, but then her eyelids fluttered, and she said, "Yes, that was it. I've done it. I've made it." He stayed the rest of the night, and in bed took her up higher steps, and each time, at the end, she went unconscious. As the sun was lighting her curtains, she said, "You're not twenty-two."

"The hell I'm not. It's hell to be that old." "You're not," she said. "You're nine. You'll always be nine." "What's that?" he said. "A slighting reference to how I do it?" "Nobody could do it, who was any older, the way you do it." She was gone when he woke, but there was a meal laid out for him and a note that read, "Thank you. Thank you for beauty." He tried often to reach her after that, but she always claimed to be busy or exhausted. He remembered the time her fiancé called, and then his brain, always behind his body by at least a season, began slowly slogging along: Was she engaged? If she'd lived with a Frenchman in his thirties, you mean he couldn't have done as much for her? or more? And then there was her admission about wanting to walk up to men on the street, and wasn't that what she'd done, more or less, with him? Did she get her kicks from pretending to each he was the first? A snapper? Or did she really flip out like that? The unconscious part wasn't an act, he was sure. He kept calling her and she finally agreed to meet him, for an hour, in the neighborhood bar. He went there early and got drunk, and watched the faces and thighs moving under the light. When she arrived and sat in the booth, in an obvious hurry to leave, he called her a liar, a liar about everything. She said she was like a child, she told him that, she warned him about that once, and then she accused him of raping her when she was practically married. He claimed she wasn't even engaged. She showed him a ring. He called it fake. They cursed one another, and it ended with her calling him a shit-face drunk, and him calling her a kike.

"It's your shot," Ellen said.

"What?"

"You've been staring at the table for two minutes. You can't be planning that far ahead."

"Right," he said, and now he had the confidence and clear eye, and the steadiness too, that comes with just enough anger and drink, and he began to slam the balls home, sinking all of hers after he'd made his own and the eight, clearing the table.

"What are you doing?" she said. "Is that the right way—"

"Forget it," he said, and hung up his cue. "Let's get the hell out of here."

He drove home wildly, squalling around curves on the county road, going eighty on the gravel roads, jerking the wheel and throwing the car into hazardous rear-end drifts, and achieved his effect: she was so terrified she sat in silence the whole way. He brought the car to a sharp, dipping halt at the back door of the lodge. She sat motionless, silent, staring through the windshield.

"All right, I have just one question to ask," he said, overarticulating because of the booze. "Just one question. And I want an honest answer. No evasive crap this time, okay?"

He listened for a long time to the sound of night insects, waiting for her to speak, and sensed that she knew the reason for his anger. "You understand?"

"Yes."

"I just want you to tell me this, just this one thing. How many guys did you put it to while you were in New York?"

"Please."

"Come on, come on, give me a straight answer!"

"Does it matter?"

"You're goddamn right!" he cried, beeping the horn as he slapped his hand down. "Tell me!"

"Please Chris."

"*Tell me*! Just tell me how many, for Christ's sake!"

She lowered her head and murmured, "Two."

"Well, two. Well, thanks. Thanks very much, dear

Ellen. That's all I wanted to know. Thank you very holy Jesus rat-shit motherfucking much."

He got out of the car and slammed the door and went into the lodge, switching on lights. He walked to the piano, grabbed up some shells that were scattered over the bearskin, loaded them in the rifle, and cocked the piece. He went to the back door and stepped outside. She was coming toward the lodge in her sad sashay, her head bowed, and when the door slammed she looked up, then stopped. Her face was pale, a white oval against the dark.

"Chris," she said, her voice tremulous. "What is it?"

"See you around," he said, and walked past her in the direction of the meadow. He heard sounds behind him, as though she were trying to speak, and then the door of the lodge closed. Silence. *Silent night, holy night* . . . The grass was black underfoot. There were stars. *All is calm, all is bright* . . . He entered the tall grass of the meadow, and made his way to the first brushpile. He sat down on a branch and faced the lodge, holding the rifle between his knees. The bedroom light went on. He saw her, through the uncurtained window, ease onto the edge of the bed, and bend over, her face in her hands. *Silent night, holy night* . . . She threw herself on her stomach and hugged a pillow to her breast. *All is calm, all is bright, round yon Virgin Mother and Child. Holy*—She rose up suddenly, as though in determination or anger, and began to undress. She threw her striped jersey toward the main room. She took off her bra.

He got up and went toward the lodge. When he came to the perimeter of the square of light that the bedroom window projected onto the lawn, he stopped. She was no more than fifteen feet away, standing at the dresser, naked, studying her face in the mirror. How many others, he wondered, had stood here this way, at one time or another, and watched her? Watched him? He skirted the illuminated area of the lawn, moving closer. The bedroom light went out. A large, slanting birch rose out of the ground three feet from the corner of the lodge. The first cha*rack* of the rifle startled him, startled the darkness, but he continued to fire until he'd emptied the shells from the magazine, five rounds, into the tree.

Lying in bed, looking out at the night palely lit with
stars, his mind still on Lynn, he was unable to sleep.
His mind replayed their three meetings, three spools
turning in unison, over and over, with diminishing
coherence and sense but with such persistence he felt he
was missing the point. He grew both angry and aroused
and the two forces locked within him as if in copula-
tion. Her black hair, her teeth showing in anger, her
teeth on her lower lip, her eyes going back in unconsciousness . . . Or was that a part of the act? No, he was
sure it happened. Or was it—? No, it made no difference if it did or not. Or did it happen only once to
women, one time or one night under signs and condi-
tions that could never be repeated? Who knew? Maybe
it happened to Ellen? In his arms? No. In New York?
Who were those two? Did she think of them as he did
of Lynn? How did they look? A face was a force to
reason with or fight. Or forget. Or—The black hair, the
teeth, the eyes, revolved again around a single center.
What? Who? No, who were *they?* Those two? Where
did they live in the city, what did they do then, what
were they doing now, what were their names? Were
they married?

"Ellen? Are you asleep?"

"How do you expect me to sleep after that?" Her

voice was pale as the night, throaty and several tones lower than usual, with fear or emotion.

He began to question her about the two. She evaded his questions, and kept saying it made no difference because there was no pleasure in it, only agony, which he didn't believe, and her evasiveness made his anger grow and lift away from the coupling force. Then she asked him if he hadn't slept with other women that year. He couldn't answer. He felt up against a blank wall. Finally he said that he had. And then, after listening a while to her heavy, irregular breathing, he said, "But you were the one that left."

"*Damn you!* Can't you get *off that?*"

"Stop screaming in my ear!"

"Can't you get *off it*? Haven't you met my grandparents? Didn't you see how they used my own parents against me? Can you imagine growing *up* under that, a child? That and their religion and 'principles,' they call them, that they forget about if it's expedient. 'Married, Ellen? You want to get *married*?' They acted *amused*! They pretended I was too young and naïve, too *stupid* to even think of such a thing. They took me apart! They put me together so they knew how to take me apart. I didn't know what I wanted. I didn't know who I was. They reduced me to *nothing*! I had to go just to get away from them. They're sick! And you wouldn't leave me alone. You were pressuring me, too. I just wanted peace, didn't any of you understand? Just some quiet. Just a few minutes' quiet to stop and think."

"So you had to go to New York?"

"Yes!"

"And you had to play around?"

"What do you want? I came back, didn't I? I love you. I came back. Do I have to live the torture of that year all over just for you? What do you want to know? What will help? Do you want to know I was out of my mind and ready to die? And I would have if I hadn't loved you and believed in your love."

"What do you mean?"

"I had pills."

"From a pusher friend?"

"A girl friend, a *girl* friend, for God's sake! And there were the rivers. I used to go to the docks and stare at them."

"Who with?"

"Myself! Myself at night! I didn't even care if I was knifed! I was alone! I didn't have you!"

He felt that the marrow had emptied from his bones, and his chest and forearms cramped with anxiety. Wasn't it wrong for pregnant women to get so emotional? She held his child. Did she? She held a child. A life. He resolved not to upset her again, to put this from his mind, but images of Lynn came to him, and images of her, his El, covered by another body, biting her lower lip as Lynn had, and he arranged and rearranged his racked frame under the covers, trying to formulate some solution, the sequence of words that would make his feelings logical and clear, and he began a fluent and moving speech of his love for her, of how it bridged the past, all that had happened, but the images returned, obscuring his words, reducing them to blur, and he saw hordes of women being raped and loving it, all of them with Ellen's face or with features of Lynn's and Ellen's body, and finally he had to get up and go out to the refrigerator and drink some ice water. And as the water poured down his throat, he felt he was a creature without substance, a transparent anxiety with burning ears that the water would run out of, and it was almost impossible to swallow.

His insides were dried from the beer and he drank too much and went back to bed feeling bloated. He tossed under the covers, half awake, half in the region of dreams, still trying to formulate the speech that would clarify his feelings and cure him of this torment. The speech seemed to lack only a minor piece, a wedge of silver, a word of ruby, to make it whole, and he searched for it with all his strength. Then he felt her body on top of him.

"Lie still," she said. "Lie still. Nothing's important except our love. Nothing else is real. You have to believe that. Nothing matters but this." She kissed him on the lips. "This."

With the pressure of her body against his body, the pressure of her lips against his lips, a sudden blackness came, and he dropped into sleep as though the back of his mind had gone out.

ELEVEN

USING ALL of his strength to do it and a little adrenaline besides, but trying to make it appear as effortless and dignified as possible because he thought she was watching him, he dragged a large piece of beached timber onto a shallow sand dune, dragged it to the edge of a small depression, and let it drop. He picked up the other end of the timber, swung it around so that it was parallel with the depression, and upwind of it, and lowered it toward the sand, slowly squatting with a straight back. Concentrating so much on form, he got one hand pinched under the timber. In a subdued panic (he had to get it out of there and meanwhile not make such a production of it that she noticed), he worked his fingers free and stood up.

Actually, she wasn't even watching him. She sat on a low boulder a few yards away, in her bikini, her long legs crossed at the ankles. They were the only people on the beach, as usual, and he was wearing street clothes and his leather jacket. It was still too cold for swimming. They should have gone somewhere anonymous and simple, like Niagara Falls or Baraboo, as he'd suggested. The gesture of coming here wouldn't appease her grandparents in the least. It would only make them feel more manipulative and powerful. Or antagonize them more. He looked toward Manitou. How far out did her grandfather own? Was the water his, too? Wasn't there a three-mile limit? He'd said to Chris, "That beach is mine, rightly, so if anybody comes along you don't like, run them off."

He kicked sand along the bottom edge of the timber. Then he got down on his hands and knees in the depression, pulled up the biggest clumps of dune grass that were growing there, and tossed them off to one side. He moved his hand in sweeping arcs across the sand, smoothing it, and lay on his back. It worked. The strong northwesterly wind blowing in from the lake was all but silenced. That and the continuous sound of whitecaps breaking on the beach (he could hardly hear them any more, either) had made conversation with her an effort, and without conversation he'd moved from anger to a point of cold detachment.

With his interlocked hands resting on his stomach, he stared up at the bright blue cloudless sky and waited for her to come to him. Every few moments, like an afterimage to a dark thought that had crossed his mind, a gull would glide into sight high above—widespread wings motionless, alert head shifting from side to side, searching, searching—and then vanish. He waited five minutes and she never appeared. Angry and impatient, he lifted himself up on one elbow and, as his head came into sight, she turned toward him as if he'd caught her at something.

"Ellen!"

She smiled and her mouth moved in an answer, but because of the distance between them and the wind, blowing into her face, blowing her hair back over her bare shoulders, he couldn't hear a word. He lay down again. After two more gulls passed overhead, and then the first streamers of a cloud, her face suddenly appeared in the expanse above him, startling in its hugeness.

"So here's where you were," she said, and sank into the sand beside him in a cross-legged sitting position, facing the lake, almost in profile.

"As if you didn't know."

"I didn't. I saw you moving some wood around, and then you were gone. I didn't know where. Really." She put her hand on his thigh. "I missed you."

"Sure."

"I did."

"Sure." He moved his leg away.

"Look," she said, and held out her hand.

In the cup of her palm there was a flat, oval rock, slightly larger than a silver dollar. Its gray surface, polished by waves, divided by hairlike white lines into interlocking hexagons, was translucent, and he could see, inside each hexagon, a black nucleus with ivory striations radiating out from an opaque center.

"See the symmetry," she said. "It's amazing. And the colors! You wouldn't think anything so perfect could come in a natural state. It's like a Miró."

He turned his head away.

"It's a Petoskey stone," she said, her voice almost lost in the wind. "I found it along the waterline."

He watched a plump, wet-looking sow bug, harried by five or six ants, crawl ponderously toward the underside of the timber, but his attention was focused in the opposite direction, toward her. Sand trickled out of his hair and ran down the back of his neck, crossing his field of concentration.

"I better go make dinner," she said.

"Sure," he said. "You go make dinner."

The sow bug lost its footing and dropped onto the sand on its back. The ants hurried down the timber in a single file and gathered around it, tentative, testing it with their antennae, backing back, advancing.

"Do you want me to stay?" she asked.

"No. You go make dinner."

"If you want me to stay, I will. But when you're like this there's nothing I can do."

"Not any more. You've already done it."

"You're being unfair," she said, but there was hesi-

tance in her voice and she seemed ready to apologize
for saying it.

"How so? It happened."

"It happened, true. But it's over."

"I just remembered something." He paused to give
her a chance to ask what.

"I just remembered something. You said that when
you went to New York, the one thing you knew in spite
of your confusion was that you loved me, right?"

"Yes."

"You said that that kept you alive there."

"It did."

"You just said that last night to shut me up."

"I did not!"

"Shit, too. One of the first letters I got from New
York started, 'Chris'—you didn't even bother to put in
the Dear—'Chris'." He cleared his throat in a falsetto.
" 'There's no denying the new freedom of spirit I feel,
and I shall not allow myself to perpetrate the false
conception, in my letters or in any of my emotions, that
things between us are the same as they were. They
aren't, and I know now they will never be.' " The way
he quoted from the letter, in a mincing voice meant to
approximate hers, hinted at the burning rage in which
he'd studied the letter, over and over, until it was
branded into his mind. "Remember that?"

She nodded.

"How do you explain that?"

She shrugged her shoulders.

"Was it after your first lay?"

"Please."

"Then how do you explain it?"

"I can't take what I was feeling then and transfer it
to now."

"But just last night you said that above everything
else then you *knew* you loved me. That sure as hell
isn't what you were saying in that letter, is it? *Is* it?"

This time she didn't nod, and all the color in her
face, as though everything in her was retreating, went.

"And when I came out to see you, you wouldn't even let me touch you. You—"

"I was still working things out."

"Is that why you asked me to leave an hour after I got there?"

"You were there almost a day."

"But you asked me to leave, by Christ, and you were so nasty about it I did."

"Swearing at me, saying you never—"

"I felt bad about that, I felt I should apologize, and I came all the way in from the airport to do it and there you were carrying on a pleasant talk with a new friend. At three in the morning."

"I told you about him. I'd just met him in the Square, and he stopped in purely by accident after you left. If you think—"

"That's not what I think! I figure you have more taste than that. I mean that you threw me out and then invited him, a goddamn stranger, in for a talk. And you threw me out *again*, with him still there, and I had to walk around those goddamn little streets at three in the morning and find a cab back to the airport. That was *love?*"

"I was just beginning to find some peace and you upset it. Him—I can't even remember his name—he was too inconsequential to affect it. But you could. And I needed peace before I could be sure I loved you."

"Last night you said you *knew* you loved me! How does that fit!"

She pushed her hair back over her shoulder, and after a long silence said, "It doesn't."

"You know what it looks like? Like you went out there for kicks—try a few new ones in for size—and got bored with that and figured I might have enough money to keep you happy, so you figured, well, since I planned to marry him once, what the hell, I might as well do it before he shacks up with a better piece."

"I was pregnant!"

"Pregnant? Who knows who from?"

"You do!"

"Hell."

"That's one thing you have to believe. You have to."

He was alarmed by the way her voice lowered and leveled off on this, as if it were a threat.

"The year was torture, you know that. It was even worse than after the accident, but it had to be lived through. I got free of my grandparents. The confusion left. The only thing that stayed was your love. It was the only real thing I had. And have."

Her statement, and the dignity with which she made it, satisfied his vanity so much he couldn't remember what he was trying to get to the bottom of. The anger went out of him and he felt closer to her. She pulled up a narrow blade of dune grass and sliced down the center of it with her thumbnail. Without moving her head, she reached over her shoulder and brushed at an insect on her back. The unguarded quality of these actions made him conscious of how near she was to being naked. That goddamned bikini.

"But you did get your kicks," he said, enraged.

"It never occurred to me that anything like that might happen."

"Then why did it?"

"At the time, you wanted me to go. You even saw me off. You were great about it. The first letter I got from you said, 'Seeing you leave with such a purpose, I don't feel left alone. After I watched your bus leave, I circled the whole town on foot until late at night, the places we'd walked, and wasn't sad.' "

It shamed him to hear this hyperbolic lie quoted back to him word for word.

"That was before I came to see you and was told to leave. It was also before you started putting it to—Oh, hell." He was done. The more he talked, giving substance to grievances and fears that were before only shadows, the worse he felt. Most of his accusations could be directed against him, and that made him feel unjust, self-indulgent, and sick with himself. The air was taking on the disturbing quality—stuffy and at the same time too bright—that it always took on when he talked blindly, emotionally, without mercy or reason, until he felt himself emerge from the blindness of the emotion as if from a disease, with a new sense of vision, seeing clearly but seeing no logic or purity in anything that had gone before or could possibly come after, and feeling too impotent and debased to care either way.

"You never deceived me about your feelings," she said.

"What's that?" He remembered the girl on the bus and felt afraid.

"You never deceived me about your feelings. You always said you loved me and wanted to marry me. If you did have any doubts, you kept them to yourself. I admired that. Maybe I felt that no matter what I did you'd be waiting."

"And by Christ you did it!" he shouted, blinded again.

She lifted her face and looked out across the lake. "I suffered for it then and you're making me suffer now. All I can say is I know I was wrong."

"Then why did you repeat it?"

She turned, her eyes large and imploring.

"Why did you *repeat* it?" he said. "There were two. I mean, there were two you told me about, so as far as I know you repeated it and repeated it and repeated it!"

"You think I'm *lying*?"

"No," he said, freeing himself from her eyes. He felt guilty for what he'd kept from her. Also, he again sensed some dark thing in the background that might be impossible to cope with if it were brought into the light.

"Because of my state of mind," she said.

"What?"

"It happened again because of my state of mind."

"What was that?"

"I felt I'd lost you. I was in agony."

Prepared to treat this with irony, he looked up and saw a tear spill over her lower eyelash and, darkened with mascara, roll down her cheek. She quickly brushed it away.

He wanted to forget all of this and simply take her in his arms. Then he remembered the speech he'd been working and reworking the night before. It seemed irrelevant after what had been said, but he decided to say it anyway.

"I don't want to think about that year or what happened during it. But it makes a barrier between us." He paused. The speech no longer seemed coherent or moving, and he tried to recall the details that had made it so.

"If there's a barrier between us, it's of your own making. I've never felt it."

"It's not that way at all!" he said, angry at her for interrupting. "I said I don't even want to think about it! But it stays there, it's in my mind, and when I think I've forgot about it, there it is again! It cuts me off from you. I have to strain my nads to get above it and sometimes I can't. And then my feelings for you are crushed. Killed. They can't get past the barrier. Can you imagine how much more I could love you if it wasn't there?"

Though he'd told her the problem instead of the speech that was meant to resolve it, it had its effect. She was crying. Good Christ, maybe now he could drop the damn subject.

"I haven't ever felt you're distant!" she cried. "But if you think about it that much in silence! If it makes you feel the way you say it does! If that's how things are, how can we ever be happy?"

He stood up. Everything around him—the sun, the sand, the water, the air—looked extraordinarily bright. The wind was blowing as strongly as before. Its sound got between him and his thought and made his head ache. He looked at the timber. Some of the sand he'd kicked along its edge had already worked loose, and the wind was blowing under the timber, drifting the loose sand into low, narrow, barely perceptible streamers. The sow bug was gone. Under its own power? Or had it been carried off? It upset him not knowing what had happened to it, and the uncertainty made him feel anxious. He wasn't sure what he had said to her or why he had said it. And what was it she had said? Was it possible that now, at least, she was his wife?

The Petoskey stone was beside her, indenting the sand where she had dropped it. With her legs drawn up, her arms around her legs, and her head resting on her knees, she was crying, her ribs showing whitely through her tanned back each time she gasped for air. He knelt beside her and tried to take her in his arms. *Mea culpa, mea culpa, mea maxima culpa* revolved and revolved in his mind as though the sentence were linked at each end. He tried to put the Petoskey stone in her hand. He lifted wet strands of hair from her cheek. He stroked her hair. "Don't," he said. "Please. We can be happy. I'm positive of that now. Don't even think about it. We can be happy."

"I don't know what to believe," she said. "I don't know what to *believe* any more!"

"Believe I love you."

"I don't know whether to believe that!"

He looked out at the lake and saw what Anna meant about seeing it on a level; it looked tipped up toward him. He felt as threatened as Anna must have felt, and wanted to run for high ground. Far out, an ore boat was moving toward the north. A gull was bobbing on a near wave. The maroon chair cushion had moved down the beach and was imbedded in sand a few yards away. Why did objects look so stark, sharply defined, dissociated from their surroundings, yet filled with unnatural significance, when seen over the shoulder of one you loved?

"Let it go, El. Like you said, it's over."

"But is it?"

"Yes. Really. Believe me."

"I want to."

"Do."

He kissed her forehead along the hairline, tasting salt (how did tears get there?), and embraced her with such strength her chest couldn't heave. She began to quiet, but his grip didn't relax, and now he felt he was holding her close for his own sake. He watched the ore boat, high at port and stern and with a long level central hull, like a barge with watchtowers at each end, move along the line of Manitou. He looked for the gull. It was gone. Then he suddenly drew back from her, and placed his hand on her shoulder in a different way.

"Somebody's coming," he said.

With the back of her forearm, she wiped away the last of her tears. A boy of about nine or ten, his blond hair tousled by the wind, his feet bare and his pants legs rolled up, was walking down the beach in their direction, trailing a branch behind him. He stared at the rocks along the waterline as he walked, studious, self-absorbed, and when he came even with them he gave a glance in their direction, shy, doe-eyed, ingenuous, questioning, and then turned his eyes back to the water as if in embarrassment. In silence, they watched him go down the beach, leaving a wavering line in the sand with the branch, a reminder of his passing. He walked along the rocky part of the beach, growing smaller and smaller as they watched, and then went around the cove and disappeared. They turned and looked at one another, holding themselves silent to preserve what they felt, and then kissed.

He stood up and took off his jacket and shirt. He sat down in the sand, pulled off his boots, pulled off his socks, stood and dropped his pants, and took her by the hand. They went running into the water, its chill making them cry out, and he dove into a wave and swam until he became accustomed to the cold, and then turned in her direction and treaded water. She dove under and surfaced close to him, her hair wet and flat against her skull. "It's not so bad," she said. "It's not that bad."

He paddled up high and a wave crashed past him. "Not if you keep moving!" he cried, exuberant from the cold.

And then, as he stared at her while she treaded water beside him, he had a sudden flash, like one of those pictures within a picture, of a miniature body treading water inside her. Oh yes. The child.

"I have to go back," she said.

"Why? It's great."

"I shouldn't stay in too long."

"Why?"

"The coldness, I guess. It's just something I know."

"Oh."

She swam toward the shore in an even, overhand crawl, and then stood in shallow water and started to walk toward the beach, taking quick side steps off sharp rocks, her knees giving as waves hit. He swam after her, still exuberant, feeling he'd mastered the water, and ran up the beach beside her. She had the blanket wrapped around her and was shivering, her neck muscles twitching, jerking her head to one side. Her lips were blue.

"I'm freezing," she said. "I'm *freezing* now!"

"There's a cure for that," he said, and reached through the blanket and grabbed the top of her bikini and pulled it down, hooking his thumbs in the belt of the briefs as he reached them, pulling both pieces down around her ankles. She stepped out of the bra and briefs and he, on his knees, kissed her.

"Is anybody coming?" he asked.

"No," she said, through chattering teeth. "No."

He stood and looked up and down the deserted beach, and then removed the blanket. He took her in his arms and laid her on the hot sand and covered her with his body, feeling the hard nubs of her gooseflesh against his skin.

"Now," he said. "Now are you cold?"

"No. A little. No, not now."

He saw sand and dune grass and felt he could count the grains of sand below the curve of her shoulder and throat, each was so individually clear as they made love, and he realized she was seeing sky, the bright blue sky he'd been staring at, and there was the feeling of freedom and openness, of sky, in her body, in its growing lightness of motion, and then all the space of sky came. They lay in silence, still linked, with the wind blowing over them. She kissed his shoulder.

"I have a confession," she said.

"What?" He felt afraid.

"There's sand in me."

"Sand?"

"Inside."

"Oh. It hurts?"

"Some. At first. I don't mind. I love it. You put it there."

. . . 2

Mea culpa, mea culpa ... The wind had slackened. The air was dark. There was something at his back and a suffusion of warmth along his stomach. He had fallen asleep on top of her. Startled, he lifted his head and found her staring at him.

"What is it?" he asked.

"I don't feel alone."

"What's that?"

"I'm not alone any more."

She kissed him. They made love again, with renewed energy, and emerged from it in a changed mood, both of them cheerful, cleansed, laughing. They dressed. She packed her things into the beach bag, and he folded the blanket and draped it over his shoulder. The bronze channel on the lake was widening as the sun went down.

"I'm starved," he said.

"We'll have steak."

"Do we have steak?"

"I got it for you."

He put his arm around her waist, and they started toward the trail.

"Oh, God," he said, and stopped short.

"What is it?"

"I must be losing my mind. I damn near forgot."

He trotted over to a leaning, weathered post, against

which he'd left the rifle propped, barrel pointing up. He slung the rifle under his arm and came back and took her by the elbow.

"Jesus," he said. "If a rain came, it could have been ruined."

... 3

He was tired of shooting at tin cans. He stalked the meadow and woods, ready to shoot the first rodent he scared up, but never saw a rat, a gopher, a red squirrel, or even a field mouse. Each evening, just as they sat down to dinner, a chipmunk with a brightly striped back streaked across the front lawn, stopped and perched on its hind legs on the stump near the dining wing, turning its quick head from side to side, and then dropped to its feet and drank rainwater from the heart-shaped hole in the center of the stump and with its nimble front paws stuffed its cheeks until they puffed with sunflower seeds (which they daily put out for it), and then streaked off to its hiding place. The chipmunk was a regular visitor, a friend almost, the only visitor they had, and he liked it. He couldn't shoot it.

He went to the edge of the bluff at all times of the day and stood or sat motionless, sometimes for several hours, but never saw the woodchuck again. One afternoon, as he was sitting there with the rifle across his lap, she came up behind him, from the meadow where she'd been watching birds, and asked him what he was doing.

"Sunning myself," he said, without turning to her.

"Don't shoot him."

"Who?"

"Our woodchuck."

"If I ever see him, maybe I'll give him a scare. Make him scoot."

"No. Not even that. Promise."

"All right," he said.

At that moment he saw, near the bottom of the wash, three birds fly toward a dead cedar and perch in its limbs. He asked her to look through the binoculars and see what they were. She looked, but said they were too far away for her to identify. He asked her if they were dark birds, and she said yes. To him, without the binoculars, they were just three ovoid shapes, like pine cones, on the thin lines of the dead limbs. He raised the rifle, sighted on one, elevated the barrel higher to compensate for the distance, and squeezed off a shot. A bird dropped, spinning down, its outstretched wings striking dead limbs as it fell.

"Chris!"

"Jesus."

"What are you *doing*?"

"I didn't think I could hit anything from this distance, really."

"How could you do it? You don't even know what it was."

"It was dark. Probably a starling."

"But how do you know? It could have been a songbird!"

"Well, God, I'm sorry."

"Sorry? It's dead!"

"It was an accident. I didn't think I could hit it."

"Then why even shoot?"

"I was just playing, for God's sake."

"Playing!"

Then she told him, warned him, that house sparrows, starlings, and crows were the only birds not protected by state law, and said that if he shot another bird without positively identifying it first, she wouldn't speak to him again, and might even report him to the authorities. She didn't want him to shoot any living animal, she said, but, if he must keep at it, she couldn't stop him from shooting the unprotected birds. Then her voice changed, and though his back was to her he could tell that her eyes had narrowed as they did when she became distant with thought, or calculating, or secretive; she said it might even be a feat, masterful of him, if he could bring down a crow, since crows were one of the wiliest of birds, brazen and fearless, and, to her, almost as noble as a hawk.

"But if you shoot one, don't ever let me see it," she said, and walked off.

It was like a challenge to him. The three crows he'd been seeing all summer worked the territory around the lodge, and whenever he heard them *caw, haw, hawing*, he ran to the piano for the rifle. By the time he'd loaded it and got outside and located them, they had usually sensed him or spotted him and flown off. He took some long, impossible shots at them, one time making one hop straight up from a limb, and only succeeded in making them more wary. He hid in blinds of ground hemlock imitating their calls, which, he learned after much listening, were actually very complex, but all the crows would do was glide over high and fast with curiosity, never perching close enough for him to get off a clean shot. He ached for a twelve-gauge so he could get one on the wing. He cursed the foliage. He told her if it weren't for the leaves and branches, he could have had thirty crows. She seemed amused.

One afternoon the three big black birds, the bastards that had become hateful to him, perched in a small tree in the front yard, near the edge of the bluff—sitting ducks against the background of the lake. He tiptoed over to the piano, loaded the rifle, eased open the screen door with its barrel, keeping his body inside, and started to draw a bead on one, but at that instant they all flapped up, *caw-cawing*, and dropped out of sight below the bluff. He emptied the rifle in their direction, the spent cartridges flying backward over the floor of

the main room. Pale and grim, he put away the rifle
and cleaned up the cartridges.

Within fifteen minutes the birds were back in the
same tree, *cawing, hawing*. He opened the screen door
and let it slam. They shifted their positions in the tree.
He went through the lodge to the back porch, picked
up a mop handle there, and walked outside and around
to the front of the building. He pointed the mop handle
at the crows, and said, "Blam! Blam!" They stayed in
the tree, tilting on its small branches, cawing at him. He
went to the front porch, took hold of the screen door,
then swung around suddenly, aiming the mop handle,
and banged the door several times. They changed their
position in the tree as though to see him better. He
went inside, loaded the rifle, and cocked it loud. They
sat motionless. He started toward the center of the
room, raising the rifle, planning to shoot through the
screen, and just as he got the stock to his shoulder the
birds were off, *haw, hawing* at him.

The three crows became a torment added to his
internal torment, and more than a torment. He stood in
the woods for hours under trees he knew to be their
lookout posts, but whenever he was in the vicinity of
one of these perches the birds never came near it. They
cawed to him from a distant perch. He sharpened up
his aim on clods of dirt, flowers, pine cones, spots of
moss, and on the gray tongues of fungus that protruded
from the trunks of trees. He could clip off small twigs
with one shot. He could fire with reasonable accuracy
from the waist. He got out his small balsa airplane, took
it to the meadow, and for several days practiced with it.
He would throw the plane on a long, circling glide, raise
the rifle, and fire at it on the wing. Once when he shot
at it this way, the plane—by a matter of luck, chance,
probability, skill (it really made little difference)—blew
into pieces in the air. He gathered up the fragments and
stared at them in sadness. His last toy gone.

She became better with the rifle also, firing at targets
and cans, and now that she was over her initial fright at

its report she was completely at ease with it, as though there were something in common between her and the weapon and she began handling it with the same thoughtful consideration, enthusiasm, and abandon with which she handled the binoculars. This chilled him, making his hair rise when she unthinkingly swung the barrel across his body, and it infuriated him, too. He had to keep repeating that it was a deadly weapon. She started taking the rifle with her on solitary walks in the woods. On the day that he lost his airplane, he was sitting on the front steps, his chin in his hands, when she returned from one of these walks and came toward the lodge. He suddenly stood up.

"Jesus," he said, moving his hand as though clawing aside cobwebs. "Watch that!"

"What?"

"I've showed you how to handle it, I keep telling you it's deadly, and here you come, swinging the end of the barrel across my face."

"The safety's on."

"That doesn't make a damn bit of difference."

"All right. I'll be more careful. I'll carry it with the barrel up."

He sat down on the steps and sighed. "Why do you do that?"

"What?"

"Why do you go out with it? What do you expect to shoot?"

"Nothing."

"Then why go out?"

"I like it," she said, and patted the stock. "It's a nice rifle. I can't understand what's wrong with Grandpa—I mean, why we never had one around before. It makes me feel safe."

His feelings about the weapon underwent a change. Now, when he walked through the woods searching for the crows, rifle ready, safety off, he had to keep forcing into the back of his mind vivid pictures of himself tripping over a hummock or hidden branch in the underbrush, sending a bullet through his leg or fore-head. Or of the breech blowing up in his hands, leaving him bloody and mutilated, mad with pain, miles from help. And even the shells, with their oily, graphitelike smell, filled him with a breathless agitation. But he made himself go out with the rifle every day, spending entire afternoons in the woods. She watched birds and sunbathed, and while she grew walnut-brown, his face took on a gray, wearied appearance. He always wore boots, long-sleeved shirts and gloves in the woods, and often fastened rubber bands around the ends of his pants legs, taking every precaution against poison ivy, but he picked up a bad case, which he doctored each night with calamine lotion. Ellen, who went running everywhere in search of birds, barefoot and bare-legged, never even got a blister from the plant.

One day he walked into the kitchen, the rifle in his hand, and saw that she'd set up an ironing board and was ironing one of his shirts. He'd come to think of clean shirts in terms of laundries, with cardboard inside and a paper band across their front.

"You iron my shirts?" he said.

"I wash them and iron them, and starch them, too."

"Medium starch."

"I'm using this." She held up a can of spray starch.

"Oh. Medium. Anyway, the reason I came in is I thought you might like to see this bird."

"You didn't shoot it?"

"Hell, no. It's right out here at the edge of the woods making a weird noise. I don't know what it is. I thought it might be rare."

"Oh, I hope it's not gone," she said, and got her binoculars and followed him out the back door to the spot where he'd seen the bird.

"There," he said. "That. Pi*aou*, pi*aou*."

"Oh, I think it's a catbird. Mockingbird family. Where is it? Can you see it?"

"There. In that small tree. The maple. In that lower limb to your right."

She located the bird and trained the binoculars on it and watched for a long time as it moved from branch to branch.

"Well?" he asked.

"I can't tell for sure. It sounds like one. But catbirds are supposed to have a red rump, and a black crown, too, I think. I can't see either on this one."

"Do you want to see it up close?"

She lowered the binoculars and looked at him. There was a curious mixture of disbelief and erotic fascination in her eyes. "What do you mean?"

"I could bring it down for you. You could study it close. Isn't that what ornithologists do?"

"Bad ones, yes. What if it's nesting here?"

"How could it be? This is the first time we've seen it, and you couldn't miss that sound."

She trained her binoculars on it again, and said, "You're such a good shot. I'm sure you wouldn't maim or cripple it."

That was all he needed. He punched the safety button on the trigger guard, raised the rifle and aimed, and when the bird was sideways to him, and motionless, shot. The bird dropped like a damp rag.

"I didn't mean for you to do that!" she cried, and ran into the woods toward the small maple. Under the tree a ground cover with broad orbiculate leaves formed a solid layer of light-green eight inches above ground level. The cover was so dense that they searched for several minutes without finding a trace of the bird. Then he noticed a big leaf spattered with blood. He edged away from it. She was circling behind him, and he heard her say, "Here. Look at this. It must be close to here." He turned. She found the bird and held it in the flat of one hand and stroked its feathers. "Yes," she said. "It was a catbird. See the red. Oh. Oh, feel. Feel." She continued to stroke it and from the way its head, which hung over the end of her fingertips, was wobbling from side to side, he assumed he'd got it through the neck. He went into the lodge, feeling nauseous, and unloaded the rifle and laid the shells on the bearskin. He pulled out the pin at the center of the rifle and removed its ejecting and firing mechanism.

That afternoon he couldn't eat lunch, not so much from the nausea as from an oppressive feeling of fullness, like the bloat of too much water after the beer, and from that day he had no appetite. His insomnia grew worse and worse and his body, operating on a logic all its own, rebelled. He started waking with the first light of the sun, startled, restless, unable to return to sleep. There were dreams of birds; birds coming down on him with talons, eagles and hawks, gray men with wings of birds who walked along the bank of a river, great black-back gulls with bodies of ashes, birds with beaks that pierced him through, birds like porcupines that flew into him at full tilt, and there was a recurring dream: He was in a small room. One wall was of glass. The room was so high in a building he couldn't see the ground. He was trapped in the room, and there was a tone and shading to the dream which let him know that the glass was there for him to fall through, or be pushed through. But he was alone in the room. Then footsteps started down a corridor toward him. The footsteps were also his. He was coming down the corridor—And each time at this point he woke sitting up, drenched with sweat, his hands still trying to push away some dark thing.

TWELVE

ZTUK, THE RIFLE went, *ztuk*, the sound of its report muffled by the wooded bluff and the expanse of the lake. Some tin cans and plastic bottles were lined in a row along the sand and Ellen was facing the bluff, in her bikini, and, with the studious concentration of a child practicing the piano, was firing at them. Chris sat in the center of the blanket, in his swim trunks, a cigarette in his hand, and watched her. *Ztuk!* She pulled back the cocking lever with caution, holding the rifle away from her at an awkward angle, glanced into the breech (why, he didn't know), eased the lever back in place, raised the rifle, barrel wavering, and finally fired. Then the slow process of cocking, which she made seem so complicated, a long ensuing silence, and then *Ztuk!* The bullets usually plowed the sand in front of her targets. He watched until he couldn't take it any more. "Here," he said, and went to her and grabbed the rifle away. He loaded it full of longs, fifteen of them, raised the barrel, feeling its end heavy with the shells' weight, and set his sights on a frozen-juice can. He fired rapidly, blapping into the can, sending it on a skittering dance, with sudden high hops, toward the trees of the bluff, chasing it along the sand until the magazine was emptied.

"God," she said. "That was beautiful."

"It's a hell of a way to waste shells," he said, and handed her the rifle and turned away and started down the beach.

"Where are you going?" she called.

"For a walk."

"You're not angry, are you?"

"No."

"Do you mind if I keep shooting?"

"No!"

He walked along the waterline, looking at the pebbles and rocks washed up, searching for a Petoskey stone. He didn't see one immediately, and gave up looking; it was too much effort. Each day his body and mind had grown weaker and weaker, from loss of appetite and lack of sleep, until he felt he could no longer perform any but the simplest of functions without overstepping his limit. The lake was calm, placid, flat as a glass table, and so clear he could see small pebbles lying between the ridges of its ribbed floor. It would be a perfect day for diving if it weren't so cold and he weren't so tired. The *ztuks*, with the long intervals of silence, grew fainter as he walked. He came to the cove and looked out at the wreck, at the pinkish-orange oblong below the surface of the water. With the lake so calm and clear, it was easier to see, and he judged it was about thirty-five feet long. His interest in it was rekindled, and he thought, Oh, what the hell, and started walking toward it through the water.

He drove and swam out to it, a distance of about forty-five or fifty feet, or more. He circled around it, his face lying in the water, his eyes open to study its wavering shape below him, and now and then he kicked up his feet and dipped under, touching its rusted hulk with his hand. It was nearly square at bow and stern and looked to him more like a barge or an old fishing tug than a tanker. Everything had been salvaged off or rotted away except the hull and the steel deck, most likely a lower deck, which had two open hatches in it. The stern was sunk deeper into the sand than the bow, but he could see a shape at the bottom of the stern that he believed to be a propeller. He took a good breath and dove down deep, the water pressure driving in his eardrums, and saw that he was right, that it was a propeller, cloverleaf-shaped, each of its three blades as big as his head. Brass. Probably a ton or so. Worth good money. He went up quick for air. He was tired of swimming around. He sidestroked back up to the bow and found that he could stand on its leading edge so that his neck was above water. He stood, gripping a metal brace with his toes, paddling his hands once in a while to keep his balance, and rested for a few seconds.

He tiptoed as far midship as he could, heading toward the nearest open hatch, which was about six feet square, and when the water level reached his nose, he filled his lungs with air, ducked his head, and dove down past shining plankton and took hold of the edge of the hatch. With a sudden movement, he pulled himself in a gliding dive into the hull. The darkness surprised him, and the water was icy inside. Sunlight coming through the hatches formed two squares of light on the sand floor. A giant shadow of his body spanned one square. He swam down, the shadow becoming more life-size and black, and started digging in the sand with his fingers, fluttering his feet to keep himself under, and felt something hard. He tugged at it, running out of breath, and finally the thing came free and he swam upward, weighted by it, keeping in the shaft of light, maneuvering carefully so that he emerged through the hatch, and broke surface.

"Ah!" he cried, relieved by the air.

He paddled to the bow, where he could stand, and saw that the thing he'd brought up was a large, open-end wrench encrusted with rust. There was no chance of throwing it to shore, the distance was too great and it was too heavy, so he held his breath and squatted down and laid it at his feet on the bow. He lifted his head above surface and took several rapid breaths, panting. He was getting cold; his legs were numb, his fingertips puckered, and his parts felt like raisins. He wondered if he should dive again. If he'd found the wrench that easily, there had to be more inside the hull, maybe something of value. He'd like to salvage the propeller somehow. For today, he decided to go down once more, and leave anything else for another time. He shoved off and floated over above the hatch, bent quick at the waist and dove down to it, and pulled himself inside and swam to the square of light at the bottom and started digging in the sand, stirring up sandy clay and sediment that turned the shafts of light somewhat murky. He couldn't find anything, he ran out of breath making some final, futile efforts, he swam to a shaft of light, rising as he went, and gave a hard downstroke to reach surface fast, and felt Ellen's ring slip off his finger. He spun around in the water, saw the glint of gold as it tumbled down the shaft of light, and started after it quick, grabbing at it, losing depth each time he did, and gave a hard kick, a last effort, all the time needing air, and slapped the ring with his hand. It went flying sideways into darkness. He dove straight to the place he saw it fall, chilled by the dark water, and patted over the sandy surface, stirring up more murk, his eardrums pained, his lungs trying in reflex to suck deep, and finally he had to push off with his foot to reach air fast, his mind on the ring, the prize of it, the terror if it were lost, and he heard a clong as his head struck steel.

The hatch, the hatch, he thought, half conscious, fighting the need to breathe, the cough he felt coming, and just as he found the hatch the cough came, water in his lungs, another cough, choking now, no air, then surface at last, where he rolled on his back, too weak to keep more than his face above water, coughing, trying to force out the water before he started to heave, each cough searing his lungs and racking and doubling his body so badly he had to thrash around to keep above water. He had no bearings. He didn't know the way to shore. He couldn't turn on his stomach and circle to look for it. There was no more strength in his arms and legs. He didn't know if his head was facing inland. There was only pale sky, his eyes burning, an ache across his crown, tributaries of fire in each lung, and no let-up in the coughing. Before he vomited and choked on it, he had to make it to shore, wherever that was, and he had to do it quick, while he still had some strength. He could come back for the ring later, after he'd rested. He turned his head and saw shore behind him. He started kicking toward it, still on his back, still coughing, doing a weak stroke with one arm until it gave out, and then the other arm, wondering when it would be safe to stand. He craned his head. He would have to go farther. Then his muscles went slack, and he thought, slipping into a daze, how much easier it would be to go under and breathe deep. And it occurred to him, as a phenomenon of wonder and incredibility, that he would be found dead in a pair of black trunks.

This gave him a waking surge of adrenaline and he started thrashing hard, realized that was senseless, wasteful, dangerous, and knew there was only one thing to do; turn and use his remaining strength to swim. If he could make it, this would be the only way. He turned, still coughing, and started a slow sidestroke, keeping his mouth away from the water. Then his right arch bent like a bow with cramp, his right calf cramped, and the leg began kicking in spasms of its own accord, tipping him out of the sidestroke, turning his face down. He lifted his head high and dog-paddled, feeling an ache in the cords of his forearms, in the cords of his palms, while the cramp took his whole leg, the pain finally numbing it—an encumbrance, a useless one, that he nevertheless had to tow behind him. The shore looked too far to reach. He was afraid the ache in his arms would turn to cramp. He made a last effort, using desperation now, the will to live and nothing more, and his toe stubbed on a rock. He stood on his good leg, bent over at the waist, unable to straighten, feeling there was weight on his back—feedsacks, stones, walls of water—and started hopping in a crouch toward the shore. He fell. He dog-paddled to keep his head above water until he could stand again. He got the good leg under him, rose on it, started hopping, and then felt a cramp start in that leg.

He threw himself forward, trying to dive, belly-flopping with a big splash, and went under for a second. He found he could touch bottom with his hands. He held his head high, his nostrils just above water level, and hand-walked and pawed toward shore and suddenly dropped, his useless legs lying in the water, his cheek resting on packed sand, neither conscious nor thankful that he was breathing air.

To lose the ring there, after three years. Her ring. *That* ring. At this place, inside that wreck, after all these years, to lose it. In his mind he watched the image, endlessly replayed, of himself thrashing around inside the hull, and it terrified him. But he had to go back. When the cramps went and his strength returned, he had to, he had to find it. Maybe in a few minutes, a few hours, maybe tomorrow. Then he was aware of a thing that he had feared and tried not to think about. Small waves were beginning to lap over him. The wind was rising and the water was beginning to move. Sand would drift, was drifting. The ring, if not already so, would soon be moved, be covered, be buried so thoroughly it could never be found.

"Goddamnit, goddamnit!" he cried, and slammed his fist against the sand. "What the goddamn hell have you done, you—" But before he could finish, there was a convulsion inside him, and he began to vomit.

... 2

Prepared for the worst, he told her about the ring. Her
face paled and took on a stony set, very much like her
grandmother's, and her lips compressed until they were
white. She started gathering her things together in the
beach bag, and he tried to explain what had happened,
how it had happened, begging her to understand and
forgive him, saying that he realized how much the ring
meant to her, and that he had almost killed himself
trying to retrieve it. Silent, she pulled on her clothes
over her bikini, picked up the beach bag and binoculars, picked up the rifle, and gave him a long, unforgiv-
ing stare, her eyes turning bright green, and then her
lips began to tremble, her jaw trembled, and in a low
throaty voice she said, "You shit." And turned away
and started up the trail.

He sat and dressed with effort, so weak he felt his
flesh was meshed with water instead of muscle and
bone, his head clamped in a band of pain. He wanted a
cigarette. She had taken them with her. He realized she
had taken the rifle, too, and stood up and his knees
buckled. He sat and stared at the water, the waves, the
waves, the whitecaps, the waves, each were repeating,
with every scroll and splash, *youshit, youshit, youshit.*
The water. He had just made it from there. The water
was safe. And now he was on the beach. He'd been on
the beach a long time.

He pushed himself to his feet and started up the

trail. He had to sit down often. He made it to the top, his legs trembling, and went into the lodge and found her in the main room on the couch, underneath a quilt. Her head was covered and turned toward the back of the couch, and the quilt rose and fell, as she let out, over and over, the lamenting wail he'd heard only once, at her grandparents' table.

He eased himself onto the edge of the couch and looked into the fireplace. The ash should be cleaned from it, he thought, with the detachment that comes with great fear for somebody else. The possum and the raccoon looked down at him, glassy-eyed. Basilisks.

He turned and put his hand on her. "El, I'm sorry."

There was no response, and he sat for a long while and watched as everything in the room turned one shade darker.

"I'm sorry," he said. "All I can do is repeat that. It's useless, I know, but it's all I can do. I know how you must feel. I know how much they—I know how much the ring meant to you. I feel as bad. Since you entrusted me with it, it's meant as much to me."

"It was—*bound*—to happen!" she cried, the back of the couch muffling the harsh way the words were torn from her. "It was—bound to happen—*some*time! I knew it. Maybe that's why I gave it to you. Maybe I was afraid *I'd* lose it. Maybe it's better lost. Maybe it's over now. But the last vestige of my past is gone. Part of me's dead."

"I'm sorry," he repeated tonelessly. "I don't know what to do."

"Don't. It was bound to happen. I didn't mean to call you—I'm sorry." Gradually, the heaving of the quilt subsided, and then she said, "I have to tell you something." She uncovered her face and turned to him. He was shocked. Her looks were usually enhanced by tears, but now her mouth was pulled down in a distorted shape, her nose was enlarged and shiny, there were spots of crimson and gray in her skin, and her eyelids were so swollen they were almost closed.

"I have to tell you this. I've always wanted to tell you, because you're the only person I know will understand, but I've never been able to. I don't even know what it means, but I feel so strongly about it I know you'll understand. You—*have* to understand."

He took her hand in his.

"It happened here. I was on the beach. I was farther up the beach than we go, swimming close to shore, and I saw a bird come out of the woods. It was a big bird, not a ground bird—I didn't know that then, I was too young—but it was walking on the ground, and I knew right away—I wasn't that old, it was the summer after the accident and I was here with Grandma and Grandpa—I knew right away something was wrong. I wasn't afraid, though. The bird was big, but it didn't scare me. I got out of the water and went toward it, and it came toward me. It was the size of a crow, at least, and black, but I still don't think it was a crow. Or maybe it was seeing it that close. I could tell it was sick. It came toward me and stretched out its wings as far as they'd reach, and I picked it up. It died in my arms. I carried it to the edge of the woods and dug a hole with a branch. Not in the sand but in soft dirt. I folded its wings against its body and smoothed its feathers back until it looked as natural and dignified as it did in real life. Its eyes were open. Then I pulled up some ferns and wrapped his body in them. He was so heavy. I wrapped the ferns around and around. Then I laid him in the place I'd dug for him. I buried him. It didn't bother me. It seemed so natural. It was the only thing to do. It was the right thing. Wasn't it? Do you understand?"

There was a long silence.

"Do you understand?"

In his mind he was still inside the hull of the wreck, trying to make the perfect, successful dive for the ring, and now, he realized there was something she wanted to hear.

"I'm sorry," he repeated.

. . . 3

Quiet would not come. Though she forgave him, and told him not to let the lost ring bother him, and said that for her it was no longer so important (indeed, she seemed to have overcome the incubus of her parents in some way, and was less troubled than he'd seen her in two years), quiet would not come. He woke each morning as the sun rose, and lay on his back and stared at the beams and bare boards of the ceiling, wondering, What was it he'd done? Where could he be found? He was locked inside layers of himself like the bones inside his flesh. He tried to imagine his way through the layers, starting at his skin and going past each layer down to his marrow. The beauty and freedom was there, in the marrow. No. It was going from his bones. Leukemia of the spirit. Now his soul was in a valve of his heart. Auricle. Pouring out into his blood. Nothing but fluid in motion. Oh, Lord, what are you doing? Where can I go?

Then he would rise from this, into what seemed reality, and think, What's this crap? It's simple. I'm me. Christofer Van Eenanam. It's on my identification. My body makes me self-evident. It has its distinctive structure, wrinkles, parts, and hair, and will not pass through walls. It's obvious where I'm going, and am.

VAN EENANAM SPENDS
HONEYMOON IN MICHIGAN

And at the same time, suspended between these ex-
tremes, he was trying to comprehend being married to a
woman who was married to him (her body crowding
closer against him as he slept), this woman bearing a
child, their child, and the three of them living together
in what is known as a family; he was trying to pene-
trate this mystery, solve this problem, break through it
and relate it to practical matters, such as money,
school, maternity clothes, mathematics, her, himself—
but he couldn't, and that made him feel even more
anxious and misplaced, because it was not only a mystery to be penetrated, it was the situation he was in at
the moment.

And over and above and between all of this was the
central problem. He sat for long periods of time staring
blankly ahead, trying to fathom it, twisting and pulling
at his hair, feeling only the oppressive fullness. He felt
that the barrier he'd mentioned on the beach had risen
again, but that wasn't it. He felt if he started talking it
would come out, but he didn't know where to begin
and was afraid of another uncontrollable flurry of
words that would hurt her. He felt up against the blank
wall. He felt something was happening. He felt they
should be communicating more. But whenever she
started to talk to him he was flooded with such anxiety
he couldn't listen. What did filter through to him—
single sentences, phrases, fragments—he hoarded, fash-
ioning his own conversations out of them.

And his replies, without his intending it that way,
became illogical, non-sequitur, and senseless. And instead of showing her his real face, the infallible barom-
eter of his most embarrassing emotions, he hid behind
masks of bravado or irony, or played the fool for her,
resurrecting all the faces—distended nostrils, cross-
eyes, duck lips, and the rest—that he hadn't used since
fifth grade. And he spoke to her not in his own voice

but from a repertoire of character voices. But with the greater part of her interest turned inward, toward the life inside her, she hardly noticed the way he was acting, and his actions became more preposterous.

And as her eyes grew rounder and her breasts grew and she slept more, he realized it was too late for an abortion, and he wondered how he'd ever summoned up the courage, or coldness, he wasn't sure which, to conceive of such a thing. He wanted to tell her of it, in an offhand, disbelieving manner, to illustrate how desperate and foolish he'd once been, but was afraid of what she'd think of him, and his lips began trembling the minute he thought of mentioning it. And he was afraid she might see some relationship between that and the lost ring, which he was reminded of each hour by the band of white skin around his finger. His mind was constantly preoccupied, yet at a standstill. It was as if he were staring inward at a blank wall, and after he'd been made to turn his attention outward, to respond perfunctorily to her, to clown, or to notice that he was in a marshy hollow with the rifle in his hand, surrounded by mosquitoes, and had better move on, it both bewildered and infuriated him to find a blank wall there.

From a suitcase he took out a book on topology (his weakest subject), a book he had vowed to master over the summer, but found his eyes focusing somewhere beyond the print. He forced himself over the strings of words on the pages (the shadow of his head getting in the way, distracting him from the print), and grew so desperate to lose himself in the material that even the words no longer made sense. He jumped up, anxious to accomplish something. He sat down again and took up the book. The wall held him away from it. He was impatient with his mind. It was making demands of him. They were incomprehensible. He tried to understand them, he spent all his energy at it, and they evaded him. They were unreal. Yet he wasted all his time trying to riddle them out. That made them seem more real. He threw the book across the room.

His appetite slackened even more, his insomnia grew worse, and his sexual appetite, omnivorous and insatiable up until now, began to taper off, and finally petered out altogether. Every time he put on a shirt, he felt hay needles lying in a prickly layer over his back. He tried other shirts, he tried all his shirts, and with each one there was the same sensation. "Did you wash m' shirts with m' work clothes?" he asked her, closing one eye and screwing up the other like Long John Silver. "No," she said. "I handwashed all your shirts and took your work clothes to the laundromat." He was about to ask her to try one on, but was afraid the sensation might be a thing he imagined, a delusion, and rather than have her discover that he was a victim of delusions, he sneaked into a closet and slipped on a shirt of hers. He didn't feel the sensation. He took off her shirt, hung it up, and went into the other room and asked her to try on one of his. "Oh, God," she said. "It feels like a welcome mat." She tried to think of what could have happened, and recalled the can of spray starch. She went to the closet, took out a shirt of hers (the one he'd tried on), and sprayed the starch over its back. She ran a hot iron over it and put it on.

"That's it," she said. "God, that's it. The starch must have gone bad somehow. Who knows how long it's been up here? I'll have to do your shirts over."

"No, naw, ha ha ha," he said, imitating Orin. "No, it's not sa bad. Stew much trouble. I'll wear these few here through till they're dirtied up. Sokay." He began to understand what sackcloth and hairshirt meant, but he wore the shirts anyway; he really didn't want her to go through the trouble, or to feel she'd spent hours over an ironing board for naught. He grew accustomed to the haylike sensation, and, in a sense, he was relieved to find a torment, among all the others troubling him, that was tangible.

He felt guilty about not opening up to her, not

showing the concern for her that he'd previously shown, but as long as the problem within him remained unsolved, demanding all his attention, her presence and her concern for him, reminding him of how remiss he was being, agonized him more. And that drove him deeper into himself. He would start up and hurry off as though to do something, but then stop and sit down, a dazed look in his eyes, and reach up to his hair and absent-mindedly twist it around his fingers.

Since he didn't know what was demanding the attention of the whole of his mind, his mind became unknown. All that was certain up until now, each shade of thought in its separate cell, all of that was nullified. The part of him that was intimately himself, the I, the calm center of all storms, the one place he could retreat to when nothing else was certain, was gone. And he began straining his consciousness outward to its most primitive, rudimentary limits, wearing it in his skin, outside his skin if he could, if possible, to keep from falling into that bottomless unknown. That dark place.

THIRTEEN

HOLDING THE RIFLE in the crook of his arm, he was in the meadow, stripped to the waist, poking around in the brushpile nearest the lodge. It was the first hot day of the northern summer. The grass was hot and streaming, it and the woods exhaling smells of wetness and ferment into the air—green and yellow smells as he perceived them. The brushpile was higher than his head but offered no shade. It was noon. The sun hung on his shoulders; there was no shrugging it. Rivulets of perspiration followed the contours of his face, bending where it was angular, more angular from the weight he'd lost. At times, as he stared into the brushpile, the crosshatch of branches seemed to suggest something he should see, which he would recognize once he saw it, and he would stop and hold himself in reverential silence and stare at the branches, waiting for the picture to assert itself and appear.

"What is it?" she asked, coming up behind him.

He swung to her, startled, crying, "Oh! Gopher! There's a gopher in here. *Under* here. I saw him go under."

"That's not what I mean."

She went to a large branch that projected from the front edge of the brushpile, and sat on it, settling herself so she faced the far end of the meadow. The binoculars that hung from her neck she sat upright on her lap.

"Tell me," she said, in a faint weary voice, her eyes straight ahead. "Tell me what it is. Please."

"What's what?"

"Why you're angry with me."

"It's hot out!"

"Not just today. For a long time you've seemed angry. Are you?"

"Why should I?"

All his interest was directed toward the center of the brushpile where the gopher was, so it took some effort on his part to stand still, out of politeness, and listen while she talked.

"I know it's hot," she said, and raised cupped hands to her forehead and drew her hair back from her face. "The heat affects me in a way it never used to. All day I've felt larger than life—omniscient in a way. Huge."

"You don't even have a belly yet!"

"A different kind of hugeness—strange, weightless, otherworldly; omniscient, I said. I'm enormous, complete in myself, a world in myself, all there is and ever was. Other than me, and you, too, since you're inside me, nothing exists. It doesn't need to. We're complete. This is completion. All day I've felt different. When I went to take my nap a strange thing happened. I was on my stomach, wide awake, and then there was nothing under me and I was falling through space and years, past now and college and the accident and childhood—I could see myself at each level—and then falling through centuries of time. There was no end or beginning. Even now I feel different. It's as if we're on one of those old maps where the world all at once ends. All there is is us, and this meadow with the trees around it, and after the trees there's nothing. There couldn't be. There's no room for it. I'm too huge."

"Right. The heat."

"You did it. You brought me back from the edge. I'll never forget what you said."

"What? When?"

" 'You have no right to want to destroy it.' "

He looked askance at her; he couldn't remember ever having said that.

"That changed me into a living thing, and it, too. The boy."

"Boy?"

"It's going to be a boy."

"What's this?"

"I just know. He feels like you."

He stared at her in disbelief. She lifted her profile and held it at a severe angle. "I don't want to think I said anything so horrible, no matter how confused I was. I didn't want to destroy it. I couldn't have. He's a part of you."

"I hope!"

"You have to believe that. If you can't believe anything else, you have to believe that. Otherwise there's no use being married or having him. There's no use being alive."

"I believe it."

"I have to feel it from you."

"You don't?"

"No."

Self-absorbed, she rose up as though she'd been speaking through somebody else, and with her eyes straight ahead started moving toward the far end of the meadow. Puzzled, disconcerted, he watched her go as if she were a thought of his walking off. He turned back to the brushpile. He heard some rustling on the other side and circled around to it. Something was moving around deeper in the pile. He started climbing into the tangle of branches, pushing them aside with his free hand, trying to catch sight of the thing making the noise. He stopped. And what if he did see something? An ivylike vine, lopped over the fork of a branch, hung in front of his eyes, swaying. Then he saw a form, a human form, her, framed in a small arch of branches. She was walking along the edge of the last brushpile.

His footing slipped and he dropped, straddling a branch. A cloud of gnats hummed close to his ear. He slapped at their mass, twisting his neck to get clear of them, and in the expansiveness of his movements he caught sight of a gull coming over the meadow.

He pressed the safety button on the trigger guard, raised the rifle, and from his insecure sitting position fired several rapid shots at the gull, leading it. Unperturbed, it glided ahead on outstretched wings, moving out over the lake.

He lowered the rifle, and saw that he was facing the far end of the meadow. He had fired in her direction. He stood up, made sure of his footing, and called, "Ellen?"

There was no sign of her.

"Ellen!"

" . . . *len*!" the woods returned to him.

"ELLEN!"

" . . . LEN, *len, len.*"

And then, announced by the pounding of his heart, by its hard dull strokes, the wall began giving way, and the beats rose in strength, gradually accelerating as he stared at the rifle, the mortal arbiter, Winchester 250, the purchase he'd made to resolve his uncertainties, the one absolute in all his confusion, death, death, *death*-death-death, *death*-death-death, *Death. His* death.

He backed out of the brushpile, bearing the rifle at arm's length, and lowered it like a dead thing to the ground, splashes of sweat dropping on its stock, and slowly stood. All this he did calmly enough, but he had only gone a few steps before he broke into a trot, repeating a litany that matched his gait, *Oh, let her be there. Let her be safe. Don't let anything be wrong with her. Oh, let her be there, let her be safe . . .* Picking up speed until he was running at full tilt, the grass slapping at his knees, turning to green blur, he passed the second brushpile and went running up the slope with the wind streaming over his face and chest, chilling the perspiration there, and with a whole new squadron of fears and uncertainties, unselfish ones, ones concerned with her well-being, following at his back, closing in on him from behind. And then, as the last brushpile flashed past, he caught sight of her. His knees gave out and he went down in the grass, sending up a spray of insects.

She'd emerged from the woods and was running toward him. He lay in the grass, too weak to get up, too anxious to lie still, rocking from side to side, saying, "El, El. Oh, El . . ."

She dropped to her knees beside him. "Chris! Chris, did you feel it, too?"

"Yes!" he cried, afraid that she sensed what he'd just been through.

"The feeling came all at once, like a wave over me, and I saw, as vivid as a picture, a half-formed thing, maimed and bloody, curled up on a sheet. Chris! Do you know what's going to happen? Do you know what I feel? We're going to lose the boy!"

The shock of it undid him. "I know," he said, because there was nothing he could do except make noise. "I *know*, I *know*."

. . . 2

Orin, for a long time, kept chuckling and shaking his head over the fellow who that Strohe girl, that nice young thing, had married. The fellow was no trouble to break in, no trouble at all, but he certainly was a strange one, that one.

. . . 3

Anna waited in vain for them to visit that summer.

CODA

THEY MOVED to Chicago in the middle of June and rented an apartment in Hyde Park. He gave up his fellowship and took a full-time job with the accounting firm. He bought a motorcycle and started working out with weights. She was alone at home during the day, and was reluctant to leave the apartment because of the bad neighborhood. She kept to the bed and read fashion magazines. The apartment, two small rooms, remained undecorated. Within a couple of months he was given a promotion and a raise. He bought a used Austin. They were on the waiting list for a studio at Marina City. In September of that year, at Presbyterian St. Luke's, she miscarried in her seventh month. The child was a boy. Documents were signed releasing his body to the hospital. In her bereavement she called her grandmother for consolation and her grandmother said, "The wages of sin, dear, is death."

EPILOGUE

FOR A LONG TIME he hadn't touched the rifle. He'd hardly been able to look at it. It lay on the bearskin rug on top of the player piano, dust gathering along its length, dulling the blue gleam of its barrel. Yet he thought of it all the time and was so conscious of its presence that when he and Ellen sat in the lodge at night, reading or watching the fire, it was as if a third person was in the room with them. Now he got up from the couch where he'd been lying, resting because of a headache, and went over to the piano and took the rifle off its top. He slid aside the doors at the front of the piano, reached into the opening where the rolls of music went, and took a box of shells from the niche he kept them hidden in. From Ellen and visitors. From himself. He counted out five shells, loaded them in the rifle, set the box back inside the piano, and slid the doors shut.

Then he stood staring at the piano keys, motionless and dazed, as though these actions had not been performed by him and he was trying to decide what to do about them. *Dear El, love, my wife. You're the only person I've ever been able to talk to and this is something I can't say* . . . He glanced around for paper and a pencil but neither was in sight. It made no difference. He'd been trying to compose the letter in his mind for the past week, but was never able to get to its end. The pain in his head—a shaft running from above his right eyeball deep into the coils of his brain—greatly increased. He took off his glasses, laid them on the bearskin, and placed his hand on the piano and rested his weight on it. His nails needed cleaning. Along the upper joints of his fingers, in the straight hair that grew between the knuckles, there were glittering pinpoints of perspiration.

He felt dirty. He knew that his hair, untrimmed, receding from his broad forehead, was oily and tousled; that his face was pale its whole length, the black sideburns emphasizing its whiteness and long lines, drawing attention to his lips (which began to quiver); and that there was a shine of exuded oil on his cheekbones, on the convex knobs of his forehead, and in the gray depressions under his eyes, goddamnit!

And his eyes would be wide, rounder and more pale-looking, with all the unresolved experience of his twenty-nine years shining behind them like fear, making him seem smaller than he was, an easy prey to attack, hesitant, mistrustful, and scared. Suddenly it was as if the black and white piano keys that stretched from one end of his vision to the other, and seemed an extension of the antipathies he felt in himself, had been hit with a fist. His head swelled with discord and pain, and he stepped back from the instrument. There was the weight of the rifle in his hands.

He turned away, went across the main room to the front door, and stepped outside, stopping at the edge of the cement landing. The afternoon was dark and overcast and a wind was blowing strongly through the leaves of the trees, tearing loose some of the brown-edged ones and lifting them off in flight. The air was cold, but it carried a moist, verdant smell. It seemed to him more like spring than the beginning of fall. He looked through the trunks of the trees to where he could see, far below, the blue of the lake. A haze hung over it, dulling its color. Off to the side of the yard, halfway between the lodge and the bluff, Ellen was kneeling in the grass, bent over something, her head obscured by the trunk of a birch. He went toward her down one of the paths that led through the tall grass, his advance rendered soundless by the wind blowing in from the lake, and stopped next to the birch, just behind her.

The dog lay in front of her knees, flattened into a curly mass, shapeless, unmoving, like a rug she'd spread on the grass to dry. She was lifting up strands of tan hair that hung damp and lifeless from its flank and was running her pocket comb through them. Her hands and fingers moved precisely, but with reserve, almost with aversion, as though they were moving over the surface of something she was reluctant to touch but whose presence she liked to tempt.

A gust of wind came over the bluff, agitating the leaves above them, and her jacket (his army fatigue jacket with the sleeves rolled up) billowed out like a sail and her hair streamed straight back from her face. She eased her weight onto her haunches, placed her hands on her thighs, and her chest heaved. The wind eased, her hair settled down lightly over her shoulders, and he could see her profile; her small brow, her straight nose and strong chin, her lips, her sparse gold eyelashes lying along the curve of her cheek.

A few feet ahead, in a ring of spaded earth, there was a seedling she had planted a few weeks before—a young maple with two opposed leaves sprouting from the tip of its stem. She seemed to be studying it. Just then a gust of wind hit and the two leaves went back like sprung umbrellas, blown into conelike shapes, wavering with the wind, their ribs showing. She watched with interest while she patted the dog. He watched her. A mild satisfied expression appeared on her face, causing the corner of her lips to lift. He made an involuntary movement, as though to touch her, and then drew back. She seemed more complete to him this way, caught in an unguarded moment, absorbed in what she was doing, unaware that she was being watched.

"I think he does it on purpose," she said, without looking up.

Her voice startled him.

"What's that?"

"I think he goes into the woods on purpose. To where these are." She held an elongated seed, the color and shape of a porcupine quill, in front of her eyes, studied it, then tossed it into the grass. She ran the comb halfway through a curl and paused. "You're getting perverse, aren't you, Winston?"

The dog lay motionless, without lifting its head or even pricking up its ears at the mention of its name.

"He loves doing things he shouldn't do," she said, and the mild expression returned to her face. "Well, it's all he has left. He's getting so old."

"Old?"

It was the first time she had admitted this.

"Well. Less lively than before."

"Less lively!"

"Tired."

She looked up and the expression of her face changed. "Oh," she said. "You're going hunting."

The island of Manitou, hardly visible through the haze that hung over the lake, was lying low and dark along the horizon. For as far out as he could see, the irregular lines of high whitecaps came following one after the other, and even from the height of the bluff he could hear, above the sound of the wind in the leaves, the deeper sound of waves breaking on the beach. He'd never seen the lake in such turbulence.

She stood up. "I thought you were going to leave without ever going out with the rifle. We have so few days left. Two, in fact."

He turned to her, his eyes dull and bewildered. "How long have we been here?"

"You know! Over a month now."

Her words didn't come through to him until a few

seconds after she spoke, so watching her face and lips was like watching a film that was out of sync "I'm not going hunting. Just down to the beach."

"Why the rifle?"

He glanced at it, gently raised and lowered it in his hands as though to gauge its weight, gave her a look that was plaintive and confused, and then, as though ashamed of it, shrugged his shoulders and started toward the trail.

"Why don't you take Winston with you?" she called.

"Let the poor thing be."

"You'll be up in time for dinner, right?"

He stopped at the end of a rail fence he'd put up that fall along the edge of the bluff, and stared at an apple that had dropped from a tree onto the trodden dirt at the head of the trail. The apple was bright green, with crimson streaks crowning its top. There were brown wormholes in it. For weeks he'd felt exhausted, and everything outside him—her, the scenery, objects, his own limbs—everything he focused on (now the apple) commanded his complete attention. It was as if this period of rest were narrowing all his faculties instead of restoring and broadening them. He had brought along some work, a briefcase full of it, which he intended to do, and was expected to do but he hadn't even opened the briefcase. His job was threatened, he knew that, but the knowledge no longer bothered him. He was a financial consultant, known in the right circles in Chicago, and he could get a job wherever he wanted. If he wanted a job. He felt her hand on his forearm.

"Chris?"

"Pardon?"

"I asked if you'll be up in time for dinner. Or do you want me to not make it till later?"

He stared at her a long time, as though he hadn't heard her question, and was about to say something striking and decisive. Then he lowered his eyes. "No," he said. "No, I just want to see the waves. Walk. I won't be long."

"It feels like it's going to rain anyway."

"It already is," he said, and pointed across the lake. Far out, above the island, there was a dark cloud with streaks of rain angling down from it.

"Should you go then?"

"There have to be more clouds and bigger clouds than that to make a real rain," he said, his voice suddenly sharp, as though the words came from a great residue of anger, an unspoken grievance. Then he became confused again, and apologetic. "I'm sorry. I mean, I don't think it'll rain here, not hard anyway, because, look, the haze is lifting from the lake. You can feel the sun. See? It's warmer. Feel?"

"What is it?"

"Nothing."

"Tell me."

"Nothing." He kissed her cheek.

"Do you still feel upset?"

"No," he said, and stepped over the apple and started down the trail. He descended at a gentle angle, and then switched back in the opposite direction, and descended again. *Dear El, love, my wife. You're the only person I've ever been able to talk to and this is something I can't say. Everything that's important we've done together, but this is something I have to do alone —I feel that and sense it but I still don't know where to begin or what's to be done. My feelings for you have grown every year, and that's good, that's how it should be—but I've always felt there was something lacking in me, something held back or not there. A dead spot. It hasn't grown, but it hasn't gone away either. It has to do with the boy, I thought. I still feel it's my fault that he died but I've always told myself he was a free spirit. That helped. And I thought if we came here, where he was alive once, inside you, and I walked over this ground, I'd feel his spirit. The ground is empty, the woods are empty, the air is empty, the sky is. A couple* *of times when I've been alone in the woods, standing quiet, a wind has surprised me and I thought I felt him close. And that's worse. Because he's not here, really, not in any sense, and never will be. I know that now. So what— So what I'm going to do—So—*And that was the point in the letter he'd never been able to get beyond.

The trail grew steeper. He leaned back for balance and clenched his teeth so they didn't jar with the shock of his heels hitting down. Soon he was in a sparse growth of trees, birches and silver maples, and then the trail straightened and went through a thicket of jack-pine and fir. Here the path was spongy, layered with needles, and bright moss carpeted the ground to his left. There were mushrooms. He slowed down, watching some frail ferns bow with the wind. It was darker in the thicket and would have been gloomy if it hadn't been for the smell of pine. A chipmunk appeared ahead of him, hurried down the trail a ways, then stopped and went up on its haunches and swiveled its triangular head to him. He kept walking toward it without raising the rifle. It dived into hiding in some brush.

Spring. Patches of shadow passing over him as he sang, "Oh, Mary, we crown thee with blossoms today, Queen of the angels, Queen of the May . . ." Moving under the budding trees, his voice blending with the voices of classmates, the boys in blue suits and white ties, the girls in their First Communion dresses. A nun walking beside them, keeping them in line, her long rosary swinging from the belt of her black habit, its beads clashing. A smell of incense and lilacs. The sun bright on the white dresses. "How dark without Mary life's journey would be! Oh, Mary . . ." The girl in the lead, a crown of flowers in her hands, turning up the walk toward the church. The altar boys turning in behind her, their cassocks with capes and sashes of gold silk catching the sun, and then the song ending. The girl pausing on the steps. The procession slowing to a halt. In the silence a nun's voice humming a pitch. Then moving ahead once more, more slowly now, singing in soft tones, "On this day, oh beautiful Mother, on this day, we give thee our love. Near thee, Madonna . . ." Up the steps, watching the polished toes of his shoes, into the coolness of the nave, gripping the purple and white lilacs his mother picked that morning. Down the dark aisle, singing still, pews going past, swinging back from his vision like spokes—colored light from the stained-glass windows lying on their seats. Ahead, off to the left of the Communion rail, the altar of the Blessed Virgin, with a set of temporary steps leading to the top of her tall statue so the girl could put the garland in place. Singing, staring at his bouquet, offering this up to his mother instead of Mary—

"Goddamnit!" he cried. The trail under him had changed into three trails, and the trunks of the trees blurred and merged as his eyes brimmed with tears.

His mother was dead. She died in the fall of the year he and Ellen were married. Ellen never met her. They didn't attend the funeral. On the day they were to leave for it, Ellen was taken to Presbyterian St. Luke's. He stood waiting on a high floor of the hospital, in a solariumlike room, staring down on Cook County Hospital, the Expressway, the black industrial plants, the smokestacks, the bowels of Chicago, when a doctor walked up, for the third time that day, and put a hand on his shoulder. "Two pediatricians worked with your boy for over an hour. They did everything possible, considering how premature he was. He was a perfectly normal, healthy child, but his lungs were too small for him to live. Your wife's fine. You'll have another."

But they never had.

The trees thinned, some last leaf shadows slipped over his face, and he squinted against the light. The heat of the sun on his forehead increased the pain of his headache. The trail grew steeper, going down at such a slant he had to hold himself in check to keep from running, and at this point the trail was no more than a ledge, sliced so deeply into the face of the bluff that an outcropping of sod brushed against his shoulder. He stopped. He was breathing heavily. He wiped the sleeve of his shirt over his face. Directly below him was a pile of sharp rocks. He let the rifle slip through his hand until it rested on its butt. He stared at the rocks, at their pointed shadows facing him, at the ground hemlock growing around them, and then he was traveling down the rest of the trail as fast as his eyes would go, flashing back and forth over the face of the bluff at the speed of sight, flying along, and finally, far below, coming up against a stand of dead cedar. The spires of their trunks showed black against the background of the lake. He was more than halfway down.

He picked up the rifle and walked along the ledge, turned a bend, passed the pile of sharp rocks, then turned and descended again, watching the gravel he kicked loose go tumbling down the trail. There was a sudden explosion, a flash beside him, and a fragment flew past his face, beating its wings, showing its white rump, and went down toward the cedars out of sight. Flicker.

It grew darker. He felt he'd entered another thicket, but the bluff here was barren; all that grew around him was a ground cover with tear-shaped leaves. He stopped and looked up. There were no clouds near the sun. He looked at the trail, at the dried grass beside it, at the slope where the ground cover grew, at its pulpy swollen leaves, its red roots lying lacelike over the clay and the clay bulging behind them, and then, once more, the landscape darkened. He shook his head, but immediately stopped; the movement brought such pain he felt his brain was swinging from a single nerve.

The shadows of the tall cedars passed over him in cool streaks, and then his heels were striking wood, making it resound with a cavernous echo, and looking down he saw in flashes, through the widely spaced planks, the deep ravine below and the rocks and logs and dead limbs piled along its bottom. He entered another thicket of pine, lost his balance, went stumbling down a steep part of the trail, saw a strip of aspens rapidly approach, crashed through them, still running, and was on the beach. The loose sand sliding away beneath his boots slowed him, the lake stretched in front of him to infinity, and the wind kept beating the sleeves of his shirt against his biceps. The waves were so high that his breath—as though the cold wall of one had crashed over his chest—caught in his throat. A black rock rose out of the water like the head and shoulders of a seal, and usually the tip of the rock showed above the top of the waves, but now when they came in they rolled high above the rock, standing in sheets as tall as he was, and then collapsed after they passed it.

He walked down close to the waterline, where the sand was wet and packed, and looked up and down the beach. It was deserted, as usual, for as far as he could see. There were no pleasure craft on the lake, no sailboats or cabin cruisers, but off in the distance, near the island of Manitou, a large ore boat was making its way toward the north, putting out so much black smoke it looked like a burning house. He kept his eyes on it, following its infinitesimal progress with interest, with reverence, until his eyes began to burn. As it neared the line of the horizon, a mirage made it seem split in two.

He watched a swell raise itself into a wave, begin to bend, curling at its top, and come cascading down over the flat retreating plane of the last wave, foaming, thundering as it fell. Then he was moving into the water, weightless, heading straight out as the next wave rose up and came toward him and then hit, the tons of water taking him under, his head knocking on the packed bottom, the rifle spiraling out of his grip, the sandy undertow rolling him, holding him under until he gave up fighting, went limp, became one with the water.

No.

A large wave crashed and spray spattered his face.

Startled, the rifle snug in the crook of his arm, he stepped back from the foam advancing toward his toes. He braced his legs. Something foreign and unclear was insinuating itself into him, taking him over. It spread through his mind like smoke, grew denser, and then, like the dark swirls in an agate, locked in place. He clenched his jaw. His heartbeat picked up and it was hard to breathe. He heard something and turned.

The dog was standing behind him, panting, its flanks heaving, its long tongue draped over the side of its jaw, dropping saliva on the sand.

"What are you doing here?"

Standing alone, it looked more enormous than ever and more ludicrous. It was a cross between a collie and another breed (a Saint Bernard?) that had bequeathed to it a broad back, heavy paws, and a blunt nose. Although she got it when she was in her teens, she still spoke to it as though it were a pup and treated it with as much affection. Shortly after the miscarriage, she asked her grandparents to have it back. The old couple had become more reserved and tolerant, and no longer interfered with their marriage. The dog was, as she said, old; it limped badly on a front paw, it coughed at night, matter ran from its eyes, and lately they had to boost it from behind to get it up the steps to their apartment. For the past year he had been trying to think of a compassionate way to put it out of its suffering.

"Why did you come down?"

He could shoot it now. The dog's eyes, bloodshot and watery, rolled up and studied him with a look of mourning and shame. Then it lowered its head, executed a slow and ponderous turn, and started up the beach, its head nodding and its wide body rocking with the limp. He felt more pity for it than affection, but sometimes he sensed that he understood something about the dog that she didn't. And what did it sense about him? Why had it walked away now? Why had it followed him? It always stayed at her side, and never made the long trip down to the beach unless she went, too.

"Winston," he said. "Why did you come down?"

The dog stopped and looked over its shoulder at him, exposing the pink tissue around its eye, and then it turned and went trudging ahead, dragging its big paws, leaving U-shaped wakes in the sand. Perhaps it had come down to die.

The dark swirls swept into his mind again, enmeshing it. He turned and started down the beach, in the opposite direction, heading toward the spring. A few days ago, when he passed the pool of the spring, he'd noticed that somebody had left beer to cool in its icy water, and apparently had forgotten it; the bottles were covered with algae, their caps were rusting, their labels coming loose. He would go there now and drink it. The alcohol would spread through his mind, dark and debilitating as the swirls, and he could pretend, for a while at least, that beer was the cause of them.

Far down the beach, a narrow point with grass-covered dunes stretched out into the water. The cove. He could see tall waves coming in at an angle and breaking on the beach there, rolling up close to the dunes. The curve of the shore caught their sound and returned it to him as an echo. It was like the sound of thunder—denser and more persistent than the sound of waves breaking beside him. Or was it thunder? He looked up and saw fat dark clouds scudding above him across the top of the bluff. A gull came sailing down the line of the beach on the high wind, its stiff wing tips tilting quick to keep it on course in the erratic currents of air. He started to raise the rifle, and then shrugged and walked on.

When he was almost to the spring, he felt pinpricks of sensation, random and chilling, on the back of his hand, then on his forehead, then his lips. It was sprinkling. The beach turned rocky, and he walked up toward the base of the bluff, stepping over driftwood and beached timbers, and followed along the bluff, keeping close to the bushes and trees, and came to the spring. The beer was gone. He cursed. He looked around. A large cedar was growing a few feet up from the base of the bluff, its trunk bent almost horizontal with the weight of its boughs, which drooped low and formed a shelter. He crawled in under the boughs, close to the scoured face of the clay bluff, and saw that an animal had dug a den down through the roots of the tree. He turned himself, propping his shoulder against the roots, and faced the lake.

It began to rain harder. The sound of the storm was muted where he lay, he was shielded from the wind, and very little rain penetrated through the boughs. Warm, enwrapped in a smell of cedar and earth, he felt for the first time in many months a semblance of peace, but at the same time a strange isolation, as though the habitable spaces of the earth had shrunk to the limits of a single room and he was alone in that room and had to be careful to keep his breath from fogging its one window. He looked at the rifle, studying the stock, the barrel, the trigger guard, the trigger. There were no thoughts in his head, no calculations or clear images, and no more confusion. It was as if his mind was cleared and ready for a final command.

He looked toward the lake. *Dear El, love, my wife* ... The pool of the spring was in front of him, only a few feet away, and he could see tiny geysers leaping straight up from its surface where raindrops struck. A finch flew down and landed on the wet rocks next to the pool, its gold body bright against the grayness of the ground and lake. Teetering unsurely on a rock, poised to fly, flicking its head from side to side, it made a quick search of the surroundings, and then, tilting back, opened its beak and gave out a musical phrase so clear and pure it pierced the sound of the storm and seemed to originate inside his own head. He put the rifle down as though it were an encumbrance to this music in him, and with a sudden flurry the bird was in the pool, bathing itself, flinging fan-shaped showers of drops from its wings. Occasionally it paused in its bathing, raised its beak to the rain, and gave out the musical phrase—a song that still seemed to originate in his mind, making it feel as crystalline and pure as the water of the spring. Then, abruptly, it was over, and the bird, drenched and heavy, went off on a low undulating flight into the trees.

The storm started to let up, and it grew lighter. First the wind slackened, and then the rain thinned, and finally it stopped altogether. He picked up the rifle, wiped his sleeve over its oiled barrel where beads of water, minute and perfectly circular, were standing, cocked the rifle, and crawled out of the shelter. He walked back up the beach and came to the foot of the trail. Several yards ahead of him a jug made of turquoise plastic, a container for bleach, was leaning against a log that lay half buried in the sand. He raised the rifle, fired off four shots, rapidly, one after the other, and they tore through the neck of the jug and thumped into the dead wood with a dull sound. He left the final round in the magazine.

He looked around for the dog, and saw it moving down the beach in the direction he had come from, heading toward the spring. Apparently they had just passed one another.

"Winston," he called. "Winston!"

The dog, its shaggy tail hanging limp, paused with its rear to him, as though its attention were focused on something distant, and then continued to walk straight ahead.

"Winston!"

It made no sign of having heard. He glanced up toward the lodge and could see, high at the edge of the wash, the rail fence, which, from where he stood, looked as if it were made of matchsticks. There was no sign of Ellen.

"*Winston!*"

The dog wouldn't even turn to look at him. It

plodded steadily ahead through the sand, its body swaying.

Oh, let it go, he thought; let it be. If it had come down of its own accord, it would go up when it wanted to. He turned away and started up the trail, but had only gone a few steps before he stopped, remembering the last shell. He crashed through the strip of aspens, walked over the loose sand to the water's edge, and stood near the seal-shaped rock. The waves were smaller now, only two or three feet high, and the darkness in the air was the natural darkness of coming night and not that of a storm. He cocked the rifle. There was nothing in front of him but the water and, fifteen miles distant, the island of Manitou. He elevated the end of the barrel, curled his forefinger around the trigger, hesitated, then let his breath go.

The expanse of water almost silenced the report. There was only a faint slap of a sound, like fingertips on skin, as he fired the last round from his waist, sending the bullet out over the open lake.

The Shattering Novel
of a Political Assassination...

by
Vassilis Vassilikos

"Unique, exciting reading . . . Vassilikos's gifts are dazzling."

—New York Times Book Review